Science for Primary School Teachers

Science for Primary School Teachers

Helena Gillespie and Rob Gillespie

 Open University Press

Open University Press
McGraw-Hill Education
McGraw-Hill House
Shoppenhangers Road
Maidenhead
Berkshire
England
SL6 2QL

email: enquiries@openup.co.uk
world wide web: www.openup.co.uk

and Two Penn Plaza New York, NY 10121–2289, USA

First published 2007

A catalogue record of this book is available from the British Library

ISBN10: 0 335 22015 0 (pb)   0 335 22016 9 (hb)
ISBN13: 978 0 335 22015 1 (pb)   978 0 335 22016 8 (hb)

Library of Congress Cataloging-in-Publication Data
CIP data has been applied for

Typeset by RefineCatch Limited, Bungay, Suffolk
Printed in Poland by OZ Graf. S.A.
www.polskabook.pl

The *McGraw·Hill* Companies

Contents

We would like to dedicate this book to our parents, Drew Gillespie, Pat Gillespie and Pauline Campion, and to the memory of Geoff Campion.

How to use this book

> We can imagine that this complicated array of moving things which constitutes 'the world' is something like a great chess game being played by the gods, and we are observers of the game. We do not know what the rules of the game are; all we are allowed to do is to watch the playing. Of course, if we watch long enough, we may eventually catch on to a few of the rules. That's the way it is, I would say, regarding the phenomena of life, consciousness and so forth.
>
> (Feynman 1963: 2–1)

The world is fabulously complex, and even the greatest scientists and philosophers, such as Feynman, struggle to explain it. Yet as human beings we continually strive to do so. As a teacher it is important to remember that science is only the human attempt to explain the world, and that it seems unlikely that we will ever fully understand what is around us. However, young children are forever curious and seeking an understanding of the world around them. It is an important part of the job of a primary school teacher to help and encourage them in this.

The inspiration for this book came from the many children and teachers we have both been lucky enough to work with over the past 15 years. Its always pleasing that science proves an interesting subject for these teachers and children, with topics like **animals**, forces and space proving particularly popular and fascinating. However, most primary school teachers are not science specialists and sometimes find it difficult to teach science and respond confidently to children's questions because of the level of their own subject knowledge. This book has been written in response to this need; it is intended to give primary school teachers, particularly beginning teachers, the subject knowledge they need to teach science with confidence as well as enthusiasm.

The primary school curriculum is undergoing significant change at the time of writing, with many schools changing the way that they approach the curriculum in response to the Primary National Strategy and other initiatives seeking to bring in a more creative and cross-curricular approach to teaching and learning. However it seems unlikely that the content of the curriculum will change much in substance, and many schools will continue to use the Qualifications and Curriculum Authority (QCA) scheme of work as a basis for their planning in years to come. The scheme is controversial, with some educationalists regarding it as limiting. However, for a teaching body, most of whom are not science experts, it represents one of many useful sources for planning creative and interesting science topics.

How to use this book

The book is split into two sections that should be used in different ways. The first section, which is an introduction to the issues of teaching science in primary schools, deals with the investigative process, the curriculum and assessment. The final, short chapter of this section is dedicated to a digest of materials that are available to support teaching of science at primary level. This section provides an introduction to the issues in teaching science in a primary school and helps teachers find more information.

Section 2 is about subject knowledge. It is structured in the same way as the National Curriculum, using the three Attainment Targets and topic headings. This should mean that once a teacher knows which objectives she or he is going to teach during a lesson or series of lessons, she or he will be able to find the relevant subject knowledge easily. If a teacher uses the QCA Scheme of Work to plan (see Table H1),

Table H1 Relating the Strands of the National Curriculum for Science to the QCA Schemes of Work and the Foundation Stage topics

Sc2: Life processes and living things	Sc3: Materials and their properties	Sc4: Physical processes
1. Life processes QCA: 1A, 2A, 3A, 4A, 6A	1. Grouping materials QCA: 1C, 2D, 3C, 3D, 4C, 5C, 5D FS: Sticky things; The beach	1. Electricity QCA: 2F, 4F, 6G
2. Humans and other animals QCA: 1A, 2A, 2B, 3A, 4A, 5A, 6A, 6B FS: All about me; Animals	2. Changing materials QCA: 2D, 5D, 6C	2. Forces and motion QCA: 1E, 2E, 3E, 4E, 6E FS: Traffic; The park
3. Green plants QCA: 1B, 2B, 3B FS: Growing things	3. Separating mixtures QCA: 4D, 6C	3. Light and sound QCA: 1D, 1F, 3F, 5F, 6F
4. Variation and classification QCA: 2C, 4B, 6A		4. The Earth and beyond QCA: 5E, 6F
5. Living things in their environment QCA: 2C, 4B, 5B, 6A FS: Spring, summer, autumn, winter		

with each unit referenced, will help in locating the right chapter. Teachers should be aware, however, that the complex nature of science means that its not easy to cover in one chapter all the science needed for a topic, and wider reading elsewhere in the book and in general about science will also help in building subject knowledge. Within the subject knowledge sections there are suggested teaching activities. These are not intended to be an exhaustive list but, rather, are things which you might try with children in your teaching. There are a number of websites referred to throughout the text and these are collected together at the end of the book for ease of reference. The bibliography relating to Section 2 will help in selecting some wider reading in subject knowledge. Section 2 contains a range of science-specific words. These appear in bold at their first occurrence and definitions can be found in the glossary at the end of the book.

How to find subject knowledge in Section 2

Use Table H1 to find the topic, area of the National Curriculum or QCA Unit you are going to teach. This will guide you to the subject knowledge that you need.

Acknowledgements

We would like to thank all the people who helped in the writing of this book and gave us support during the lengthy process. Special thanks go to Caroline Nair, Brian Mortimer and Anne Oakes who read through initial drafts, checked the science and offered suggestions to improve the text, and to Anne Oakes' sons who offered suggestions from a pupil's perspective. Thanks are also due to all our teaching colleagues at the University of East Anglia (UEA) and Wymondham High School as well as to all those we have taught over the past 15 years and have made our jobs so worthwhile. Last but not least we would like to thank our families for their continued support and encouragement throughout all our endeavours.

SECTION 1

Learning and teaching science:
the investigative process

1

How children learn about science

Learning about the world

From their very first hours babies are developing ideas about the world around them, how things look, taste, smell and feel and what things sound like. These initial experiences with the senses continue to develop as babies become toddlers and then into the pre-school years, where learning about the world begins to be formalized in the 'Knowledge and understanding of the world' area of learning in the Foundation Stage curriculum, and then, once into Key Stage 1, into the subject we call science. This natural flow of learning may not be obvious to those of us for whom the word 'science' conjures up laboratories and test tubes, but essentially learning about the world and how it works is something that all **humans** are involved in, right from the very beginning of their lives. The aim of this section is to examine some of the early learning experiences of children and how this lays a foundation for the later learning we call science.

This section is also where we will tussle with one of the most confusing ideas in science education, namely, the confusion which arises out of the word 'science' itself. In terms of the school curriculum, science is both the content of the science lesson (in effect the subject knowledge) and the process by which the learning takes place (in effect the science investigative process). In good science learning children will be doing both of these things. They will be learning about the world around them and how to find out more about it. The National Curriculum formalizes both these meanings of the word, with the first Attainment Target (Sc1 Scientific enquiry) setting out the requirements for teaching and learning the process of science, and the other three attainment targets representing the three areas of science, **life processes** and living things (Sc2), **materials** and their properties (Sc3) and physical processes (Sc4). These areas of science are also known as, respectively, biology, chemistry and physics, and while these subject names are less frequently used at primary school level, they still feature in some secondary school curricula and in further and higher education. These distinctions between the disciplines in science are, however, not a foolproof way to categorize the subject and there are many aspects of science knowledge that blur these traditional boundaries. There are also aspects of science learning that cross into other areas of the curriculum, especially design and technology, geography and mathematics.

Attempting to define a neat and tidy body of knowledge that we can say encompasses what young children should know about science is difficult for all the reasons put forward above. It is also difficult to say what children will know about science and how to find things out when they start in primary school. It is a grave mistake to assume that children have no understanding of science when they begin in a nursery or reception class. In my experience, in fact, children have a complex and interesting, if idiosyncratic, understanding of the world around them when they first come into school. Therefore a good teacher will build on this, unpick it, develop it and add to it as a child makes progress.

Children learning to investigate

Children's investigative learning is a complex process. Teachers need to support learning in a number of ways, including developing questioning and willingness to engage in open-ended enquiry.

The importance of questioning

In order to help children develop investigative skills it is important to choose the right approaches to teaching. Good science teaching has much in common with good teaching generally, and well-planned lessons which are based on a proper assessment of children's prior knowledge and understandings are important. A teacher will also want to select from a range of teaching strategies. In their book, *Teaching Young Children*, McNaughton and Williams (2004) set out a range of 'general teaching techniques', many of which could be applied to the teaching of science. One particularly important aspect of science teaching is questioning. The nature and structure of questions is particularly important if teachers are to get the most from the questions they ask and encourage children to adopt a questioning approach themselves. McNaughton and Williams discuss a range of questioning techniques that can stimulate children's higher order thinking skills (McNaughton and Williams 2004). It is important for teachers to plan carefully for questioning, and when doing so they should consider:

- whether an open or closed question is appropriate
- how to structure the question, thinking about its length and the vocabulary used
- whether the question should be directed at one child, a group or asked to all present
- the type of answer anticipated and responses to the answer which will support children in responding in future.

The scientific enquiry process

Scientific enquiry is at the heart of good science teaching. The process is set out in the scientific enquiry (Sc1) Attainment Target of the National Curriculum. There are a number of ways to characterize the scientific enquiry process. This is discussed in more depth in Chapter 2, where the two elements of the process, experimentation and investigation, are discussed. Some might argue that the enquiry process is exclusive to science, but it might also be considered that the process has elements of good teaching approaches that can be applied to other curriculum subjects. In their chapter on developing investigative thinking skills in children (Jarvis and Woods 2002), investigative skills are discussed in the context of science, design and technology and mathematics. The examples of investigative projects given, making a fruit salad and planning and making a wild garden, are genuinely cross-curricular and demonstrate that some investigative skills can be taught in this way. This is also borne out in the Foundation Stage curriculum, where the early skills of investigation and exploration are taught in the context of the knowledge and understanding of the world area of learning that encompasses several National Curriculum subjects.

For children to learn effectively through investigation a teacher must carefully consider:

- to what extent the children are able to work independently to come up with their own ideas and plan their own work
- the nature of the teacher interventions which may need to be made
- whether the investigation has specific outcomes or can be open-ended
- which resources will be needed
- what is a realistic timescale in which to carry it out.

Jarvis and Woods (2002) go on to discuss the stages of the science investigatory process. These stages are also discussed by Coltman (1996) and are evidenced in an individual child's development discussed by Arnold (2003). Although there are some differences between the number and names of the stages, the themes and ideas behind them are similar. Coltman also makes the point that when young children are undertaking investigational work they cannot be expected to carry out the whole process independently, but should learn the skills in individual activities and begin to link them together only when they are confident. A list of activities that children might engage in when carrying out an investigation include:

- asking and answering questions
- thinking what needs to be done
- planning a 'fair test'
- predicting what might happen
- observing
- exploring
- describing
- explaining and articulating ideas
- collecting and organizing data
- recording and measuring

- hypothesizing about results
- evaluating the process
- drawing conclusions
- assimilating new and existing understandings.

Teachers need to carefully plan which of these to make the focus of their teaching when planning an investigation.

Science teaching and meeting individual needs

In her book, *Observing Harry*, Cath Arnold (2003) charts the progress of one child between his birth and the age of 5. His developing understanding of the world can be traced as he plays and talks about the world around him. Toys such as his train set feature in his developing understanding, as do the **Sun** and the **Moon**. We can see how his understanding develops:

> Like other young children, day and night are probably the first divisions of time of which Harry becomes aware ... At age 4 Harry notices the moon is out on the way home (it is still light). Harry has two ideas: 'Might be it likes to be out in the light' or 'might be it thinks it's still night'. (Arnold 2003: 136)

In this short excerpt we can see that Harry is developing some interesting ideas about the world, but at present his ideas are not correct. Each child will develop their own ideas about such phenomena, and it is very important for teachers to listen to and understand children's ideas in order to unpick them and develop understanding. It is not appropriate to simply tell Harry he is wrong about this. He will find it much easier to assimilate ideas which begin where he is at the time and working through talking, experiences and stories to help him develop his understanding of this difficult concept.

The principle of matching science teaching to individual needs is also important when working with children who have special needs in science. The sensory nature of science learning has already been discussed. For children whose ability to appreciate the world around them is limited because they have a sensory impairment, it is particularly important to tailor their science learning experiences to meet their needs, making the most of the senses they use the most. In addition, it is important for children with language or learning difficulties that science is as practical as possible, so children can develop an understanding of science at their own level.

Children who have English as an additional language may also need their science programme to be tailored individually. This may mean that, where available, talk takes place in their home language as well as English, although it is wrong to assume that translation into their home language guarantees that children will understand the concept.

It might seem daunting for a teacher to meet a variety of individual needs at once, but there are a number of simple principles that a teacher can follow to support their teaching and make it as accessible as possible to all learners:

- Use resources and demonstrations as well as explanations.
- Allow for practical tasks in small groups.
- Encourage children to play with toys which extend scientific understanding.
- Use other adults in the classroom carefully to support groups and individuals.
- Plan for science carefully, especially when planning questions and vocabulary to be used.
- Consider carefully the role of recording ideas in science lessons.

Children and misconceptions about science

We have seen how Harry has misconceptions about why the moon can be seen in the daytime. Teachers need to tackle such misconceptions through talk and practical teaching of accurate ideas. But to do this effectively teachers must understand how misconceptions develop. There are four main reasons why children develop misconceptions:

1   Language-based misconceptions – these develop because sometimes language is used inaccurately by adults. A common example of this is where the words 'melt' and 'dissolve' are used interchangeably, for example, the idea that a sugar-cube 'melts' in a hot cup of tea. In addition, sometimes words themselves are confusing; for example, many children confuse the words 'mammal' and 'animal' because they sound similar and so think that fish and birds are not animals.

2   Inaccurate information from adults – adults have a surprising number of misconceptions about science. In addition, they sometimes tell children things that are inaccurate because they think it will be easier on the children. For example, when children see an empty snail shell an adult might choose to tell them the snail has 'moved house' rather than that it has met its demise and become a meal for a bird. Although adults might think they are being kind, scientific accuracy is preferable!

3   Fact and fiction – many stories, especially for young children, give 'human qualities' to objects and animals, which do not have them. For example, a ball rolling away from a child down a hill might be called naughty, when all that is at work is gravity. From Thomas the Tank Engine to Doctor Who, fiction is fun but full of inaccurate science. This is not to say that children should not enjoy fiction, but that teachers should be aware of the problems that fiction can cause, and try to address misconceptions in their teaching.

4   Problems with the abstract – the biggest problem with children learning about forces is that they are invisible. For example, a duck floating still on a pond may appear to have no forces acting upon it because it is not moving, but in fact the two forces of upthrust from the water and gravity are balanced to keep the duck on the surface. Many teachers find explaining abstract ideas such as the presence of invisible forces difficult but, if planned for carefully, such ideas can be introduced to young children.

Teaching young children science: a summary

A good teacher of science will:

- listen to what a child says about the world around them
- ask questions and stimulate a child to think for themselves
- provide a wide range of opportunities to learn about science
- be able to demonstrate and explain scientific ideas effectively.

Stages of development in science learning

Foundation Stage

In the Foundation Stage, children's experience of scientific concepts and learning should be through play-based learning. This will take place in their school or nursery setting, at home and in the wider world. The best early years teachers help children link and understand all their experiences of science in life.

At school or in the nursery setting, there need to be a wide range of opportunities provided for children to learn about science. Examples of these might include:

- outdoor play
- play with vehicles
- large play equipment like slides or swings
- water play
- sand play
- messy play with paint and glue
- cooking.

At this stage children are likely to explore ideas physically rather than talk about them or respond to questions, although many children will try to develop their ideas by asking 'why' about a whole range of things which they experience. Teachers at this stage should not shy away from explaining ideas to children using correct scientific vocabulary, but these verbal explanations are unlikely to make as much impact on a child's development as practical and physical play activities.

Key Stage 1 and Key Stage 2

In Key Stage 1, children should still need the opportunity to 'play' and engage in practical learning. Good teaching at this level involves the teacher working alongside the child to develop scientific ideas and concepts. Teaching should be focused on helping children develop independent skills in the scientific investigative process. The best way to approach this is to develop the skills in a planned way, giving children increasing independence over the decision-making when carrying out an investigation. It is tempting, as a teacher, to try to support children in ways which enable them to 'get the right answer' in science experiments, but in truth children can learn as well from their mistakes as they do from 'getting it right'. The investigative process, the heart of good teaching, at this stage is discussed elsewhere in this chapter.

In addition, children quickly develop their understanding of science subject knowledge at Key Stages 1 and 2. It is important for teachers to give correct explanations to back up children's practical experience.

Good primary school teaching also includes cross-curricular work, and science learning will often be combined with other subjects, especially design and technology and geography.

Beyond Key Stage 2

Once children start the secondary phase of their education their experience of science changes. Science will be less practical and cross-curricular as learning is increasingly focused on abstract concepts and teaching has to fit in with established secondary phase pedagogies. However, practical science is still a very important part of children's education at this stage.

Assessing science learning

In the past ten years the influence of assessment procedures in the primary phase has had a significant affect on teaching. Good teachers want the pupils in their classes to achieve high standards and make regular progress in their learning. Assessment for learning (AfL) has two main roles and forms in the primary classroom. First, there are assessments that are made by teachers to inform their day-to-day planning of teaching. Second, there are assessments that are made to enable teachers to compare and communicate pupils levels of achievement. The methods of assessment for these two purposes are different. More information about AfL can be found at the comprehensive website www.qca.org.uk/7659.html.

Assessing for teaching

Teachers need to make assessments of their pupils' progress as they teach science topics. These may be in many forms, for example:

- informal notes of children's comments
- assessments against learning objectives
- running records of progress in the investigative progress.

Effective ways of making these kind of teacher assessments will depend on the teacher and the type of lesson as well as on the pupils. Shirley Clarke (2005) gives useful advice on how teachers can make formative assessment useful and meaningful in the primary classroom.

Formal assessment procedures

There are three stages at which children's science learning is formally assessed during the primary phase. The first of these is the Foundation Stage Profile which is completed during the reception year. The second is at the end of Key Stage 1 in the form of teacher assessments against National Curriculum levels. The third is at the end of Key Stage 2 in the form of tests and teacher assessments against National Curriculum levels.

The Foundation Stage profile assesses children's acquisition of skills in the 'Knowledge and understanding of the world' area of learning. These assessments are discussed with parents and used in schools for benchmarking pupils' future progress. The description of a child's attainment at the end of the Foundation Stage is as follows:

> Communicates simple planning for investigations and constructions and makes simple records and evaluations of her/his work. Identifies and names key features and properties, sometimes linking different experiences, observations and events. Begins to explore what it means to belong to a variety of groups and communities. (QCA/DfES 2002: 48)

At the end of Key Stage 1 teachers are required to make an assessment of children's level in science against the National Curriculum level descriptors. These descriptions, printed at the back of the National Curriculum document and online at www.ncaction.org.uk/subjects/science/levels.htm, synthesize the scientific enquiry process and science subject knowledge into one set of level descriptions for science. In the teacher assessments and tests that determine the levels awards to children in science, the assessment is 'weighted' in favour of their skills in the investigative process. Requirements are as follows for the teacher assessment of a National Curriculum level:

> A subject level for science will be calculated automatically when the levels for the individual attainment targets are entered into the school's management information system. Where it is not possible to calculate an overall level because of absence or disapplication from more than one attainment target, the software will generate the code U, unable to determine the attainment target. Weightings remain unchanged from previous years.

> * Scientific enquiry (Sc1) 3
> * Life processes and living things (Sc2) 1
> * Materials and their properties (Sc3) 1
> * Physical processes (Sc4) 1. (QCA 2007)

At the end of both Key Stage 1 and Key Stage 2 teachers will use their records to make an assessment of children's levels of understanding of both subject knowledge and the investigative process. The assessment is weighted 50 per cent of level for scientific enquiry and 50 per cent for subject knowledge. To do this effectively a teacher should keep notes on children's attainment against the National Curriculum level descriptions over the course of their Year 2 in school.

At Key Stage 2, there are two science tests that examine children's understanding of the science enquiry process and subject knowledge. The nature of these tests is described on the QCA website:

Pupils' marks from both tests will be aggregated to calculate their overall science level. Tests A and B have 40 marks each, giving a total of 80 marks.

Pupils are allowed 45 minutes for each science test. Questions may be in the context of any of the science attainment targets and there may also be discrete Sc1 questions.

Teacher assessment will continue to be the only method of assessing aspects of Sc1 that involve practical skills and interpreting and evaluating pupils' own data. (QCA 2007)

The nature of these tests and the use of the data produced is a controversial issue for many teachers. For many years there have been those who disagree with both the principle and the practice of testing pupils during the primary phase. However, it seems unlikely that there will be the political will to abolish these tests in the near future and good teachers need to adapt their practice to make the processes as useful as possible to teaching while trying to keep pupil and teachers' stresses as low as possible.

2

Planning for teaching and learning: the process of scientific enquiry

At the heart of good science teaching and learning is the process of scientific enquiry. It is as important for young children to learn how to investigate scientific ideas as it is for them to learn the subject knowledge. This can be confusing for beginning teachers, especially those who do not have a scientific background. 'Science learning' can mean two things: first, it can be the acquisition of subject knowledge and, second, it can mean learning the process of investigating and experimenting in science.

Experiment or investigate? The processes of science enquiry

The scientific enquiry can be in the form of a guided experiment or an open-ended investigation. An experiment would be a specific scientific activity in search of a particular outcome. An experiment might involve the following:

- a defined process
- a prescribed way of finding out
- observing and comparing results to what was expected
- repeating activities to validate them.

The investigative process can comprise a combination of the following:

- asking and answering questions
- thinking what needs to be done
- planning a 'fair test'
- predicting what might happen
- observing
- exploring
- describing
- explaining and articulating ideas

- collecting and organizing data
- recording and measuring
- hypothesizing about results
- evaluating the process
- drawing conclusions
- assimilating new and existing understandings.

It is important not to view the experimental process and the investigative process as the same thing. They are both important parts of the science enquiry process, but they have different methodologies and are taught in different ways. In an experiment, the teacher will define the processes which the children undertake to find the answer to a prescribed question using a predetermined method. In an investigation, the learning is more open-ended with the children having more opportunity to explore their own ideas. It is not appropriate to make value judgements in terms of teaching about these processes. It is too simplistic to say one is 'better teaching and learning' than the other as they fulfil different purposes. An experiment is likely to give children a practical demonstration of a theory or idea, whereas the investigative process allows children to start with their own ideas.

Science enquiry in the Foundation Stage

There are two early learning goals in the 'Knowledge and understanding of the world' area of learning. These are, like the rest of the Foundation Stage curriculum, set out as skills for the children to learn rather than content or subject knowledge. Table 2.1 gives examples of these. The earlier skills are at the top of the table, and as children's understanding develops they are likely to be able to progress to the skills further down.

The science enquiry process and the National Curriculum

The first attainment target of the science National Curriculum – Science 1 Scientific Enquiry, sets out the investigative and experimental skills that children should learn. They are organized under three headings which, if the children were to work through them in order, would enable the children to undertake a scientific enquiry. These are set out in Table 2.2, with examples of teaching and learning opportunities.

Topics and the QCA scheme of work in science

The teaching of science in many primary schools has been shaped by the QCA scheme of work for science (www.standards.dfes.gov.uk/schemes2/science/?view=get). However since the Primary National Strategy was launched in 2003 there has been a policy to move away from the single-subject teaching this promotes into a more cross-curricular and creative approach to teaching science in schools. At the time of writing, however, the impact of this policy change has been limited in schools (OFSTED 2005a). In reality most primary school teachers are not science specialists and the

Table 2.1 Skills in exploration and investigation in the Foundation Stage

Skill stepping stones from the Foundation Stage guidance	In a Foundation Stage setting children might do this by . . .
Show curiosity and interest by facial expression, movement or sound	Jumping in puddles, running sand through hands, calling an adult to look at a woodlouse in the wildlife area
Explore objects	Playing with playdough, shaping and reshaping it
Show curiosity, observe and manipulate objects	Watching another child on a swing, then having a go themselves, using feet to push
Show an interest in why things happen and how things work	Rolling a car down a slope repeatedly on a toy garage
Describe simple features of objects and events	Talk about what happens when it snows
Sort objects by one function	Choose clothes which will be waterproof to wear outdoors on a rainy day
Examine objects and living things to find out more about them	Study the changes in tadpoles in the school pond
Talk about what is seen and what is happening	Describe what happens to an ice lolly on a hot day
Notice and comment on patterns	Explore paint-mixing, noticing how more watery paint takes longer to dry
Investigate objects and materials by using all of their senses as appropriate	Taste, smell and feel different fruits and describe them
Show an awareness of change	Make bread, commenting on how it rises and changes when baked
Look closely at similarities, differences, patterns and change	Observe the changes in the weather throughout the year – comment on changes
Find out about, and identify, some features of living things, objects and events they observe	Learn the names of some of the plants and animals in the school wildlife area
Ask questions about why things happen and how things work	Ask questions about the differences between people, animals and plants they observe

QCA scheme, or other pre-prepared science materials are used. In the 2004/05 OFSTED report into primary science, these limited changes are noted:

> Science is still taught in most schools as a separate subject. QCA research shows that this is so in 64% of schools in Years 1 and 2, 77% in Years 3 and 4 and 79% in Years 5 and 6. The impact of the Primary National Strategy (PNS) on science has been slight. (OFSTED 2005b)

Table 2.2 The scientific enquiry process and the National Curriculum for Key Stages 1 and 2

	Objectives from the National Curriculum	Examples from the primary classroom
Key Stage 1 programme of study	*Ideas and evidence in science* 1) Pupils should be taught that it is important to collect evidence by making observations and measurements when trying to answer a question	Keep records on the growth of different plants over a term
	Investigative skills 2) Pupils should be taught to: Planning a) ask questions b) use first-hand experience and simple information sources to answer questions c) think about what might happen before deciding what to do d) recognize when a test or comparison is unfair	Plan a fair test to investigate how to stop foods decaying. Consider what they know about foods beforehand and identify and control the variables
	Obtaining and presenting evidence e) follow simple instructions to control the risks to themselves and to others f) explore, using the senses of sight, hearing, smell, touch and taste as appropriate, and make and record observations and measurements g) communicate what happened in a variety of ways, including using ICT	Over a series of investigations be able to choose the best ways to collect and present data, given some examples by the teacher, for example: a table, a picture, a digital photograph
	Considering evidence and evaluating h) make simple comparisons and identify simple patterns or associations i) compare what happened with what they expected would happen, and try to explain it, drawing on their knowledge and understanding j) review their work and explain what they did to others.	Talk about what happened during experiments, noticing patterns and offering simple explanations, for example: the larger parachute took longer to float to the ground because there was more air pushing up inside it
Key Stage 2 programme of study	*Ideas and evidence in science* 1) Pupils should be taught: a) that science is about thinking creatively to try to explain how living and nonliving things work, and to establish links between causes and effects b) that it is important to test ideas using evidence from observation and measurement	Begin to offer hypotheses about simple scientific ideas they encounter, for example: what happens to various sweets when they are put in the mouth – melt, dissolve, and so on

(Continued)

Table 2.2 (Continued)

Objectives from the National Curriculum	Examples from the primary classroom
Investigative skills 2) Pupils should be taught to: Planning a) ask questions that can be investigated scientifically and decide how to find answers b) consider what sources of information, including first-hand experience and a range of other sources, they will use to answer questions c) think about what might happen or try things out when deciding what to do, what kind of evidence to collect, and what equipment and materials to use d) make a fair test or comparison by changing one factor and observing or measuring the effect while keeping other factors the same	Be able to identify the variables in planning a simple test or experiment, for example know that to test the best growing conditions for a tomato plant only one aspect of the growing conditions should be changed in each example
Obtaining and presenting evidence e) use simple equipment and materials appropriately and take action to control risks f) make systematic observations and measurements, including the use of ICT for datalogging g) check observations and measurements by repeating them where appropriate h) use a wide range of methods, including diagrams, drawings, tables, bar charts, line graphs and ICT, to communicate data in an appropriate and systematic manner	Use a datalogger to log the sounds made by various musical instruments, check that the instruments are being tested at the same distance and played in the same way. Use the graphs created to draw explanatory diagrams
Considering evidence and evaluating i) make comparisons and identify simple patterns or associations in their own observations and measurements or other data j) use observations, measurements or other data to draw conclusions k) decide whether these conclusions agree with any prediction made and/or whether they enable further predictions to be made l) use their scientific knowledge and understanding to explain observations, measurements or other data or conclusions m) review their work and the work of others and describe its significance and limitations.	When talking afterwards about an investigation, consider what happened and draw conclusions about how effective and fair the test was, for example: after using a datalogger to compare heart rates after exercise, think about the other factors which effect heart rate

But the report goes on to note some cross-curricular links are being made:

> There are now more often references to literacy in schemes of work but less frequently are opportunities for numeracy work identified, as discussed below. However, as teachers have become increasingly confident they have incorporated more cross-curricular elements and subject links into their science teaching. For example, there is now greater attention to the ways in which science can contribute to pupils' spiritual, moral, social and cultural development, and useful links are made to design and technology and geography. (OFSTED 2005b)

Whichever approach teachers take to planning to teach science effectively, they should ensure that:

- learning opportunities are as practical as possible
- objectives in terms of both scientific enquiry and subject knowledge are clear
- teachers' explanations are clear
- cross-curricular links are utilized
- recording of the activities is meaningful and adds something to the process
- over the course of a topic there are a range of practical activities, some of which give pupils opportunities to investigate their own ideas.

3

Finding help with teaching and learning in science on the Internet

The Internet is both a blessing and a curse as far as science education goes. There are a variety of really helpful websites for science teachers, some of which are listed below.

Online curriculum documents

Curriculum documents are available in printed form and most schools keep these. They are also available to buy in hard copy through bookshops. However, the programme of study for each subject and at each key stage can be accessed free on the Internet through www.nc.uk.net. The advantage of using the National Curriculum online is that embedded in the pages are hyperlinks to support and advice for teachers, such as links to inclusion advice and ideas about how to include information and communications technology (ICT) in teaching activities. To support developing assessment practice, the level descriptions for each subject are also available online alongside the programme of study. The documents can also be accessed as .pdf or .rtf files at www.nc.uk.net/nc_resources/html/download.shtml.

The QCA Scheme of Work is available on the standards site at www.standards.dfes.gov.uk/schemes3/. There is also advice about how to adapt and develop the schemes of work to meet the needs of the school.

The Association for Science Education

The Association for Science Education is an organization for those who teach science and it is a useful source of advice and help for members. Details can be found at www.ase.org.uk/. As well as courses and publications, the website is a useful source of downloadable booklets and information about subjects such as inclusion in science teaching and learning outside the classroom.

Science at home and in school

The BBC website provides a wide range of good quality and reliable science content of the web. Using this site with pupils helps to make useful links between learning at home and learning at school.

The human body site (www.bbc.co.uk/science/humanbody/) allows children to learn about their bodies in interactive ways as well as being a useful source of facts. In setting homework about the body (or other science topics), teachers can use the BBC website as a source of information.

The BBC site www.bbc.co.uk/sn/ is also a useful repository of up-to-date science information, such as pictures of recent events like eclipses or weather events. The regular Springwatch television series is also supported by extensive web-based materials which can be used in environmental projects.

The BBC schools website (www.bbc.co.uk/schools/websites/4_11/site/science. shtml) is also very useful to teachers, as it links to BBC programmes as well as to useful teaching materials, simulations and revision guides for pupils.

The quality of the games and activities is particularly high and many teachers use these on their interactive whiteboards as a way of introducing scientific ideas or assessing pupils' learning at the end of a lesson.

Other useful websites

The *New Scientist* website, linked to the publication, is a useful archive of science questions and answers. These are designed for adults, but could be useful to teachers with specific science questions. www.newscientist.com/lastword.ns.

Dr Universe is an American based Internet site which answers questions in a more child friendly way. www.wsu.edu/DrUniverse/Contents.html.

A comprehensive source of science information is wikipedia. Although this is editable, it is usually accurate and teachers may find its definitions useful when researching Science topics. http://en.wikipedia.org/wiki/Main_Page.

There are also some useful websites that can support learning in specific topics. Useful ones for popular primary school topics include the following. Most of these websites contain dense text that might be unsuitable for primary school children. They also have useful images and, in some cases, education resources which are specifically designed for children.

The Food Standards Agency for information about human **nutrition** and food science. www.food.gov.uk/.

The National Aeronautics and Space Administration (NASA) for information about space topics and space travel. www.nasa.gov/.

The Royal Society for the Prevention of Cruelty to Animals (RSPCA) for information about animals and animal welfare. www.rspca.org.uk/education.

SECTION 2

Subject knowledge for primary school teachers

4

Life processes

National Curriculum: Attainment Target Sc2, Strand 1 (KS1: 2.1a–1c, KS2: 2.1a–1c)
QCA Schemes of Work: Units 1A, 2A, 3A, 4A and 6A

Curriculum requirements

Life processes are taught discretely as part of the Key Stage 1 (KS1) and Key Stage 2 (KS2) programmes of study, while at Key Stage 3 (KS3) and Key Stage 4 (KS4) the various life processes are studied in more detail in the context of other topics (for example, green plants and humans as organisms) and through the idea of **cells** and their functions. The amount of subject knowledge here is relatively small but introduces the important processes that unite living things.

The National Curriculum for Science programme of study states that at KS1 pupils should be taught the differences between things that are living and things that have never been alive; that animals, including humans, move, feed, grow, use their senses and reproduce; to relate life processes to animals and **plants** found in the local **environment**. At KS2 this is developed and they should be taught that the life processes common to humans and other animals include nutrition, movement, **growth** and **reproduction**; that the life processes common to plants include growth, nutrition and reproduction; to make links between life processes in familiar animals and plants and the environments in which they are found.

Cells: a brief introduction to the building blocks of life

Although cells are not explicitly mentioned in the KS1 and KS2 programmes of study, they are fundamental to all living things and, as such need to be mentioned early on.

The simplest of living things consist of just one, single cell, while more complex organisms, such as humans are multicellular. Thus the cell is regarded as the smallest unit of life capable of an independent existence. Figure 4.1 shows a simple version

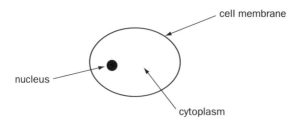

Figure 4.1 Simplified diagram of a typical animal cell

of a typical animal cell that will be familiar to all pupils by the end of KS3 (the cells that line the inside of our cheeks are very much like this and it is common for secondary school pupils to extract and look at their own cheek cells under a microscope). The name cell originates from the seventeenth-century observations made by Robert Hooke, a contemporary and rival of Isaac Newton. When studying cork under his microscope, he likened the small spaces he saw to the cells in which monks lived in a monastery.

Figure 4.1 shows three basic parts to the cell:

the cell membrane – which lets substances the cell requires in and waste out

the cytoplasm – a jelly-like substance which is where the processes occur that keep the cell alive; for example, **respiration**

the nucleus – the cell's control centre where the genetic information is kept as DNA (*Note*: this often erroneously described as 'the brain of the cell'; this is not an idea that should be encouraged as it creates a misconception that pupils can carry with them for the rest of their school life – the notion of a control centre should be perfectly adequate, without the need to refer to a brain – far more complex than a cell nucleus!).

Not all cells, of course, are like this. Complex organisms are made of many cells of differing types, each with their own particular job. Groups of the same cells bound together are known as tissues (such as muscles and nerves), while organs are composed of a number of tissues working together for a particular function or functions.

Cells with different functions have special features that allow them to perform that function (for example, sperm cells have tails so that they can swim to meet an egg cell ovum). Plants have cells that can also produce food by photosynthesis (see Chapter 6, 'Green plants').

Living or not? The life processes

It is generally regarded that there are seven signs of life. That is, there are seven things that all living things (organisms) have in common (from bacteria to plants to animals) and the question as to whether something is living or not is tested against these seven life processes. They are:

1   Nutrition/**feeding**.

2   Growth.

3   Movement.

4   Respiration/**breathing**.

5   Reproduction.

6   **Sensitivity**.

7   **Excretion**.

Some pupils may suggest death as one of these processes, but although living things will eventually die, this cannot really count as a sign of *life*. Life processes are discussed briefly here and in more depth in the context of plants and animals in Chapters 5 and 6.

1 Nutrition

All living things need to take in substances to survive. Animals feed to obtain most of this nutrition (although many can produce some nutrients, for example, humans can produce vitamin D in their skin, when it is exposed to sunlight). Plants obtain their nutrition from the air and the soil. The process of photosynthesis in plants enables them to produce a basic form of food, glucose, and they obtain minerals through their roots from the soil (see Chapter 6 for more detail here). All living things need nutrition to provide them with the raw materials they need to grow, produce new cells, replace old cells and produce important chemicals for cell processes. When organisms are deprived of essential nutrients they develop symptoms of this deficiency. Examples are plants becoming yellow through lack of the mineral magnesium that is needed to produce chlorophyll, and humans developing scurvy when they have a lack of vitamin C in their diet. Essential nutrients are those that an organism cannot produce itself, so it needs to obtain them from another source. For instance, humans need to eat a variety of sources of protein to obtain the raw materials (called amino acids) they need to make the proteins they need for their bodies. We can make some of these amino acids, but not the *essential* ones. There are also some essential fatty acids (like omega 3) that we need to obtain by eating organisms that produce these fatty acids themselves.

2 Growth

All living things grow, even when they are mature. Immature organisms grow new cells to enable them to grow to their mature size. This is achieved through cell division. The nucleus of a cell contains the genetic information necessary to produce others of its kind. When new cells form, this nucleus makes a copy of itself and then divides to form two new cells. This type of cell division is known as mitosis (see Figure 4.2). These new cells may be used simply for growth or to provide new cells to replace old and damaged ones.

Even mature organisms show growth, for example, human fingernails and hair.

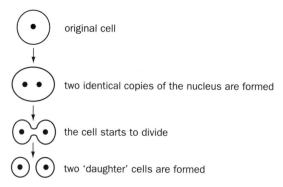

original cell

two identical copies of the nucleus are formed

the cell starts to divide

two 'daughter' cells are formed

Figure 4.2 Cell division (mitosis) simplified

3 Movement

All living things move to some extent and this is perhaps most obvious with animals. Plants, however, do move as well, for instance, when buds open. Many plants also follow the path of the Sun through the sky during the day. Movement is important for gathering nutrition and to evade **predators**. Movement can also be internal, such as the movement of the heart muscles or the muscles that push food through the digestive system. The energy for much of this movement comes from respiration.

4 Respiration

Respiration is a means of releasing energy from food (see also Chapter 6). Respiration occurs in the mitochondria – structures that are found in the cytoplasm of cells. Aerobic respiration requires oxygen and is the reason why humans and other animals breathe, to extract the oxygen they need from air and to get rid of the carbon dioxide produced by respiration. The food normally used is the sugar, glucose. Aerobic respiration can be summarized with a chemical equation:

$$\text{glucose} + \text{oxygen} \longrightarrow \text{carbon dioxide} + \text{water} \quad [+ \text{energy}]$$
$$C_6H_{12}O_6 + 6\,O_2 \longrightarrow 6CO_2 + 6H_2O \quad\quad\quad\quad [+ \text{energy}]$$

The energy released is used for a variety of chemical and other processes, including digestion and movement. So called *warm-blooded* animals (homeotherms) use some of this energy to maintain their body **temperature**. It should be remembered here that plants respire aerobically as well. They do this all the time, but during the day, when they are photosynthesizing, they produce more than enough oxygen to provide what they need for respiration.

Organisms can also respire anaerobically (without oxygen). This releases less energy than aerobic respiration and so organisms that can do both will tend to respire aerobically as much as possible. Humans can respire both aerobically and anaerobically. When we exercise, the oxygen supply can be insufficient to supply our energy needs through aerobic respiration alone. Hence we start to respire anaerobically as well. This can be shown with another chemical equation:

$$\text{glucose} \longrightarrow \text{lactic acid} \quad [+ \text{energy}]$$
$$C_6H_{12}O_6 \longrightarrow 2C_3H_6O_3 \quad [+ \text{energy}]$$

The lactic acid produced builds up in our muscles and starts to make them ache. Once we rest, we only need to use oxygen at a lower rate again. Reacting further with oxygen to produce carbon dioxide and water, releasing more energy and completing the respiration breaks down the lactic acid. Panting after exercise is the body's way of obtaining enough oxygen to remove the lactic acid made, and the oxygen needed to do this is known as the oxygen debt.

A number of organisms only respire anaerobically, such as yeast. Yeast (a type of fungus) obtains energy from glucose without oxygen, to produce carbon dioxide and ethanol (alcohol). This is what occurs during fermentation:

$$\text{glucose} \longrightarrow \text{alcohol} + \text{carbon dioxide} \quad [+ \text{energy}]$$
$$C_6H_{12}O_6 \longrightarrow 2C_2H_5OH + 2CO_2 \quad [+ \text{energy}]$$

It is this process that we exploit in bread-making and brewing. As the yeast feeds on sugars released from the flour, bubbles of carbon dioxide get trapped in bread dough, making it rise (the alcohol is evaporated off during the baking process). When beer is brewing, the energy released makes it feel warm and, when making champagne, some of the yeast is transferred to the bottle to allow a second fermentation, the carbon dioxide made forming the bubbles in the wine (the source of food here are sugars in the malted beer barley or the grape juice used).

Breathing is how organisms take in air for respiration. In the strictest sense this is really only limited to animals with lungs. The lungs are the organs that some animals possess (mammals, birds, reptiles and adult amphibians) to extract oxygen from the air and to release carbon dioxide into the air. Other organisms exchange oxygen for carbon dioxide in other ways (for instance, the gills of fish). While this still might be thought of as a kind of breathing, it is not really an appropriate term for organisms like plants and single-celled organisms such as bacteria. As such it is more correct to say that respiration is one of the seven life processes rather than breathing, which is probably why it is not named explicitly in the KS1 and KS2 programmes of study, as the notion of respiration is difficult for younger children to relate to – you are aware that you are breathing, but not that you are respiring.

5 Reproduction

Without reproduction living things would not survive more than one generation. Single-celled organisms such as bacteria reproduce by simple cell division (see the section on 'Growth' above). This type of reproduction is known as asexual reproduction, where there is only one parent organism. Plants can also reproduce asexually as well as sexually (see Chapter 6), where two parent organisms are needed – male and female. The purpose of reproduction is to maintain the population of a particular

species. As living things get older they function less well and show signs of the negative effects of their environment such as damage to tissues, and so on. Reproduction allows a copy of the genetic material of an organism to be passed on to a new generation. Indeed, many scientists believe that the aim of reproduction is simply to ensure the survival of DNA. More on human reproduction will be covered in Chapter 5, 'Humans and other animals'.

6 Sensitivity

Sensitivity is an important function of organisms that helps them to survive in their environment. Plants are sensitive to gravity, hence their roots grow downwards and they can obtain water (for that is where it will usually be found). They are also sensitive to light, which is why their leaves point towards the light. In these cases gravity and light are stimuli. Stimuli are often chemical in nature as well, such as the **gas molecules** our noses are stimulated by when we smell something. The five human senses that we all come to learn have helped to ensure our survival over thousands of generations:

sight	– to see danger; to see prey
hearing	– to be alerted to predators/prey
smell	– to be alerted to predators/prey; to avoid, potentially dangerous, food that has gone off
taste	– avoid eating food that has gone off; to spit out poisons
touch/feeling	– to know when we have injured ourselves/to know when our body temperature is in danger of rising/falling.

7 Excretion

Excretion is simply the removal of waste. All organisms produce waste substances that they need to get rid of. The build up of such waste can be hazardous to the cell and the organism it is part of. Examples of this include the removal of carbon dioxide made by respiration. Carbon dioxide is weakly acidic and if it were allowed to build up the resulting increase in acidity would affect the chemistry of the cell and the structure of proteins within it. Humans and other mammals produce a substance called urea in the liver when dealing with nitrogen-containing compounds such as the amino acids produced when we digest protein. This urea would slowly poison us if it were allowed to build up, so is removed by the kidneys, mixed with water and other waste chemicals and passed out of the body as urine.

Strictly, excretion is the removal of waste from *cells*, that is, the removal of unwanted chemicals produced *in cells*. Thus the removal of faeces from the body is, strictly, not excretion. This is because faeces contain the remains of the food taken into the digestive system of an animal, which the animal could not digest. As such it has not been produced in a cell or even entered one. The correct term for the removal of this undigested waste from the body of an animal is egestion. Indeed, if we consider the digestive tract as, essentially, a long space inside us stretching from the mouth to the anus, the undigested food that leaves has never truly entered our body.

Life processes in humans and other animals

Before we start here there is one point that must be made absolutely clear, namely, that *humans are animals*. It is not surprising that children get this fact wrong from their everyday experiences, but it is a misconception that should be sorted out early on.

Teaching activity

To get across to younger children the idea that humans are animals, try sorting activities with groups of plastic animals or pictures that include humans. When giving children pictures or plastic animals to sort, always make sure that you are giving them the right animals to meet the criteria of the sort. For instance, sort by the following criteria which emphasize the similarities (and the differences) between humans and other animals:

- has legs from no legs
- has babies from lays eggs
- has fur from has scales.

The focus at KS1 is that animals, including humans all move, feed, grow, use their senses and reproduce. This is the same at KS2, although the wording used implies that we see these as actual processes, hence the use of a term like movement rather than move and nutrition rather than feed. Although, of course, one can refer to the other life processes, that is, breathing/respiration and excretion, they are not highlighted in the programme of study probably because they are more complex. It is important to recognize that these are processes that *animals* clearly demonstrate; hence it is vital to pupils' understanding of what an animal is that we use examples that encompass as many different animals as possible. Good examples to highlight here are fish, insects and other invertebrates. Children often only consider mammals and vertebrates, although fish (which are vertebrates) often present a problem here. Invertebrates are often also not regarded by children as animals, so using these as examples is useful too. Woodlice are often a good choice for study as they are easy to find and demonstrate the five processes implicit in the scheme of study well.

Teaching activity

Set up habitats for invertebrates in the classroom, woodlice and worms work particularly well. Children should research the animals' needs before setting up the **habitats** and bringing the animals in from the wild. Children should be encouraged to respect these animals and treat them kindly and carefully. When the project is over the animals should be returned to the wild where they were found.

Life processes in plants

Plants also present a problem in the minds of children, who do not necessarily regard them as living. This, again, should be stressed as early as possible, despite the fact that it is only in the KS2 programme of study that the life processes of plants are studied in greater detail. The focus here is on growth, nutrition and reproduction, and this is perhaps best demonstrated by the pupils actually growing plants from **seed**, nurturing them, watching them develop **flowers** and then the next generation's seeds; something that can be done quite effectively with plants such as beans. Nutrition is, perhaps the hardest idea here as we cannnot actually see the plants make their food, but we can emphasize the fact that plants develop leaves, which contain the food they produce (by photosynthesis – see Chapter 6) and animals in turn eat as a source of food and that seeds contain a food store which is why animals, including humans, eat seeds, nuts, pulses, and so on. The role of soil, compost and fertilizers (natural and man-made) can also help the idea of plants gaining nutrition from other sources. Indeed, a Venus flytrap is a nice example of plants obtaining nutrition from other sources.

Identifying life processes in the local environment

Early on in their education pupils will find it easier to relate ideas to their everyday experiences, so it is good to look at the local environment when exploring life processes. Many pupils will have pets or have a friend or family member who has a pet. Many of us have plants in our homes and a garden, which are all sources of experience. At school a class may also contain plants and pets that can be related to. Some schools are lucky enough to have gardens, a nature garden area or even a pond. Even without these things it is possible to seek out living things in the school environment, be it weeds between paving stones, mosses and lichens on walls, or insects and other invertebrates under stones. All these are good places for study in the local environment. Consideration can be given as to why certain things live in certain areas and relate this to living processes and, conversely, why living things are less abundant in other areas.

Linking life processes to an organism's environment

At KS2, work on the local environment can be extended to areas outside pupils' direct experience. Children will be aware of many different types of animal and plant at this stage and have some awareness of the environment that some of these organisms live in. Living things are adapted to the environment they live in, their *habitats*.

Adaptation

The word *adaptation* can be misinterpreted if it is not fully understood. Organisms do not adapt themselves to their environment, rather they have developed special features (adaptations) by the process of **evolution** that mean they can survive better in a particular habitat. The French scientist Jean-Baptiste Lamarck, who invented the word *biology*, believed that animals actually developed their adaptations themselves, then passed these advantages on to their offspring. The most celebrated of these 'Lamarckisms' is the lengthening of the giraffe's neck so that it was able to reach food in the tall trees of its habitat in Africa. This is an idea that has persisted from time to time and stems from a misunderstanding of the evolutionary process – indeed, Soviet

Russia officially embraced this idea in favour of Darwin's ideas on evolution until the 1960s. Darwin's theory of evolution states that organisms do develop adaptations but essentially by chance. Darwin's theories are underpinned by the idea of *natural selection*, often referred to as *survival of the fittest*. Darwin proposed that organisms change over millions of years. They do not adapt themselves, rather some individuals will be born with certain differences and if these differences prove to be an advantage in some way then these organisms will have an edge and be better able to compete with others. This will increase their chances of survival and, so, their chances of reproduction. These advantages will then be passed on to their own offspring who will, in turn, be better competitors themselves. As time goes by, these gradual changes develop into the adaptations that we see, often though they may only really become an advantage when the environment undergoes dramatic change and suddenly these differences will help those that have them to survive better that those that do not. For instance, some birds may have been born with slight webbing on their feet. This may have increased over many years from one generation to the next. Perhaps then the environment changed and became wetter. Those birds with the webbing will now have an advantage as they can swim better through the water that has appeared than those without the webbing. Thus the web-footed birds are better at getting food in this changed environment and are more likely to survive and reproduce (they are, inadvertently better adapted to this new environment), while those that do not have this special feature will find it harder to compete and may die out or move to a new habitat.

It is possible to discuss the adaptations of a wide range of organisms that pupils do not necessarily have direct experience of but that they know about from other sources. Fish have gills that allow them to breathe underwater, while many terrestrial animals have lungs. Indeed, amphibians have external gills (that can be seen) in their initial phase of growth (tadpoles, newtpoles, and so on), but lose them later when they mature and start to live out of the water and use lungs to obtain much of their oxygen. Birds have developed wings to allow them to move around more in search of food, evade predators and nest in trees; however, some have lost the ability to fly when the need for wings has become less important, for example, the dodo which, before European humans arrived in Mascarene Island, near Madagascar, had no natural predators to evade. 'Warm-blooded' animals that live in colder climates tend to be larger than their relatives in warmer climates, as a larger size means they are better at retaining body heat.

It is possible to look at examples of adaptations and relate them directly to the seven life processes (Table 4.1).

Humans and adaptations

It is, of course, quite possible to discuss the adaptations of humans to their environment, for instance, darker skin colour to enable better survival in habitats where exposure to sunlight is greater (this reduces the harmful effect of ultraviolet rays on the skin). However, care should be taken as the intellectual ability of humans has meant that we are able to survive in environments that we are not best suited to. In essence this is an adaptation, as our ability to reason and solve problems has evolved to allow us to colonize even the most hostile of habitats. Most of the ways in which we

Table 4.1 Relating adaptations to life processes

Life process	Examples of adaptations
Nutrition/feeding	Giraffe necks; different types of bird beak; cows can obtain nutrition from grass but humans cannot
Growth	Plants grow towards the light; many animals grow and mature quickly
Movement	Predators can move quickly to catch prey and prey can run fast to evade predators; some plants can follow the movement of the Sun during the day
Reproduction	Short life cycles to maintain population; shells around birds eggs and jelly around amphibians eggs for protection; internal fertilization to increase chance of successful fertilization; more offspring produced than will survive to maturity
Sensitivity	Plant roots responding to gravity; good sight, sound and smell for predators and prey
Excretion	Animals in hot climates producing solid urine/faeces to avoid losing too much water
Respiration/ breathing	Gills in fish; aquatic mammals' ability to hold their breath for long periods of time; use of anaerobic respiration when oxygen supply is low (for example, when running to evade a predator)

have adapted to such places are not physical. For instance, we can survive under water for short periods using diving equipment and have developed tools and agriculture that help us to farm for food. The major adaptation of humans is that we take much longer than any other organisms to reach maturity (that is, there is a long time between birth and the ability to reproduce), to allow us to develop the use of our brains through education. We will find in other areas of biology that consideration of humans and their behaviour is very different to other animals so caution is needed when considering humans in natural processes.

Links to teaching

More teaching activities

Good plants to grow in the classroom include sunflowers, tomatoes, strawberries, beans and houseplants such as spider plants. The best practice is to grow these throughout the year in the classroom rather than waiting for a 'plants topic' to occur in the curriculum map.

Animals find the classroom environment stressful and, although it is good practice to bring animals into the classroom to study, it is important for teachers to encourage respect for *all* animals. Therefore if woodlice, tadpoles or other invertebrates are borrowed from the wildlife area, they should be looked after and replaced as soon as possible.

Taking note of the changes of the seasons is important in learning about life processes. It is also important to compare different habitats and, where possible, visit woods, forests, beaches and lakes.

Other things to do and try

- Show pupils pictures of a number of living and non-living things. Ask them to sort them into living and non-living, justifying their choices.
- Walk around your school and search for living and non-living things.
- Show pupils a video clip of plants moving in response to sunlight.
- Using pictures or models pupils could match 'mothers to babies' (adult animals to their offspring).
- Show pupils pictures or plastic models of a range of animals and get them to look for their adapted features and think about why they have them.

TOP TEACHING TIP

Because plants and animals take a long time to change and grow, it's important to take opportunities to learn about them throughout the school year. Short topics on living things can be important in focusing children on the ideas but they need to experience them throughout the year.

Some common misconceptions

- Plants are not living.
- Plants do not move.
- Plants make food from the Sun.
- Plants get food from the soil.
- Humans are not animals.
- Fish and invertebrates are not animals.
- Adaptations occur because an organism has to survive in a particular habitat.
- Organisms which look alike superficially are the same biologically, for example, worms and snakes might look similar but are very different biologically.

AMAZING FACT

As with all science, there are exceptions to general rules. Most plants have roots and need some sort of soil to grow. One interesting and unusual plant is an 'air plant' that has no roots and lives without soil. These plants, from the **genus** *Tillandsia*, get what they need from the air around them.

5

Humans and other animals

National Curriculum: Attainment Target Sc2, Strand 2 (KS1: 2.2a–2g, KS2: 2.2a–2h)

QCA Schemes of Work: Units 1A, 2A, 2B, 3A, 4A, 5A, 6A and 6B

Curriculum requirements

Humans as organisms are taught at all key stages of the National Curriculum. At KS1 and KS2 this is in the context of *humans as animals* and considers humans and other animals together. Currently in the KS3 and KS4 programmes of study, humans as organisms is dealt with more discretely and, as a result, in more detail. Even in light of the changes at KS4 and the proposed changes at KS3, the importance of human biology is unlikely to diminish at these later key stages. The content at KS1 and KS2 is quite large, builds on the content of life processes and is another important basis for further study.

The National Curriculum for Science programme of study states that at KS1 pupils should be taught to recognize and compare the main external parts of the bodies of humans and other animals; that humans and other animals need food and water to stay alive; that taking exercise and eating the right types and amounts of food help humans to keep healthy; about the role of drugs as medicines; how to treat animals with care and sensitivity; that humans and other animals can produce offspring and that these offspring grow into adults; about the senses that enable humans and other animals to be aware of the world around them.

At KS2 the various strands of study are divided up more discretely into the five key themes of *nutrition*, where they are taught about the functions and care of teeth, the need for food for activity and growth and the importance of an adequate and varied diet for health; *circulation*, where they are taught that the heart acts as a pump to circulate the blood through vessels around the body (including through the lungs) and about the effect of exercise and rest on pulse rate; *movement*, where they are taught that humans and some other animals have skeletons and muscles to support and protect their bodies and to help them to move; *growth and reproduction*, where they are taught about the main stages of the human life cycle; and *health* where they are taught about the effects on the human body of tobacco, alcohol and other drugs, and how these relate to their personal health and about the importance of exercise for good health.

The main external parts of the bodies of humans and other animals

From the outset it is important for pupils to realize that humans *are* animals and, despite any differences, humans share many characteristics with other animals.

Indeed, it is these similarities and differences that are used to identify and distinguish different types of animal and how they are classified. Again, the distinction between what is meant by living and non-living is important here as well (see Chapter 4, 'Life processes').

The main parts of the human body include features such as limbs, parts of limbs, the head, the thorax (chest), the abdomen (area below the chest) and the sense organs (ear, eye, tongue, nose and skin). These may then be compared with other animals. This will be easier when considering other mammals and may become more difficult with other animals such as invertebrates. Pupils may not realize that wings are, in fact, modified limbs or that the tail and fins replace the limbs in fish.

The use of pictures and models may be useful here, as will other pupils in the class when they compare each other. The latter will also help pupils to realize that even the same types of animal have differences. Obvious differences between humans are eye, hair and skin colour. It can later be emphasized that differences also occur between other animals of the same species, for instance the difference between the coats of dogs and cats. Pupils should be asked to communicate these ideas. This can be done verbally, through model-making, annotation of pictures and drawing and annotating their own pictures. Also, use can be made of actual animals to help in this process, either by bringing them into the classroom, observing them in their natural habitats or through visits to farms and zoos.

Treating animals with care and sensitivity

A number of children will have pets of their own, or may encounter animals as part of their everyday lives in other ways (for example, by living on a farm). They will already be aware of the idea that we, as a society care for certain animals; feeding them, ensuring their health, and so on. However, they are probably also aware that there are some animals that humans do not seem to care for and may even harm. Sometimes this harm will be an innocent act, such as inadvertently killing a worm when gardening or accidentally treading on a snail after rainfall. Sometimes, however, the harm will be a deliberate act, such as killing ants, rats and garden pests. Because of this children may already have their own ideas on the 'value' of certain animals over others.

As such we are dealing with important moral issues here. As far as teaching science occurs it is important to realize that, more often than not, scientists are passive observers of living things. This is seen in wildlife programmes where injured animals are not treated by their human observers. However, it is also important to teach children that all animals have a right to life and this is especially true when we take them from their natural habitat to study them, for instance, when pond-dipping or examining the behaviour of invertebrates in **leaf** litter. At no point should we deliberately attempt to harm such animals and this includes ensuring their safe return to their natural habitat as soon as possible. This may, of course, be in spite of what they have learnt out of the school environment. Advice and support is available from the Royal Society for the Prevention of Cruelty to Animals (RSPCA) at www.rspca.org.uk

Life processes

Nutrition

The general role of nutrition for all living things has been discussed in Chapter 4 of this book. As far as the KS1 programme of study is concerned the emphasis is on food and water as vital for life for all animals (including humans) and the role that a good diet has in one's health. Most (if not all) will appreciate that animals cannot stay alive without food or water, but quite why that is the case is another issue. They will also be aware that other animals need food and water for the same reasons, and this will be very obvious to those that have pets of their own. It will be less obvious how certain invertebrates such as woodlice feed, although many will know how spiders trap in their webs the food they eat.

Different animals obtain their nutrition from different sources. **Herbivores** feed only on plant material, often the leaves which are packed with starch made from the glucose produced by photosynthesis. It is often a lengthy process digesting the nutrients from plant matter, which is itself of fairly low nutritional content compared with animal matter. As such, large herbivores are grazing animals that spend much of their life eating. **Carnivores** feed only on other animals and may go for long periods of time between meals as their food is rich in nutrients. Often the distinction between carnivores and herbivores is simplified to those that eat *meat* and those that do not, although this can create confusion later (meat essentially being muscular tissue) and it is best to avoid the use of this word. **Omnivores** are animals that obtain nutrition from both plant and animal matter. Humans and pigs are good examples of omnivores, although this can create confusion if the subject of vegetarianism is brought up. Humans have the ability to make choices about what they eat, however as a species we are all omnivores.

Food is essential for growth, for energy, for movement and for staying healthy. This is true of all animals. In addition, mammals and birds use a lot of the energy content of their food to maintain their body temperature. The main nutritional constituents of food are carbohydrates, proteins, fats (or lipids), vitamins, minerals and water. The main functions of these nutrients is summarized in Table 5.1.

In addition, some foods contain a lot of *fibre*, which is made from complex carbohydrates such as cellulose. Some animals (such as humans) cannot digest this fibre, but some (such as cows) can. As food is digested the **particles** become so small that they become dissolved and it is difficult for this **liquid** to pass along the digestive tract. In humans the fibre provides solid material to help the digesting food to move through the digestive system.

Table 5.1 The functions of the essential nutrients in humans

Nutrient	Function	Good sources
Carbohydrates	Energy	Sugary foods such as fruits and jams; starchy foods such as bread, pasta and rice
Proteins	Growth and repair of body tissues	Meat, fish, soya, eggs
Fats/lipids	Energy, insulation	Dairy products, eggs, lard, margarine, vegetable oils
Minerals	Each mineral has a specific function such as *iron* for producing red blood cells; *calcium* for production of bones and teeth; *sodium* to maintain blood pressure	*Iron* from red meat and dark green vegetables such as spinach; *calcium* from dairy products; *sodium* from salt
Vitamins	Each vitamin has a specific function such a *vitamin C* to help produce certain body tissues; *B vitamins* for growth; *vitamin D* to help bone formation	*Vitamin C* from citrus fruit and cabbage; *B vitamins* from yeast and wheat products; *vitamin D* from eggs and cod liver oil
Water	Water has a variety of functions such as digestion, temperature regulation through sweating, transporting substances around the body, enabling chemical reactions to occur in the body, and so on	Most foods contain some water, although the best source is simply drinking water

A healthy diet comprises a range of foods that provide all these essential nutrients in the amounts needed by an individual. Too much of one nutrient can lead to health problems, as can too little (malnutrition). The actual quantities needed vary from organism to organism and from individual to individual. There is some government guidance on suitable levels of vitamins and minerals and general healthy eating (the Food Standards Agency website, www.food.gov.uk, provides some useful data). A person with a very active job will require more energy-rich foods such as carbo-hydrates; a pregnant mother may require more iron and folic acid in her diet. Children are still growing and so need a healthy, balanced diet to ensure that growth is not hampered. There are many health issues here, especially in the developed world at present for example, obesity in our children. These are partly dietary issues, such as the high levels of sugars and fats in many youngsters' diets, but also issues relating to exercise which is discussed further in the 'Health' section of this chapter. However it is important to remember that there is nothing wrong with eating some of the more controversial foods (such as fried foods, sweets, fizzy drinks, and so on) provided that they are *part* of a balanced diet and not eaten exclusively and to excess.

At KS2 there is also a requirement for pupils to learn about the function and care of teeth. It is important that this is dealt with at this time as pupils will be shedding their deciduous (milk) teeth and gaining the teeth they will need to use for the rest of their lives. Figure 5.1 shows a cross-section through a typical human tooth. Humans have four types of teeth: incisors at the front for cutting food, canines behind the incisors for gripping meat, and premolars then molars for chewing food. The main function of teeth is to break food down into small enough pieces to swallow. In addition saliva is produced by the mouth's salivary glands, which coats the food pieces, making them easier to swallow and to start digesting starch by the action of a digestive enzyme called amylase present in the saliva.

Teeth

Teeth are coated in a hard substance called enamel, which prevents damage. This enamel can, however, become damaged by the action of acids in the mouth (saliva is alkaline which helps to neutralize moderate levels of acidity). The most common source of enamel damage is plaque. This consists of bacteria, which live in the mouth, which feed on the sugars in foods. As they feed they produce an acidic by-product, which attacks the enamel. Once the enamel has been corroded away the acid attacks the bone-like dentine below. If this continues then a cavity will develop allowing bacteria to enter the tooth pulp and this will start to decay. Preventing this decay in the first place will ensure healthier teeth. Brushing with a suitable toothpaste removes the plaque (and pieces of food that are a potential food source for the plaque), but needs to be done at least twice a day as not all the bacteria are removed and will quickly reproduce. Tartar is unremoved plaque that has been calcified. Toothpaste is slightly alkaline to help neutralize acids but is also abrasive (as is a toothbrush) so pupils should be warned against too vigorous brushing as it may damage their gums. Removal of plaque also helps to prevent infections of the gum, which can lead to the loosening of teeth in the gum. In addition, pupils should appreciate that they ought to use their own toothbrush to prevent cross-infections. Since the bacteria in plaque feed on sugars, sugary food can contribute greatly to tooth decay. Pupils should there-fore be able to make decisions on which foods are potentially bad for the health of their teeth.

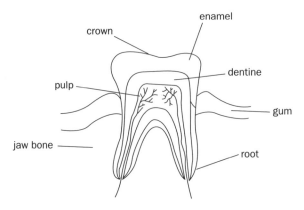

Figure 5.1 The structure of a human tooth

Finally, in the context of other animals, it is important to remember that not all animals have teeth and those that do may have different teeth as they eat different foods. Herbivores do not eat other animals so have no need for the canines that carnivores and omnivores need for gripping prey and tearing at meat. Herbivore teeth are subject to a great deal of wear through constant chewing and, consequently, may continue to grow throughout their lives. Also it should be remembered that when an animal loses its teeth it can no longer feed and therefore will die – humans of course have remedied this with false teeth, but not all humans have access to dental care.

Teaching activity

Children can make models of their own teeth using red and white plasticine. They need a mirror to inspect and count teeth, and they should be encouraged to shape and name the teeth appropriately. If you are able to get hold of the skulls of different animals, they can try modelling then comparing them with their own teeth.

Circulation

The circulatory system is the human body's transport network. It is through the circulatory system that substances are carried to and from all the cells of the body to maintain those cells.

The main parts of the system are the blood vessels (arteries, veins and capillaries), the heart and the blood itself. Blood is pumped around the body by the heart which is actually a double pump (hence the two parts to the sound of a heartbeat). A simplified diagram of the heart is shown in Figure 5.2. Beware, anatomical drawings

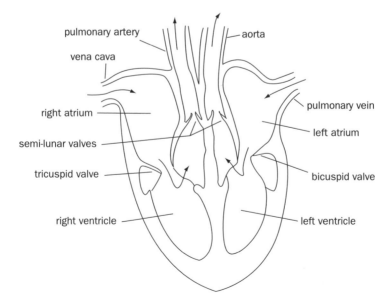

Figure 5.2 The structure of the human heart

are usually drawn as if we are viewing the person from the front, hence the left and right labels seem reversed.

Contrary to popular myth, the heart is not on the left of the chest, but in the middle, behind the sternum (breastbone). However the left side is larger than the right as it has to pump blood to everywhere in the body except the lungs, which are supplied with blood by the right side. The right-hand side of the heart receives blood from the body into the right atrium (or right auricle). This blood is deoxygenated blood, which is blood low in oxygen content since it has given up its oxygen to the body's cells on its journey around the body. This blood is therefore high in carbon dioxide which the cells have released into the blood from respiration. The blood then moves down into the right ventricle which has thick muscular walls which contract to squeeze the blood out of the heart into the pulmonary artery. The pulmonary artery leads to the lungs where the blood exchanges its carbon dioxide content for oxygen in a process known as gaseous exchange (Figure 5.3). At this stage the blood is flowing through much smaller blood vessels called capillaries, which have walls that are one cell thick. This allows the carbon dioxide and oxygen to pass through easily in their respective directions. The capillaries surround small air sacs in the lungs called alveoli which are at the end of tubes called bronchioles. This network of tubes join to the two bronchi which connect the lungs to the trachea (windpipe), which in turn leads out to the mouth and nose. The lungs cannot move themselves to draw air in and out of the lungs, rather they inflate and deflate due to changes in pressure caused by the contraction and relaxation of the diaphragm muscle at the bottom of the chest cavity and the intercostal muscles around the ribs. When we breathe in, the muscle movement causes the chest cavity to expand and the air pressure is reduced inside, so that air from outside rushes in. When we breath out the reduction in the size of the chest cavity increases the pressure in the lungs and the air is forced out. It is often wrongly assumed that we 'breathe oxygen in and carbon dioxide out'. In fact about 78 per cent of the air we inhale and exhale is nitrogen (which we cannot use), about 21 per cent

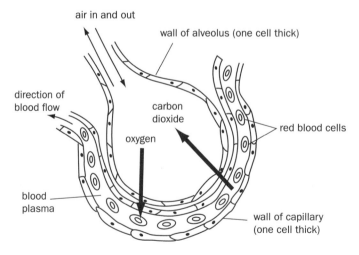

Figure 5.3 Gaseous exchange in the lungs

of inhaled air is oxygen and 0.03 per cent is carbon dioxide. When we exhale there is still about 17 per cent oxygen in the air we breathe out, with the missing 4 per cent replaced by carbon dioxide and water vapour. This is why blowing on a dying fire can help it relight – if we exhaled pure carbon dioxide then it would extinguish the fire!

Once the newly oxygen-rich blood (oxygenated blood) has passed out of the lungs it returns to the heart. This time it enters the left side through the pulmonary vein and into the left atrium (left auricle). The blood then moves down to the left ventricle to be pumped out, to the rest of the body through the aorta (the body's main artery). A series of valves in both sides of the heart maintain blood flow in the correct direction and open and close at particular points in the pumping cycle to maintain the correct blood pressure. The aorta divides into smaller arteries which each lead to different areas of the body. These include the carotid artery to the head, the hepatic artery to the liver and the renal artery to the kidneys. Arteries contain blood at high pressure, since it has been pumped directly from the heart, so the walls of arteries need to be thick to withstand this pressure. Blockages in the arteries due to fatty deposits can restrict the flow of the blood and lead to damage to the circulatory system, including the heart itself. The blood in arteries is also oxygenated (the exception being the pulmonary artery to the lungs from the right side of the heart). Arteries divide into smaller arterioles, then capillaries. Every cell of the body is near a capillary, since it is only through the thin walls of capillaries that useful substance and waste substances can be transferred to and from cells. Blood flow through these narrow capillaries is slow to allow time for maximum transfer of these substances. Organs are full of these blood vessels (they are the blood vessels that you see in your eyeball). As blood passes out from organs the capillaries start to join together, eventually resulting in the veins. Veins carry the now deoxygenated blood back to the heart. As the blood flow is much slower, after having travelled through the capillaries, its pressure is lower. This means that there is in increased risk of the blood flowing in the wrong direction, especially as much has to work against gravity to get back to the heart. As a result, veins have valves inside them that prevent this potential backflow. The blood finally re-enters the right atrium again, through the vena cava, before setting off on its journey again. The heart has its own blood supply via the coronary blood vessels and is made of a special type of muscle known as coronary muscle, which needs this constant blood supply to keep beating. Unlike other muscles, say in the legs, it cannot afford to tire and only when this blood supply is blocked will it start to hurt (angina) like other muscles when they are starved of oxygen.

If the blood vessels are the 'roads' of the circulatory system transport network, then the blood is the traffic. Blood consists of four major components:

- plasma – the liquid part of the blood, mainly water and containing dissolved substances
- red cells – to carry oxygen
- white cells – to fight infection
- platelets – to aid in the formation of blood clots when a blood vessel is cut.

Plasma is the transport medium for a number of substances such as digested food molecules, carbon dioxide and hormones (chemicals that act as messengers from one part of the body to another). The colour of red blood cells is due to a chemical called haemoglobin which allows them to pick up oxygen molecules when flowing through the lung capillaries, and deposit them later into cells requiring oxygen. Inhalation of carbon monoxide is dangerous as the haemoglobin can also pick up the carbon monoxide molecules, however, they cannot subsequently release the molecules, effectively preventing the cells from performing their function as they can no longer pick up oxygen. Red cells are unusual in that they have no nucleus. This is because they are produced by other cells in the bone marrow. They die and are replaced every six weeks or so.

White cells attack foreign bodies in the blood which are potentially harmful, such as bacteria and viruses. They can do this in a number of ways, for example, by engulfing and digesting the invader or creating antibodies to attack the foreign body. If a blood vessel is cut then there is a chance that bacteria and so on can enter the wound, hence a blood clot forms over the damaged area to help prevent this and to prevent the loss of too much blood. This is brought about by a number of different, complex events. Essentially the platelets, on exposure to air, cause a chemical dissolved in the blood plasma called fibrinogen to change to an insoluble protein called fibrin. The fibrin forms as fibres which create a net which catches the red blood cells as they flow out of the wound. Eventually these trapped cells dry and harden into a scab which plugs the wound and prevents foreign bodies entering the blood vessel at the cut.

One final, important, function of the blood in humans is to distribute heat around the body to maintain body temperature.

The circulatory system of other vertebrates is very similar to that of a human; with perhaps fish being the most different (they have a single circulatory system). Most other animals (with the exception of some very simple ones) have circulatory systems as well but the way in which they function varies from organism to organism.

A pulse is caused by a pressure wave moving through an artery as blood is pumped through it. We can feel a pulse when the artery is close to the surface and the most common places for taking a pulse are at the inside of the wrist (on the side where the thumb is) and at the neck (the carotid pulse through the carotid artery) against the side of the windpipe. Many people (not just children) can have great difficulty locating their pulse and this should not be done with the thumb as it has a slight pulse itself. Since it is caused by a heartbeat, the pulse indicates the rate at which the heart is beating which is usually around 70 beats per minute when resting, although this will vary from individual to individual and depends on other factors such as temperature and so on. When we exercise our pulse rate increases, meaning that our heartbeat has increased also. As this can be experienced directly, it is something that is easily learnt; what is harder is why this happens and many KS4 students still have difficulty with this. As stated earlier the blood is the body's transport system. It provides cells with what they need including oxygen and glucose to obtain energy by respiration (see Chapter 4). When we exercise we use up the oxygen and glucose in the blood *at a greater rate*, hence the blood needs to circulate faster to provide muscles with the extra amounts that they need to sustain movement. As a result the heart beats faster to increase the supply of blood to the muscles and hence the pulse rate increases. As the levels of oxygen and glucose drop they need replenishing and this drop is detected by a part of the brain called the hypothalamus. Hormones are released into the blood to stimulate the release of more glucose from the liver and the breathing rate increases to raise levels of oxygen in the blood; this also results in the need for greater blood flow and increased heartbeat and pulse rate. Once the exercise is over and the body comes to rest, it continues to work faster until normal levels are restored and eventually the pulse slows to its resting rate.

Movement

Movement in humans and other vertebrates is achieved through the use of muscles and the skeleton. Some movement such as the beating of the heart and the movement of food through the digestive system essentially involves just the action of muscles. However, large-scale movement of body parts such as the limbs involves muscles causing bones to move.

Pupils may be familiar with the names of some of the bones of the human body, especially if they have been unfortunate enough to break any of them, and some of the major bones are shown in Figure 5.4.

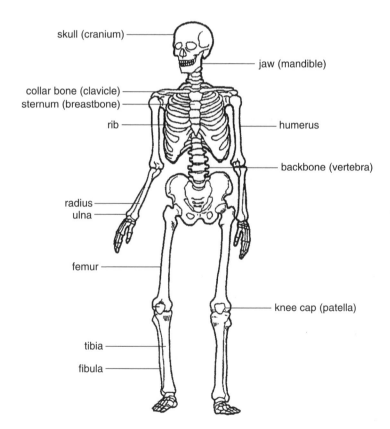

Figure 5.4 Major bones of the human body simplified

The skeleton in vertebrates performs three main functions:

- protection of major organs
- support for the body as a whole
- movement.

Bone is a living tissue which contains cells. It consists of strands of a protein called collagen and deposits of minerals such as calcium carbonate and calcium phosphate. The latter give the bone its rigidity and hardness, while the collagen provides tensile strength and flexibility. Bones have a blood supply and nerves, and some bones contain marrow where blood cells are produced. When developing in the womb, a child's skeleton is made of cartilage (the pinna of the ear and the end of the nose are made of cartilage) and this more flexible material is replaced as a child develops. Some fish only have skeletons made of cartilage. The mixture of different substances in bone increases its strength and it is often compared to composite materials such as reinforced concrete and carbon-fibre reinforced plastics. Bones are utilized in the body to protect organs; the skull protects the brain, the ribs the lungs, the sternum the heart and the bones of the spine protect the spinal cord running inside them. Bones, of course, can break, but their composite design prevents total breaks unless they encounter very large forces. This is similar to a car windscreen which is rather like a sandwich with glass on either side of a softer, plastic material. If the outer glass breaks, the inner layer prevents that break continuing into the interior layer of glass.

Vertebrates are animals which have an internal skeleton with a backbone. Humans, as mammals thus belong to this group. The strong skeleton thus provides a framework for the body, supporting its external features and its internal organs, which are attached to the skeleton. Often this is taught by considering what we would be like without a skeleton. While this is perfectly valid, the idea that 'we would just be a blob without a skeleton' is an idea which persists in many pupils' brains and presents problems later (this would not be a suitable answer in a KS3 standard assessment task). Hence the emphasis should always go back to the idea of what it *does* do rather than what would happen if we did not have one, that is, it supports the body or 'holds it up'.

The places where bones meet are called joints. In some cases these joints are fused at an early age, such as in the skull, preventing movement. However, some joints allow movement to occur. The bones at the joint are held in place by fibrous tissues called ligaments. They also have smooth cartilage at the ends of the bone where they meet the other bone(s); this reduces friction, allowing the bones to move smoothly and without wear, so preventing damage and pain. Some joints also contain a membrane that contains a liquid called synovial fluid which also acts as a lubricant for the moving bones. Muscles are attached to the bones by tendons and it is the contraction and relaxation of these muscles that causes the movement. Muscles work in pairs (called antagonistic pairs) since it is only when they contract that they actually move the bone. When a muscle contracts it shortens and bulges outwards (this can be felt when one holds the biceps muscle as the forearm is raised towards the shoulder). This contraction pulls on the bone the muscle is attached to, causing it to move one way.

The paired muscle is relaxed as this happens to allow this movement. For the bone to move in the opposite direction, the first muscle relaxes and the other one in the pair now contracts, to pull the bone the other way. In effect the bones are acting as levers, pivoted at the joints. This can be demonstrated very easily with the movement of the forearm, caused by the action of the biceps and triceps muscles (see Figure 5.5).

The elbow is the joint here and only allows an up and down movement (that is, in one plane). Some children may dispute this but when one prevents movement of the wrist and shoulder joints it is shown to be the case. The elbow and the knee joint, which display this type of movement, are called hinge joints. The hip and shoulder joints are called ball and socket joints due to the fact that one bone has a rounded end that fits into a socket in the other bone of the joint. These require more than one pair of muscles and allow movement in all directions. Other joints, such as those in the hands and the feet, are known as gliding joints, where the bones slide over each other.

There are, of course, other vertebrates besides humans – all the mammals, birds, reptiles, amphibians and fish – and while there will be some key differences to their skeletons there will also be many striking similarities. Children are amazed that when they look carefully at the skeleton of a whale that its flippers look like hands, which is essentially what they are, albeit modified. Many are also unaware that some vertebrates actually have skeletons, especially some reptiles such as snakes and tortoises and amphibians such as frogs and toads. This can be rectified by letting pupils see the skeletons of a wide range of vertebrates, either the actual skeletons or pictures of them.

Invertebrates do not have this type of internal skeleton, and different types of invertebrate have different ways of replacing them. Arthropods, such as insects, crustaceans and arachnids for instance have a hard outer layer called an exoskeleton (exo- comes from the Greek for outside), with softer, flexible areas to allow movement at the legs and other moving parts. This exoskeleton performs all the functions of the skeleton of a vertebrate and is shed and replaced as the animal grows. Some have no form of skeleton at all, such as molluscs, although many molluscs have shells for protection (for example, snails).

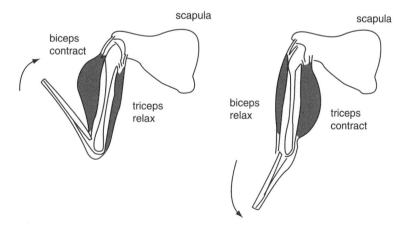

Figure 5.5 The movement of the forearm

Health

The need for a balanced diet to maintain health has already been described. In addition to this, exercise plays an important role in a healthy lifestyle. Regular exercise ensures that we use the food that we eat efficiently, especially energy foods such as carbohydrates and fats, which would otherwise be stored in the body if more are taken in than are needed. Too little exercise means that these reserves build up and can lead to being overweight. This in turn can lead to other problems, especially with the heart and circulation. Exercise increases muscle bulk and raises the metabolic rate of the body so that we process more energy foods even at rest and less are stored and laid down as body fat. Even an hour or two of moderate exercise a day helps maintain levels of physical fitness and this can be achieved through day-to-day activities such as walking and gardening. Also, as one becomes fitter, it takes less time to recover after exercise, as the body becomes more efficient at taking in oxygen and delivering blood to the muscles.

In addition to the notions of exercise and a good diet being important for health, the National Curriculum also focuses on the issues surrounding drugs. At this stage more of the emphasis is on legal rather than illegal drugs. Drugs are chemicals that have an effect on the body. This may be a physical or a mental effect or a combination of the two. Children are most likely to encounter them first hand in the form of medicines and this is the main emphasis at KS1. Drugs of this kind tend either to act on a part (or parts) of the body (for instance, to relieve pain, lower blood pressure, relieve the symptoms of asthma, and so on) or they are taken to fight infections (for example, antibiotics to kill bacteria). Most pharmaceutical drugs require a prescription from a doctor and may have dangerous effects if taken by someone who does not require them. It is important that pupils realize this early on and it is a message that they will hopefully have received from their home lives already. The notion of not eating things unless we know what they are is important here and is a good general rule for life, not eating berries or **fungi** unless we know they are safe being a similar idea.

At KS2 these ideas should be reinforced and complemented with further ideas. The action of pharmaceutical chemicals on the body, even when prescribed properly, may lead to side effects such as drowsiness or stomach upsets. In addition, it is important that the instructions for dosage are followed carefully. It is the liver that processes the drugs as they enter the bloodstream and too much of a drug at any particular time (an overdose) may damage the liver. It may also have an adverse affect on other organs of the body and possibly lead to death. It is also important to see a course of medicines through to the end. This is especially true of antibiotics. Since these 'wonder-drugs' were first used they have, over time, started to become less effective as a result of overuse (they kill bacteria so there is no point prescribing them for a disease that is not caused by bacteria) and the fact that many patients do not always complete their course. As such some strains of bacteria are becoming immune to certain antibiotics. The antibiotic is likely to cause the death of the weakest bacteria first, gradually affecting the stronger ones as a course of drugs is taken. If, however, a course of drugs is not completed then there may still be a number of these stronger, more resistant bacteria left. As these bacteria reproduce they are likely to pass on this resilience to their offspring so the population as a whole becomes more resistant to the effect of the drug.

At this stage, the idea that there are drugs that people use when they are not ill is also introduced. Pupils will be aware of smoking tobacco and drinking alcohol and some will also be aware of the use of illegal drugs. Clearly people must do this for a reason as excessive use of such drugs can have adverse effects on health, and this can therefore be a tricky area to tackle when teaching, for a number of reasons. Pupils may not recognize these as drugs, but the nicotine and other chemicals in tobacco smoke, alcohol and the chemicals in narcotic drugs all have an effect on the functioning of the body. They are also addictive in that the body is tricked into thinking it needs a steady supply of the chemical in question, when in fact it does not and it is this false need for the drug that leads to cravings and withdrawal symptoms. There is plenty of good information available on the effects of these different drugs and a good source is the National Health Service (NHS). It is also important that they get good information at this stage as they are likely to encounter many of these substances fairly early in their lives.

Growth and reproduction

Growth and reproduction are two of the characteristics of living things and have been discussed briefly in the 'Life processes' section in this chapter. Growth of some kind occurs throughout life (hair and nails being good examples) but is, of course, most noticeable with immature animals. Humans actually mature over a much longer period than other animals and this has to do with learning and development of the brain. A mature animal is usually regarded as one which can reproduce, although often some additional development occurs after this time before most growth stops. Many changes occur during this time with, perhaps, the most obvious being changes in **weight** and size or height, although this will not necessarily occur at the same rate for all individuals, as is apparent with humans. Rate of growth is affected by a number of factors, some genetic and some environmental (such as diet) and is controlled by hormones released into the bloodstream from the pituitary and thyroid glands. It is important to remember that size does not always indicate age. Some animals also have definite stages in their lives when they change quite radically, such as the pupal and adult stages of insects and tadpoles developing into frogs.

One of the most important changes that occurs when an animal matures is developing the ability to reproduce. The changes that cause this happen during puberty. Human reproduction is sexual, meaning that two parents are involved and this is common with most animals and many plants (see Chapter 6). Each sex produces sex cells (gametes) which in animals are sperm cells (male) and ova (female). Each cell contains a nucleus with half the genetic information needed for a new organism, and so the two cells need to join so that their nuclei can join (fuse). For this to happen, sexual intercourse must take place. During sexual intercourse sperm cells are released from the *testes* (see Figure 5.6) and combined with other fluids to form semen that passes out through the penis. The semen is deposited in the vagina and the sperm start to swim to locate the ovum (egg). Ova are released from the ovaries approximately every 28 days and travel down the *fallopian tube* (or oviduct) towards the *uterus*

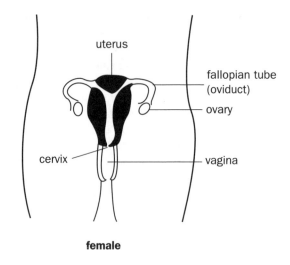

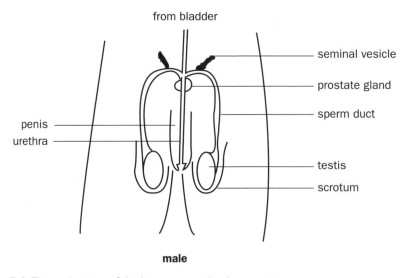

Figure 5.6 The main parts of the human reproductive system

(or womb). The sperm swim through the uterus and then divide to swim up the two fallopian tubes. If an ovum has been released the sperm surround it and attempt to get inside. When one sperm manages to do this and its nucleus joins with the ovum's nucleus, the ovum is *fertilized*. A layer forms around this newly fertilized ovum, which is now called a *zygote*, to prevent any further sperm cells from entering. This new cell now has all the genetic information to create a new individual and starts to grow and divide into new cells. These are all similar at first but gradually start to develop in different ways. As time goes by the embryo develops into a foetus and after about nine months the baby is ready to be born. The growth that has started in the uterus now continues. For the first few years the children will only have their primary sexual characteristics but from about the age of 11 they start to develop their secondary sexual characteristics as they go through puberty. Once puberty is over and their reproductive organs are fully functioning, the life cycle is complete and can start over again with the production of new offspring.

The senses

The senses are how we, and other organisms, detect our surroundings. Without them survival becomes harder and there is no doubt that the senses are part of our body's protection system. It is sometimes not always clear that our senses have this function but they act as a sort of early warning system to alert us to dangers and help us to make informed choices about our actions.

There are five senses: sight, smell, hearing, taste and touch. Each sense has its own specialized sense organ to detect particular stimuli. The information gathered by the sense organs is transferred to the central nervous system, which then acts on the information received. The central nervous system consists of the brain and the spinal cord. As a general rule, the spinal cord tends to process information connected to involuntary actions, so-called reflex actions. The brain does this as well but also processes information about more complicated actions as well. The central nervous system will then send information along nerves to muscles where a suitable response is achieved. A simple example of this is the reflex action brought about by hitting the area just below the knee. The receptors here are the nerve endings in the skin which respond to pressure exerted on them. A nerve impulse is sent along the neurones (nerve cells) that have been stimulated (the sensory neurones) and arrives at the spinal cord. Cells in the spinal cord respond to this and another impulse is sent through a relay neurone, which is connected to another neurone, the motor neurone. This motor neurone then sends an impulse to the muscles in the leg, causing them to move and the lower leg jerks forward. This series of events is known as a reflex arc and while it is hard to see how this aids survival, it is also the mechanism which causes someone to remove their hand from hot objects and controls the size of the pupils in the eyes in response to differences in light (but this latter example is relayed by the brain). These impulses along the neurones are electrical in nature and only travel in one direction. The neurones act like wires and are insulated (rather like electrical wires) by a fatty covering called myelin.

Pupils should be able to identify the various sense organs associated with each sense: the eye for sight, the ear for hearing, the nose for smell and the tongue for taste. Touch is more difficult, with the nerve endings in a variety of places in the body, although the skin is one organ that they should be able to consider.

Sight

The eye (Figure 5.7) is a complex organ that detects light; both its intensity and colour. Muscles in the eye control its movement in the eye socket, the shape of the lens and the size of the hole in the iris (the pupil). Light enters through the transparent cornea and passes through a liquid called the aqueous humour. This starts the focusing of the light by causing light rays to converge. The light passes through the

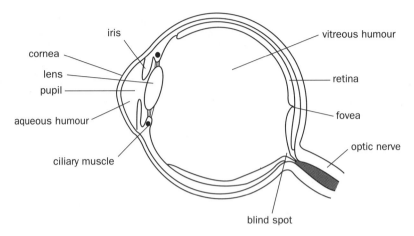

Figure 5.7 The human eye

pupil, which is a hole in the iris. The size of the pupil is varied automatically through muscle action in the iris, widening in low light. This is a nice exercise for pupils to try with each other by looking at each other's eyes having removed their hands after a period of having their eyes shut and covered by their hands. Of course, it is potentially hazardous to deliberately shine light in the eye to see the pupil get smaller and this should not be attempted. The light then passes through the lens. The lens shape can be altered by the ciliary muscles, which relax when viewing far objects, causing the lens to *flatten* and contract when viewing near objects, causing the lens to *fatten*. This is known as accommodation and results in a sharply focused image on the back of the eye. Wearers of spectacles and contact lenses cannot achieve this sharp focus without them, with those being short-sighted unable to focus clearly on distant objects as the lens focuses the light too soon in the eye and those with long sight unable to focus clearly on close objects as the light never achieves focus in the eye. The light is focused onto the light-sensitive layer of cells on the back of the eye, called the retina. This has cells to detect light intensity (rods) and cells to detect colour (cones). The retina produces electrical impulses that carry their information along the optic nerve to the brain. The place where the optic nerve is attached to the eye (and the blood vessels enter) lacks these cells and so is known as the blind spot. Two forward-facing eyes allow us to have two slightly different views of the world around us that the brain combines to produce a three-dimensional image. Hence the loss of the use of one eye means that judging distance is difficult. This 3-D vision is common to predators as it is an advantage for hunting. Animals that are prey tend to have eyes on the sides of their head thus sacrificing this three-dimensional vision for all-round vision; a rabbit is a good example here. (Note that the function of the eye is also considered in Chapter 14, 'Light and sound'.)

Hearing
The ear (Figure 5.8) is composed of three parts, the outer, middle and inner ear. The outer ear comprises of a flap known as the *pinna* and the *ear canal*. The pinna is

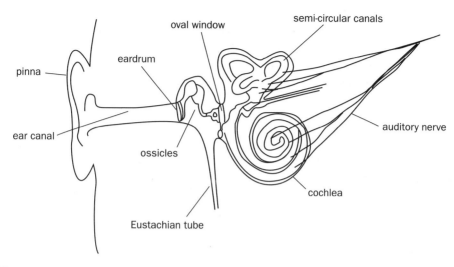

Figure 5.8 The human ear

designed to direct sound waves into the ear canal. At the end of the ear canal is the eardrum. Sound waves enter the ear canal as vibrations of air particles. This vibrating air causes the eardrum to vibrate, so passing the vibrations on to the middle ear. The middle ear is an air-filled cavity containing three small bones (the *ossicles*). The first of these (the *hammer*) is connected to the eardrum and so vibrates as the eardrum vibrates. These vibrations are passed to the second bone (the *anvil*), which in turn causes the third bone (the *stirrup*) to vibrate. The stirrup then taps against the end of the cochlea, at a point called the oval window, which causes fluid in the cochlea to vibrate. As this fluid moves it moves small hair-like parts, called cilia, which produce electrical impulses that are carried to the brain along the auditory nerve. If any part of this series of events fails to work properly then the result is hearing loss or complete deafness. This can happen in a variety of ways, for instance, a blockage in the ear canal, a tear in the eardrum, infection and damage caused by prolonged exposure to loud sounds. Pupils may have experienced their ears popping. This is caused by differences in air pressure between the outer and middle ears. When this occurs pressure is placed on the eardrum and it feels uncomfortable. Moving the jaw allows the Eustachian tube to open and close. This is connected to the back of the mouth and allows air either in or out of the middle ear to restore equal air pressure, relieving the pressure on the eardrum and allowing it to function correctly. This in turn results in restored clarity of hearing and the characteristic sound as the Eustachian tube opens and closes. As with eyes, two ears allow for a three-dimensional sound that allows one to detect where a sound is appearing to come from and, to some extent, distance. The function of the ear is also considered in 'Light and sound' (Chapter 14).

Taste

The tongue's role in the sense of taste is due to the taste buds that cover its surface. As with other senses, these produce nerve impulses that are transmitted to the brain and respond to chemicals on the tongue. The tongue only responds to four tastes; sweet, salt, sour and bitter (see Figure 5.9). Sweet and salt tastes are perhaps easiest to associate with foods, with sour and bitter often being confused. Sour effectively means acidic and bitter can be best understood by considering the taste of coffee and the taste of a paracetamol tablet. Drinks like bitter lemon are actually sour and bitter, the sourness from the lemon and the bitterness from the quinine added to it. Taste is a good example of our sense protecting us. We know that foods that are sweet, such as fruits, are ready to eat when they taste sweet and when we need energy it is sweet food that we crave. Salt is vital for life and obtaining it is important, so it has always been necessary to know which foods are salty. Sour tastes are often associated with foods that have gone off (such as milk) and hence may harm us, while many poisonous foods have a bitter taste. These four tastes clearly do not account for the full taste experience that we obtain when eating foods and, in fact, much of what we think of as taste is actually smell, which explains why we do not seem to 'taste' things as well when we have a cold.

Teaching activity

The relationship between the senses of taste and smell and how they influence the way we experience food can be explored with 'blind' taste and smell testing. A good example of this is testing different flavours of squash, first by smell, then by taste. This can either be done blindfold or food colourings can be added to the diluted squash to disguise the colour. Teachers should check with parents about food allergies before conducting any taste testing!

Smell

As already stated, smell contributes to much of what we call taste. Like taste, the sense of smell is stimulated by chemical molecules in the olfactory organs of the nose. We can distinguish between thousands of different smells, and the molecules that cause them are thought to fit into the different receptors in the upper part of the nose. If a substance is odourless it is because it cannot be detected by these receptors. In

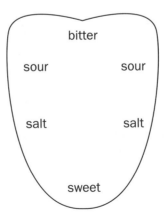

Figure 5.9 The human tongue

addition, over short periods of time we may become less sensitive to a particular smell, which explains why we may cease to detect a particular smell in a confined space. This may be a defence mechanism of a sort. Detecting certain smells alarms us to danger, for example, a wound that has gone septic or a poisonous gas. In addition, we and other animals can respond to the smell of chemicals called pheromones that are emitted by animals to send chemical messages to others (like hormones do inside the body). Pheromones play an important role in the mating behaviour of animals.

Touch

This is perhaps the hardest sense to describe, simply because we cannot see the receptors that are associated with it. There are receptors in the skin which are sensitive to pressure and temperature and send signals to the nervous system for it to act on. These sensors are found at the end of sensory neurones (see above). This is important to survival as it helps the body to avoid damage and alerts the body to any damage which has been caused. Hence pain is part of the sense of touch. Touch also allows us to interact with our physical environment, such as when picking up objects and treating fragile objects with care. Some areas of the body are more sensitive that others as they have more nerve endings, such as the lips and the fingertips. Other places have fewer nerve endings, such as the soles of the feet, probably as they will be subject to more opportunities for stimulation than other parts of the body and to avoid too many unnecessary responses.

Links to teaching

More teaching activities

The human body and bodies of other animals can be compared using pictures. Throughout a topic on animals children could keep scrapbooks of pictures they collect or draw of animals. The pictures could be sorted and categorized, for example, a page of 'different sort of legs' could include pictures of humans, giraffes and millipedes.

Other things to do and try

Pulse meters for dataloggers are available and very useful when teaching about the circulatory system and the effect of exercise on pulse rate.

TOP TEACHING TIP

Teaching about the senses needs to be approached with some thought. Some children may have deficits in some senses and it is important for teachers not to make value judgements or compare children's ability to see and hear. However, there are some interesting investigations which can be done with the senses, for example, 'blind' taste testing of crisps (it is very difficult to differentiate flavours if the nose is held while tasting).

Teaching about health, reproduction and drugs as medicines can raise some sensitive issues. It is not appropriate to approach these issues in a judgemental way, as teachers must remember that many children do not have control over many aspects of their lives. An example of an unsuitable activity is to ask children to compare the contents of lunchboxes. Aside from excluding children who have free school meals from the activity, many children might like to have a healthier lunchbox, but they have to accept what their parents give them. Links with personal, social and health education (PSHE) sessions may be helpful in discussing issues related to health.

Some common misconceptions

- All blood vessels are veins.
- Humans are not animals.
- Insects and other invertebrates are not animals.
- Fish are not animals.
- Light leaves the eye rather than enters it.

AMAZING FACTS

The three bones in the middle ear are the smallest in the human body.

Women have 2½ more pain receptors than men.

The human heart creates enough pressure to squirt blood 30 feet when it pumps (the length of a classroom?).

A cockroach can survive for nine days without a head before it starves to death.

6

Green plants

National Curriculum: Attainment Target Sc2, Strand 3 (KS1: 2.3a–3c, KS2: 2.3a–3d)
QCA Schemes of Work: Units 1B, 2B and 3B

Curriculum requirements

Green plants, as a topic of study in the National Curriculum, is visited in all four key stages (their links to other organisms being made more explicit at KS3 and KS4 with a change of name to '*Green plants as organisms*'. As such this makes this aspect of science teaching a fundamental one.

The National Curriculum for Science programme of study states that at KS1 Pupils should be taught to recognize that plants need light and water to grow; to recognize and name the leaf, flower, stem and root of flowering plants, and that seeds grow into flowering plants. At KS2 this is separated into two sections:

Growth and nutrition, where pupils should be taught the effect of light, air, water and temperature on plant growth; the role of the leaf in producing new material for growth; that the root anchors the plant, and that water and minerals are taken in through the root and transported through the stem to other parts of the plant.

Reproduction, where pupils should be taught about the parts of the flower and their role in the life cycle of flowering plants, including pollination, seed formation, seed dispersal and germination.

The importance of plants

The importance of plants themselves lies in their ability to make their own food from non-living materials. Therefore all other living things depend on them either directly or indirectly for their own food. The process of plants making their own food, *photosynthesis,* is one of the first key biological processes that many pupils learnt about in any detail and it appears in the KS2 programme of study, albeit unnamed. The food that plants produce is glucose, a sugar. Leaves are often described as 'food factories' as this is where most of the photosynthesis takes place. Glucose is made from carbon dioxide from the atmosphere and water from the soil. The energy that is required to transform, chemically, these two substances into glucose is obtained from sunlight (although artificial light will also provide the necessary energy as well). It is important at this stage to focus on a couple of issues of language here, since it is the Sun's *light* that is required, whereas some pupils (and indeed many adults) erroneously refer to plants requiring *the sun* – which is wrong and the cause of many a lost mark in tests and examinations in later years. In addition, it is also incorrect to say that plants *make food from sunlight/the sun* since the glucose is actually made up of the **atoms** that were in the carbon dioxide and the water. The sunlight itself is absorbed by the *chlorophyll* found in the plant's cells. Chlorophyll is a green pigment. This means that it will absorb all colours of light *except* green light, which it reflects, hence the plant looks green. Each colour of light has a different amount of energy associated with it and the green light's energy is not used. Photosynthesis can be summarized by a chemical equation, shown here in both word form and chemical form (that is using symbols and formulae):

$$\text{carbon dioxide} + \text{water} \xrightarrow[\text{chlorophyll}]{\text{light}} \text{glucose} + \text{oxygen}$$

$$6CO_2 + 6H_2O \xrightarrow[\text{chlorophyll}]{\text{light}} C_6H_{12}O_6 + 6O_2$$

This chemical equation shows us that six molecules of carbon dioxide will react with six molecules of water to create every molecule of glucose. Six molecules of oxygen will also be produced and some of this will be used by the plant for processes such as respiration and the surplus released into the atmosphere. The light and chlorophyll appear around the arrow of the equation as they are needed but not used up, as with the chlorophyll, or not a chemical, as with the light.

Plant cells

One of the most important key themes in biological sciences is that of cells. Prior to KS3, teaching and learning tends to focus on bulk features of organisms, such as organs and other, larger parts, for example, flowers. From KS3 onwards this is still important, but taught with cells as the building blocks of these features. Many pupils may have had some experience of cells by the end of KS2 and, since they are so fundamental, it makes sense to discuss plant cells here.

Figure 6.1 shows the standard diagram of a typical plant cell that most pupils will come across when they first start to study them. This is a simplification of what the cells are really like, but is the basic standard cell up to General Certificate of Secondary Education (GCSE) level. This is closest to one of the palisade cells, found in the leaf of a plant and responsible for most of the photosynthesis. Other cells have their own unique features that allow them to perform their specific functions, such as the root hair on a root hair cell for the absorption of water and minerals. Root hair cells also

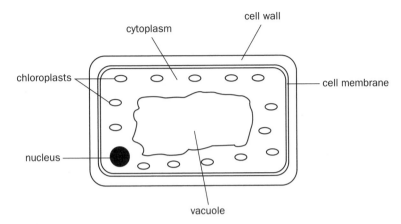

Figure 6.1 A typical plant cell

contain no chlorophyll and so are not green. This is because sunlight will not be able to reach them as they are below ground and the production of chlorophyll would be an unnecessary waste of the plant's resources.

The major parts of a plant cell are:

- the cell wall – a rigid structure of cellulose (a substance made by linking together thousands of glucose molecules) which provides support for the cell
- the cell membrane – a sort of liquid covering for the cell contents that is select-ively permeable (lets only certain substances in and out of the cell)
- the nucleus – contains the cell's genetic material and controls the cell's processes
- the vacuole – essentially a hole, which is where the cell sap is contained
- the cytoplasm – a jelly like fluid where the cell's life processes take place
- chloroplasts – where the chlorophyll for photosynthesis is stored.

Most plants are multicellular, that is, they are made up of many cells, with different versions of the cells for different functions. Single-celled plants such as single-celled algae can photosynthesize like more complex plants, but are often classified with other single-celled organisms as *protists*.

The basic structure of a flowering plant

Most of the work done in schools concerns *flowering plants*. On a simple level, we can classify plants into *flowering* (for example, grasses, orchids and daisies) and *non-flowering* (for example, mosses, ferns and conifers) varieties. One problem arises here in that from their day-to-day experiences, many pupils do not realize that a flower is just part of a plant, they see 'flowers' as a whole plant. They also do not realize that many trees produce flowers, which stems from our use of the word blossom when referring to the flowers on trees. In addition, few realize that *grasses* produce flowers because they do not look like the image of a flower that children grow up with (they do have flowers, which hayfever sufferers will attest to when they find themselves among the hairy-looking fronds that make up many a grass flower).

Figure 6.2 shows the basic structure of a flowering plant, consisting of:

- the leaves – where the majority of the photosynthesis takes place, so providing the food necessary for growth and other life processes; for the exchange of gases between the plant and the atmosphere; for the loss of water (transpiration)
- the flower – for sexual reproduction
- the stem – for support of the leaves and flowers and for the transport of water, minerals and food through the plant. This transport system consists of specialized cells that line up to form tubes through which materials can pass. Water is transported through *xylem* vessels and food through *phloem* cells
- the roots – for taking in water and minerals and to provide anchorage.

The growth of plants

Like all living things, plants need protein for growth. Chemical processes within plant cells allow them to produce these protein molecules, using the glucose from photosynthesis, water and minerals obtained through the roots as raw materials. As such, the supply of these is crucial for healthy growth. Plants need a good supply of water, carbon dioxide and light energy for photosynthesis to provide the organic matter that can be converted into protein. They also need oxygen for *respiration*. Respiration is another of the fundamental processes that plants and all other living thing need to carry out to survive. Essentially it is a means of releasing energy from stored food. This can be aerobic respiration (which requires oxygen) or anaerobic respiration (which

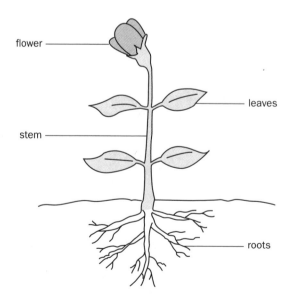

Figure 6.2 The basic structure of a flowering plant

does not require oxygen). Aerobic respiration provides more energy (this time, in the form of heat) than anaerobic respiration and for most organisms this is the preferred process. Like photosynthesis, this aerobic respiration can be summarized with an equation:

$$glucose + oxygen \longrightarrow carbon\ dioxide + water \quad [+ energy]$$
$$C_6H_{12}O_6 + 6O_2 \longrightarrow 6CO_2 + 6H_2O \quad [+ energy]$$

Interestingly, this is chemically the reverse of photosynthesis, with only the form of energy that is different. Respiration occurs in the mitochondria – structures that are found in the cytoplasm of the cell (such structures that have specific jobs within cells are called *organelles* – the nucleus is another organelle). The energy derived from respiration is used to drive the chemical reactions that occur within cells and in obtaining minerals from the soil.

Water is also essential for many other processes connected to growth besides photosynthesis. Chemical reactions within cells occur in water-based solutions. Protein molecules are often held in shape by attractive forces, called hydrogen bonds, which can be exerted by water molecules. Water is also important in the transport of materials around the plant and a vital part of the plant's support mechanism. Without a skeleton, plants rely partly on the fact that water-filled cells are under pressure (called *turgidity*) for some of their support – fail to water a plant adequately and it will wilt as this pressure is lost. This support helps the leaves to present a large surface for the absorption of sunlight.

Temperature is also a factor in plant growth as the chemical reactions that are part of all life processes, including growth, are themselves temperature dependent. As in all living things, plants contain enzymes, made up of protein molecules, which work at their most efficient within a certain temperature range. Too cold and the enzymes only work very slowly; too hot and their structure breaks down and they are said to become *denatured*. Hence plants grow very slowly when the temperature is cold, something born out by the fact that we do not have to cut the grass in winter.

The common way of showing the effects of light, air, water and temperature on plant growth is by comparing plants that have a 'normal' amount of these variables with those that have 'lack' of them. Thus plants that are well watered, have a plentiful supply of air and sunlight and are kept warm grow well. Those lacking these requirements do not grow well. This can be extended by comparing with plants grown in a greenhouse. It should be borne in mind though, that a good result can only be achieved by having a number of plants in each sample, due to natural variations between individuals.

Teaching activity

Try growing plants in different conditions, for example in the dark, without water, in the fridge. Most teachers use cress and bean seeds for this but sunflower seeds are equally effective for a change, as well as putting mature plants (such as spider plant offshoots) in different conditions.

Mineral nutrition

Minerals are naturally occurring chemical compounds. Living things require a small, but constant supply of these substances for a variety of life processes. Although plants can make their food (that is, glucose), they need to take in minerals, which they do through their roots. The term 'mineral' can be a little confusing to the non-scientist – how many of us visualize obtaining nutrition from an iron bar to gain our daily intake of iron? What we are actually taking in are iron atoms that are joined, chemically, to other atoms in the form of a compound (iron tablets typically contain iron sulphate, where the iron is joined to sulphur and oxygen atoms). A variety of chemical elements are essential for life, each needed for a specific function. Plants, for instance, require magnesium atoms to produce chlorophyll molecules. These minerals can be obtained naturally from the soil. They get into the soil by a variety of means, for example, dissolving from rocks, the rotting of dead organisms, waste products such as urine and faeces.

One of the most important minerals for growth is nitrogen. This is because it is needed to produce protein molecules for plant structures and enzymes. Despite the fact that air is approximately four-fifths nitrogen, plants cannot use this directly and have to absorb nitrogen in the form of nitrates (nitrogen chemically bound to oxygen as nitrate ions NO_3^-). Nitrates form in the soil naturally via the action of lightning causing atmospheric nitrogen and oxygen to react, from decaying organic matter and by the action of bacteria in the soil and in the roots of leguminous plants such as peas and clover. Thus nitrate formation can be encouraged by the spreading and digging in of manure and compost and by allowing fields to lie fallow so that, for instance, clover can grow. Nitrates can also be added through the use of chemical fertilizers that contain nitrogen compounds. This leads us to another common misconception that plants can obtain *food* from the soil. Certainly they obtain mineral nutrition from the soil, but the idea that they obtain food is incorrect (they make their food by photosynthesis). This misconception is reinforced by the use of the term *plant food* for fertilizers, commonly used by gardeners.

Plant reproduction and seeds

Unlike humans and most other animals, plants have the ability to reproduce *asexually* as well as *sexually*. Asexual reproduction requires only one parent organism and is how simple organisms such as bacteria reproduce. There are, in fact, a number of different mechanisms by which asexual reproduction can occur. This includes simple cell division, where single-celled organisms make a copy of themselves, then divide into two new cells (such as bacteria) and what is known as vegetative reproduction, which muliticellular plants can undergo. Examples of vegetative reproduction include the formation of eyes on potatoes and runners from plants such as strawberry and spider plants. These growths result in new plants, which are *clones* of the parent plant, which means that they are *genetically identical*. This has been used widely in horticulture to produce new plants with identical characteristics of their parents. Asexual reproduction has its advantages, for instance, for plants that are well suited to their environment. It is also quicker than sexual reproduction. However, it can lead to genetic weaknesses and such plants may be very susceptible to changes in their environment.

Sexual reproduction, on the other hand, involves two parent plants. As such it does not produce clones, but offspring that contain genetic information from both parents. This can be an advantage as genetic weaknesses become less likely and the offspring can often cope better with changing environments. One way that plants reproduce sexually is with flowers; as such these are called *flowering plants* or *angiosperms*. The flowers of such plants contain the reproductive organs of the plant, each plant has a different flower, but they all contain the same basic structures. A simplified diagram of a typical inset-pollinated flower is shown in Figure 6.3, with the function of each part summarized in Table 6.1.

For sexual reproduction to occur the *pollen* grains from one flower have to be transported to the flower of another plant and this is called *pollination*. Pollen can be transported by the wind blowing it from the exposed stamen of one plant to another's flower or by animals such as insects inadvertently picking up pollen from one flower, and then depositing it in another as they search for *nectar* – produced in flowers to

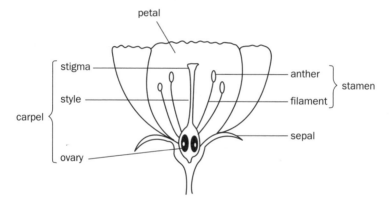

Figure 6.3 The flower of a typical insect-pollinated flowering plant

Table 6.1 The functions of the parts of a flower

Part of flower	Function
Petal	Attracts insects by colour and scent
Sepal	Protects the developing flower when in bud
Carpel	The female reproductive organ
Stigma	Part of the carpel which collects the pollen
Style	Part of the carpel between the stigma and the ovary; a pollen grain grows a tube through the style to deliver its nucleus to an ovule in the ovary
Ovary	Part of the carpel where the female sex cells, the ovules, are stored
Stamen	The male reproductive organ
Anther	Part of the stamen where the male sex cells, the pollen, is stored
Filament	Part of the stamen, the stalk which supports the anther

encourage the insects in. The flowers of insect-pollinated plants consist of brightly coloured petals, which attract the insects towards the flower. The process of pollination is, however, subject to many failures, much more so for wind-pollinated plants, which, as a result, produce more pollen than insect-pollinated plants. Indeed, some plants increase their chances of success by temporarily trapping insects inside their flowers to allow greater opportunity for the pollen to be picked up or deposited in the right place.

The pollen is the male *gamete* (or sex cell) and is the plant equivalent to sperm in animals. Like all gametes it contains half of the genetic information to produce a new organism and its nucleus must join with that of a female gamete, the *ovule*. The ovules are contained within an ovary in the carpel. A pollen grain is adapted so that it can stick to the stigma of a carpel. It then grows a tube (the pollen tube) into the style of the carpel, which delivers the pollen nucleus to the ovule, so that the two nuclei can join. Once the two nuclei have joined the ovule has been *fertilized* and now contains a full set of genetic information. It is this fertilized ovule that becomes a seed, which will contain an embryo of the new plant, a store of food so that it can *germinate* and a tough outer coating called the *testa*.

It is the embryo inside the seed that will grow into the new flowering plant. For this to happen the seed must be *dispersed*, that is, leave the parent plant. Different species of plant have developed different mechanisms for this *seed dispersal*. Some develop fruits that contain the seeds. When an animal eats the fruit, the seeds that are not broken up, pass through the animal's digestive system (protected by the indigestible testa) and are dispersed in the animals faeces. Others may be dispersed by the wind (such as dandelions, and sycamores with their winged seeds), some are encased in a coating that attaches itself to the body of an animal (such as the burdock) and some may explode from pods (such as lupins). This process is important as it allows the new plant to move away from its parent, so that the two will not be in direct competition when the new plant starts to grow.

Once the seed has been dispersed, if it has found a suitable place to germinate the embryo plant inside will start to grow. Germination is the initial growth of the new plant, as it uses up its food store. It occurs when there is an adequate supply of water and air (the latter to provide oxygen for respiration), and if it is not too cold. Again this can be proved by experimenting with seeds, having one batch in 'normal' conditions as a control, with the other batches being deprived of various things. It is good to prove here that light is not essential for germination, in fact the seeds often grow much quicker (albeit with yellow leaves) as they use up their food store in an attempt to reach the light they need for further growth.

This then is the last stage in the life cycle of a flowering plant, before the new plant itself reproduces (see Figure 6.4).

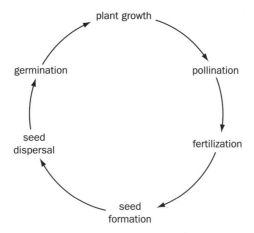

Figure 6.4 The life cycle of a flowering plant

Links to teaching

Teaching activities

Experiment with newly germinated bean plants to see how their roots are sensitive to gravity. Try moving them as they grow to see what effect this has on the direction in which the roots grow.

Grow a variety of plants in the classroom throughout the year, and encourage pupils to take responsibility for looking after them. Try growing plants from cuttings and bulbs as well as from seed. Grow cacti and spider plants, which make small plants without flowering first.

Other things to do and try

With the help of enthusiastic and knowledgeable members of the wider school community, set up a gardening club.

TOP TEACHING TIP

Use trees as examples when discussing plants. Children are just as familiar with them as they are with other plants

Some common misconceptions

- Plants are not living.
- Seeds are dead.
- Plants do not move.
- Plants make food from the sun.
- Plants get food from the soil.
- Fertilizer is plant food.
- Flowers are plants.
- Insects 'know' they are pollinating plants.
- Pollination is the same as fertilization.
- Trees are not plants.
- Seeds will not germinate in the dark – we plant them underground!
- Plants breathe in oxygen and breathe out carbon dioxide.

AMAZING FACT

Acorns are less that 2 cms in length, but oak trees can grow up to 50 metres tall.

7

Variation and classification

National Curriculum: Attainment Target Sc2, Strand 4 (KS1: 2.4a–4c, KS2: 2.4a–4j)
QCA Schemes of Work: Units 2C, 4B and 6A

Curriculum requirements

Variation and classification is important at all Key Stages of the National Curriculum. At KS1 and KS2 the emphasis is solely on these two aspects, with inheritance included at KS3. Currently in the KS4 programme of study, classification is of less importance (although becomes important once again at A level) and the focus is on the mechanism of inheritance and other factors which cause variation and on the process of evolution.

The National Curriculum for Science programme of study states that at KS1 pupils should be taught to recognize similarities and differences between themselves and others, to treat others with sensitivity and to group living things according to observable similarities and differences.

At KS2 pupils should be taught to make and use keys, how locally occurring animals and plants can be identified and assigned to groups and that the variety of plants and animals makes it important to identify them and assign them to groups.

Variation

Variation in this context simply refers to the differences between living things. All living things exhibit variation as a result of their genetic make-up or what happens to them throughout their lives. Sometimes these variations may be few in number, such as the differences between different humans (especially if they are related), or many, such as the differences between animals and plants.

Indeed, a suitable starting point for discussing variation would be the differences between people. Obvious differences are sex, eye colour, hair colour, skin colour, curly or straight hair, hair length, height, weight, and so on. (The list may end up quite large, despite the fact that we are all of the same species!) It is also important to be aware that some children will be very conscious of their appearance, height, weight, and so on, and this is where 'treating others with sensitivity' comes in. Ultimately the professional judgement of the teacher is important here concerning which variations may be studied in more detail in terms of measuring some of these variations or recording them in charts, and so on.

Once humans have been looked at, the differences between other types of organism can be explored. Indeed, it is these differences that help us to identify other organisms as we rapidly ask a number of questions, subconsciously, to make a decision on what the organism we are looking at is. We often identify different trees by the shapes of their leaves and we distinguish insects from other invertebrates by the fact that insects have three pairs of legs. This will be considered further in the section on classification below.

The causes of variation

Variation is caused by two major groups of factors, *inheritance* and *environment*. For some variations it is easy to identify which is the cause, but for others it can be less obvious, and it is often a combination of the two.

Inherited variation is a result of the genetic information that has been passed on from parent to offspring. Characteristics such as eye colour, (natural) hair colour, the shape of some facial features (for example, the nose) and blood group are inherited. The nucleus of each cell in an organism contains this genetic information. In most organisms this information is found on structures known as *chromosomes*, of which humans have 46, 23 inherited from each parent. Chromosomes are made of long, complex molecules of a chemical called *DNA* (deoxyribonucleic acid). We can think of DNA molecules as being rather like a ladder, twisted into a spiral shape known as a 'double helix'. The 'rungs' of this ladder are made of pairs of chemicals known as *bases*. There are four types of base and each is known by a letter that corresponds to the initial letter of the name of that base: G, C, T and A (guanine, cytosine, thymine and adenine). These bases always pair up in the same way to form the rungs of the DNA ladder – G with C and T with A – and the sequence of these paired bases along the DNA molecule form a code, rather like the bar code we find on goods bought in shops. Different sections of the DNA contain the code for producing different proteins in the body and thus determine the make-up of the body. These different sections of DNA are called *genes* and each gene controls a different characteristic of the body, either on its own or in combination with one or more other genes. When an organism reproduces, it makes copies of its chromosomes and these get passed on to their offspring. Hence human sperm and egg cells (ova) contain a nucleus comprising copies of the parents' genes on 23 chromosomes. If a sperm fertilizes an ovum, the nucleus of the new cell (the zygote) contains the full 46 chromosomes, with genes from both parents. It is the combination of the genes inherited that determines the characteristics of the offspring. There are other mechanisms for passing on genetic information but they are too complex to consider here.

The process described above is what happens in sexual reproduction and this process increases variation, since the nuclei of different sperm and ova will contain a different combination of genes – which explains why siblings have different genetic characteristics from each other. Identical twins, however, have the same genetic characteristics as each other as they resulted from a single fertilized egg that split in two, with each part developing separately. Organisms that reproduce asexually pass on a copy of their whole nucleus and genetic information to their offspring, hence parent and offspring are *clones*, meaning they are genetically identical.

However, even identical twins and clones can exhibit variation between each other. This is because *environmental* factors also have a role to play in variation. Examples of this cause of variation are many. Availability of food, exposure to disease, the effects of sunlight, ionizing radiation and chemicals in the environment can all lead to variations. Hence identical twins will have different birth weights if one receives more food than the other in the womb, and plants with a common parent, which were a result of asexual reproduction, will vary depending on the amount of sunlight and water they receive. A suntan is a good example of environmentally caused variation, where the skin produces a chemical, melanin, to help protect it from ultraviolet light from the sun. This is only temporary as the natural levels of melanin in the skin are controlled by genes; having a suntan does not change one's genes. In very extreme circumstances, exposure to radiation or chemicals may cause genes to alter. This is called *mutation*. Any change to a gene will affect how it works. Many mutations are harmless, some may prove to be beneficial, for example, in the process of evolution, and some may prove to be harmful, such as those that lead to cancers.

Classification

Humans like to classify things, it helps us to study them in detail and to identify how new discoveries fit into our existing understanding. The sheer number of living things means that we can study them more effectively if we have classified them first. It also helps to establish when a new species has been discovered. One of the problems here is that there are a number of ways in which we can classify organisms; indeed, the systems employed can vary between modern books and other resources which discuss the subject. The major discrepancies, however, tend to be for some of the more obscure members of the living world such as micro-organisms and the subtle differences between the different levels of hierarchy in the classification system, and will not really impact on the learning of pupils at primary level. As such, we will start simply then move on to one of the major accepted methods for classification.

A very basic way to classify living things is into three basic groups: animals, plants and other organisms. This last of these is wide ranging as it includes a variety of organisms as diverse as fungi and bacteria, but as the emphasis at KS1 and KS2 is on plants and animals, so as long as the pupils accept that fungi are not plants, there should not be a problem. Classification, or *taxonomy*, works on a hierarchical system based on the characteristics of different organisms. Organisms are grouped because they share similar characteristics. As these initial groupings are refined the amount of variation becomes smaller and smaller until we reach the level of species. Indeed, even at this level, as we have already seen, there is still a lot of variation between individuals.

One of the most commonly employed classification systems (see Figure 7.1) starts by dividing all living things into five *kingdoms*:

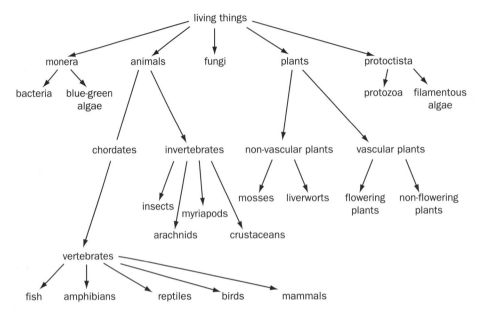

Figure 7.1 Classification simplified

Animals   Plants   Fungi   Monera   Protoctista

The key variations looked for in kingdoms are at the cellular level. Monera include bacteria and blue-green algae which have no true nucleus (or other organelles) in their cells and protoctista include other simple organisms such as *amoeba* and filamentous algae which have cells with a nucleus.

Below each kingdom we have the level of phylum (sometimes called division), then class, order, family, genus and finally species (indeed, sometimes we can subdivide species into subspecies) and the variations as we progress down this hierarchy often become more apparent as physical differences with the body of the organism and the functions of its parts. The general definition of a species is where individuals can successfully mate to produce *fertile* offspring. Sometimes closely related species can produce offspring together but these will not be able to reproduce themselves. A common example here is the mule, which is the infertile offspring of a horse and a donkey. At genus level we have groups of very closely related species for example horses and donkeys as mentioned. The organisms in families are not as close as those at genus level and a good example here are the cat family. The variation at order level and above is much greater and includes much larger and more diverse groups of organisms.

As an example of how this hierarchy works we could take humans:

Kingdom: *animal*
Phylum: *chordate/vertebrate (actually a subphylum of chordate)*
Class: *mammal*

Order: *primate*

Family: *hominid*

Genus: *homo*

Species: *sapiens*

Much of the work carried out by pupils at KS3 concerns the classification of animals, first into vertebrates and invertebrates and then into the various classes of these animals. At primary level much will be concerned with the differences between animals and plants, which can then be extended further by considering different groups of animals and plants, however, there is no expectation that pupils should recall the specific names of these groups. This can be achieved through the use of pictures, models and live specimens and considering their differences and similarities. Consideration of animals and plants in the local environment is also stressed in the programme of study for KS2 and this can be done quite simply by observing various plants and animals such as garden plants, local wild plants, birds, insects and even pets.

One problem that children often have with grouping anything (not just living things) is that they focus too much on differences at the expense of similarities. As such they may be reluctant to place an animal in a group because it has one obvious difference despite the fact that it has many more similarities with the other animals in the proposed group. A good example here might be not placing snakes with other reptiles and grouping them with worms, purely on the basis that a snake has no legs. This assessment of characteristics and their relative importance needs, in the writer's experience, to be taught explicitly to pupils.

Keys

Keys are very effective tools for identifying things, in this context living things. At KS2 pupils should be taught how to use keys and how to make their own. Keys essentially involve a series of questions to which there are only two possible answers. As one progresses through the key the number of possibilities is reduced until the answer is reached. Keys generally take one of two basic forms, either a series of written statements leading to either another question or the answer, or a more visual approach rather like a family tree. The latter is likely to be more accessible to those with problems with interpreting lines of text and has the advantage that it can be followed through physically with a finger until the answer is reached.

Teaching activity

A good way to introduce keys is to use one to identify members of the class, or develop one with the class to do the same when teaching pupils how to make their own key. A successful key will have unambiguous questions that swiftly lead to the correct identification. Pupils can use or develop keys to identify animals and plants that they have studied in their local environment or animals and also other animals and plants that they know of. The next stage is to use keys to identify more unusual organisms which is a skill they will need to take beyond KS2.

Figures 7.2a and 7.2b show the two types of key being use to identify the same six organisms.

Studying variation and classification

As has already been stated there are numerous ways of studying variation and classification from considering the differences between fellow pupils and animals and plants in the local environment. Use of school nature areas and ponds can be made but it is still possible to study local animals and plants without such areas as living things are everywhere, even in the most built up of areas. Annotating pictures of animals and plants to highlight their characteristics can be useful and this can be extended to consider why they have these characteristics (see also 'Linking life processes to an organism's environment' in Chapter 4). Use of models produced by pupils and plastic toys of animals can also be useful, the latter especially so as pupils can physically group the figures, then regroup as necessary. There is also the opportunity here for cross-curricular work with mathematics and geography as obvious examples.

More advanced ideas

Beyond KS2 the mechanisms for passing on inherited characteristics and other related ideas are studied in increasing detail. Pupils often find it surprising that different breeds of dog actually belong to the same species, in fact a poodle has more in common genetically with an alsatian than a wolf does, appearances can be deceptive! Different breeds of dog have been developed over a very long time by a process

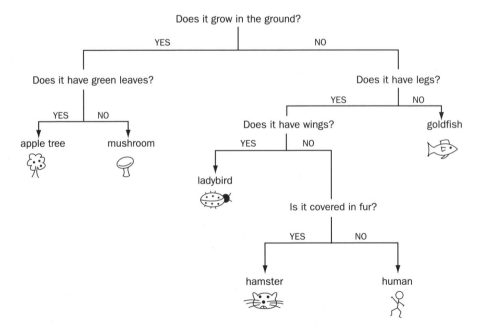

Figure 7.2a Example key 1

1) Does it grow in the ground?	....YES – go to 2
	....NO – go to 3
2) Does it have green leaves?	....YES = apple tree 
	....NO = mushroom
3) Does it have legs?	....YES – go to 4
	....NO = goldfish 
4) Does it have wings?	....YES = ladybird 
	....NO – go to 5
5) Is it covered in fur?	....YES = hamster 
	....NO = human 

Figure 7.2b Example key 2

known as selective breeding. This involves choosing an organism and deliberately breeding it with another to produce offspring with desirable characteristics of one or both of its parents. This has occurred for as long as humans have domesticated animals and plants for their own use. Plants can be selectively bred to produce higher-yielding or better tasting crops or for a particular colour of flower. Livestock can be selectively bred for meat or milk production and horses for racing. The reasons why this process works were only realized relatively recently with the science of genetics. The hope is that certain genes will be passed on from one generation to the next. However, gene transfer can be somewhat of a lottery which drives people to choose breeding partners from an ever-decreasing number of individuals, to increase the chance of the desirable characteristics being inherited. The downside of this restriction of the *gene pool* is that the risk of passing on faulty genes also increases as the amount of variation decreases. This was very apparent with the interbreeding that occurred in the royal families of Europe, the classic example being the increases in haemophilia in the descendants of Queen Victoria. Victoria was a carrier of this gene and passed it on to some of her offspring. The gene in question is found on the X chromosome which also plays a role in sex determination. As a female she had two X chromosomes, the other without the faulty gene so she did not suffer from the disease. However, a male inheriting the faulty gene will have haemophilia as males have an X chromosome and a Y chromosome and the Y chromosome does not carry the equivalent gene to counteract the faulty one. Hence this faulty gene was passed on to numerous male members of Europe's royal families as Victoria encouraged her children and grandchildren to marry into them.

New developments in gene technology mean that it is possible to add genetic information to cells to achieve desired effects. The creation of Dolly, the cloned sheep, involved passing all the genetic information from Dolly's 'mother' into the nucleus of an egg cell which had had its genetic material removed. Hence Dolly was a clone of her parent with all her parent's genetic characteristics. Genes can also be implanted into the cells of crops to give a variety of desired characteristics such as longer shelf life, greater yields and resistance to disease and herbicides. Genetic engineering is currently a very controversial issue but an even-handed consideration of the facts is important. If it were not for the fact that it is possible to implant the human insulin producing gene into certain bacteria then millions of diabetics across the world would not be able to have access to the amount of insulin they need to stay healthy.

In contrast to selective breeding, evolution (see also 'Linking life processes to an organism's environment' in Chapter 4) results from a natural form of selection. The fact that an organism has a certain characteristic is often genetic, hence these genes are likely to be passed on to the organism's offspring. When these inherited characteristics are useful, they help the organism to survive successfully enough in its environment so that it is able to reproduce before it dies; hence the genes have a chance to be passed on again. Less successful organisms will become fewer in number and may even become extinct. Small variations that occur from one generation to the next can build up over thousands and millions of years until the descendants are so different from their ancestors that we can say that they are a new species. Much longer periods of time were needed to produce the variation that exists at higher levels of the taxonomic hierarchy, hence the further you go back, in theory, the fewer taxonomic groups there will be. In addition, the percentage of common DNA in many species points to them originating from only a few simple forms of life and, perhaps even from only one organism. Evolution takes many paths and surprisingly few are successful, as the fossil record of extinct organisms shows us. Indeed, the organisms that we know through fossils are only thought to represent a tiny fraction of those that have existed since life started on the planet. There is, and has been, therefore, huge variety in the living world and classifying it all is no mean feat!

Links to teaching

More teaching activities

Sorting activities are important for children to develop an understanding of how things can be sorted. The best way to start with very young children is to sort animals by observable characteristics, for example, animals with legs, animals with no legs. After this, teachers can then begin to introduce scientific ideas such as where an animal lives (sea or land) or how they have their young (eggs or babies). This can be done with pictures or with plastic model animals.

Other things to do and try

Information and communication technology can be used for sorting and categorizing plants and animals. Databases can be built up over the course of a topic. A good way to introduce children to the idea of databases and what they can do is with the Top Trumps card game that can be played and then adapted for categorizing plants and animals.

TOP TEACHING TIP

The best place for children to learn about living things is to get out and look at them in their natural environment.

Some common misconceptions

- Fungi are plants.
- Plants are not living.
- Humans are not animals.
- Insects and other invertebrates are not animals.
- Fish are not animals.

AMAZING FACT

Humans originated in Africa, but now the homo sapiens species has adapted and lives all over the world where we have adapted to different environments.

8

Living things in their environment

National Curriculum: Attainment Target Sc2, Strand 5 (KS1: 2.5a–5f, KS2: 2.5a–5g)
QCA Schemes of Work: Units 2C, 4B, 5B and 6A

Curriculum requirements

The subject matter of this section forms the beginnings of the interdependence strand identified by the national framework for science. Study at KS1 tends to focus more on the local environment, with consideration of other habitats becoming important at KS2. The National Curriculum for Science programme of study states that at KS1 pupils should be taught to find out about the different kinds of plants and animals in the local environment; identify similarities and differences between local environments and ways in which these affect animals and plants that are found there. They should also be taught to care for the environment. At KS2 the various strands of study are divided up into three main areas: *adaptation* where they should be taught about the different plants and animals found in different habitats and about how animals and plants in two different habitats are suited to their environment; *feeding relationships* where they are taught to use **food chains** to show feeding relationships in a habitat and about how nearly all food chains start with a green plant; *micro-organisms* where they are taught that micro-organisms are living organisms that are often too small to be seen, and that they may be beneficial or harmful. In addition they are expected to be taught about ways in which living things and the environment need protection.

The subject of the environment can be an emotive and controversial one and is of increasingly greater concern around the globe. As such, it is one of the most important areas of science in relation to current and future affairs and offers debates that current and future generations need to be well informed about if they are to face up to some of the challenges that undoubtedly lie ahead.

Environments and adaptation

The word 'environment' can have different meanings at different levels from the whole of the **Earth** to small parts of it. The *physical environment* refers to the actual structure of the Earth such as the types of rock found there and the formation of that rock (for example, a cave). This, together with other conditions such as climate are what constitute the wider environment and it is the result of all these factors which initially determines which organisms can survive there. Indeed, the organisms within an environment also contribute to it. *Ecology* is the study of the *interdependence* that exists between living things and between living things and their environment. Places where organisms live are called *habitats*. Some habitats are natural while others are artificially created by humans. This distinction can be useful but it should be remembered that the activities of humans can affect so-called natural environments, and remarkably few places are unaffected by human activity. There are a huge number of different habitats on the planet and the differences between habitats and their environments affect the types of organisms we find there. Local environments can be found everywhere, a garden, under a leaf or a stone, walls, window sills and plant pots. A good example of an easy to find local habitat is leaf litter (areas under-neath trees and shrubs where leaves have fallen) and the organisms that live there do so because they survive well in that habitat. Hence we find woodlice and millipedes which feed off the leaves and other decaying vegetation that makes up the bulk of the leaf litter, but we also find predators such as centipedes which will feed off other animals living there. Such animals thrive in the damp, cool and dark conditions found there. Indeed, we can use a simple device called a choice chamber to show that woodlice prefer darkness to light conditions. When comparing habitats, both local and otherwise we should look to see what conditions make up its environment as this will affect what organisms can survive there.

Living things are adapted to live in their own environment and this has already been explored in Chapter 4. Without these adaptations they would not be able to compete successfully for resources such as food, water, breeding partners and light with plants. This idea of competition is studied in later key stages and is a major factor in survival and population size. Studying the adaptations of organisms is an important part of understanding why they live where they do, and this can be done by describing the features of these organisms, the make-up of the environment they live in and then comparing the two. Classic examples include the comparisons between land- and water-based animals, and between animals and plants that live in hot and cold climates. In addition, organisms have to cope with daily and seasonal changes to their environment and the latter is especially apparent in a temperate climate such as that in the UK. Hence: animals tend to reproduce so that their young are born in the spring when the climate is warming up and more food becomes available; some animals may hibernate or migrate during the winter when less food is available; and some trees lose their leaves in winter when there is less light and free water available for photosynthesis, thereby compensating for by the reduced amount of food that can be provided for the tree.

Feeding relationships

The idea of interdependence, mentioned earlier, is also important when considering the feeding habits of animals. Plants and animals are sources of food and so the organisms within a habitat are dependent on one another for this food, and their ability to compete for it affects the population size of each organism within that habitat. At KS2 the main focus is on identifying these feeding relationships with simple food chains. This is later built upon at KS3 and KS4 by considering how food chains are linked and how we can quantify these relationships by considering, first, population size and then the amount of food energy available. Food chains (see Figure 8.1) basically show us what eats what within a particular habitat. They generally start with a plant, which is known as a producer because it produces its own food. Some food chains may start with micro-organisms which can, like plants, photosynthesize (see Chapter 6) and some which produce food from other sources, like the bacteria which live around volcanic vents on the deep sea bed and utilize the sulphurous chemicals there to make food. Such food producing organisms are called *autotrophs* (organisms which eat others for food are called *heterotrophs*), although it is only the plants that we really need to consider at this stage. The plants at the start of the food chain are eaten by animals known as primary consumers. These may in turn be eaten by another animal, known as the secondary consumer, which itself may be eaten by a third animal, the tertiary consumer. It is possible that this could continue but food chains containing four or more consumers are rare and where they do occur it is likely to be in the sea where the primary producers and primary consumers are microscopic organisms.

It is important that each organism is linked with a series of arrows that are shown the correct way round, from producer to primary consumer to secondary consumer, and so on. This is because what they actually represent is the flow of energy through the food chain, and it can be a hindrance to later study if this is not done correctly from the start. One way to remember this might be to consider that the arrow shows that the various organisms end up inside the others when they are eaten. The animal at the end of the food chain is often referred to as the top predator although it should be remembered that this may not be a *carnivore*, it may be an *omnivore* and even, in some cases, a *herbivore* (see Chapter 5 for definitions of these terms).

Of course, food chains are only simplifications. Many animals eat a variety of food and most plants and animals have several 'predators'. Food chains can be linked together as a **food web** and when this is done (at KS3) it helps to see how this interdependence works. Not all the energy of a consumed organism ends up as part of the body of the animal that has eaten it, so for a food web to be sustainable there must

grass   rabbit   fox

Figure 8.1 A simple food chain

be more food available at the start with the amount of food decreasing as one progresses along the food chains. This can be quantified in two ways. First, one can use a pyramid of numbers. This is rather like a bar chart which has been rotated through 90° and centralized. It is produced by considering the population of each organism along the food chain as in Figure 8.2. Pyramids of numbers can quickly show if the food chain can sustain itself. Each level is called a *trophic level* and the number of organisms at each trophic level should decrease as you go up the diagram. We can also show how a change in the population at one trophic level could affect the others as in Figure 8.3; where the number of organisms in the second trophic level (the primary consumers) has decreased, causing an increase in the number of producers (as fewer are eaten) and a reduction in the number of secondary consumers (because they have less food available). Pyramids of numbers do have their drawbacks as they do not indicate the size of an organism and thus the amount of food it either provides or needs. Hence we use pyramids of biomass (biomass being the **mass** of the organisms in the food chain) to overcome this. A classic example is shown in Figure 8.4, which shows that a single oak tree has enough biomass to sustain a number of animals despite the fact that a pyramid of numbers might indicate otherwise!

Micro-organisms

The name 'micro-organism' reflects the size of these living things as they are usually too small to be seen unless viewed through a microscope, although large colonies can

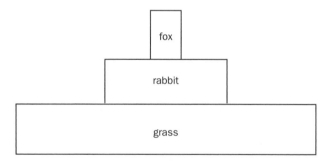

Figure 8.2 A pyramid of numbers

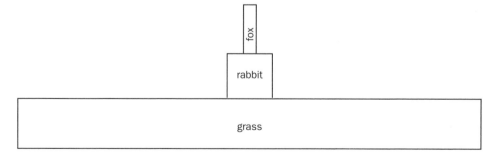

Figure 8.3 Changes in population in a pyramid of numbers

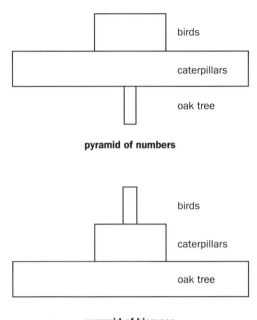

pyramid of numbers

pyramid of biomass

Figure 8.4 Comparing a pyramid of numbers with a pyramid of biomass

be seen with the unaided eye. There are a great variety of micro-organisms, including bacteria, viruses, yeasts, protozoa such as amoeba and some algae. Micro-organisms grow best in certain conditions where they have a source of food, warmth and oxygen (although some, such as yeast, can exist without oxygen).

The QCA Scheme of Work focuses on the micro-organisms that cause disease, those that cause decay and those which are used in food production, such as yeast. Micro-organisms are everywhere, including large numbers on and in the human body. Many are harmless in the populations that we are exposed to but some can be hazardous to health and these are called *pathogens* and commonly referred to as *germs*. Many diseases such as chicken pox, colds, measles, mumps, rubella and athlete's foot are caused by micro-organisms. They attack cells and may produce toxic chemicals which make us feel unwell, such as salmonella bacteria from food poisoning. Tooth plaque consists of micro-organisms that cause tooth decay and gum disease. Cleanliness, using bleaches, cooking food thoroughly, and so on reduces the risk of disease by removing or killing the micro-organism concerned. It should be remembered though that reheated food might be harmful as, although it may kill the bacteria that have regrown during storage, it will not destroy the toxins they have produced. When we are infected by a pathogen, our body's immune system attempts to destroy the invading micro-organisms but this takes some time and that is why we suffer the symptoms of the disease while we are fighting it. Sometimes we may need extra help to destroy bacteria and this can be done with the use of anti-biotics (these do not work against viruses) such as penicillin, itself a mould, another micro-organism.

Micro-organisms such as moulds also cause the decay of foods and this can be studied in the classroom, albeit under strict supervision and with reference to the appropriate health and safety guidelines. Decay itself is an important process that allows organic materials to be recycled. Sometimes these are broken down into inorganic materials that can be reused by plants, such as nitrogen compounds. The nitrogen cycle is not studied at primary level but is an important area of study at later key stages, especially KS4. Plants need to absorb nitrogen as nitrate compounds and these are produced mainly by bacteria in the soil and in the root nodules on leguminous plants (like clover and beans). Bacteria also produce other nitrogen-based chemicals such as ammonia, and even convert nitrates back into nitrogen gas that is released into the atmosphere. Decay of dead organisms therefore adds fertility to the soil and this can be managed to produce compost for gardening.

Teaching activity

The way in which food substances decay can illustrate the effects of micro-organisms and an interesting investigation is to study the rates of decay of different foods, for example, different fruits.

Micro-organisms are also used in food production. Cheese and yogurt making utilize the controlled action of bacteria on milk and the chemical changes that occur in the milk allow it to be preserved for longer in these forms. Indeed, blue cheeses take this a stage further as the blueness is due to colonies of bacteria that add to the flavour of the cheese. Often milk is pasteurized (named after Louis Pasteur who devised the process and who was a leading figure in proving the existence of micro-organisms), which kills many of the more dangerous bacteria in the milk (some, however, do remain which is why, even sealed milk bottles will eventually go off). Ultra-heat treated (UHT) milk is heated to a higher temperature and for longer than pasteurized milk thereby killing all the bacteria so that the milk has, effectively, an indefinite shelf-life). Yeast is a fungus that is also used for baking and brewing. It feeds on sugars in food and respires anaerobically (see Chapter 4), producing alcohol and carbon dioxide. In baking, the carbon dioxide gas bubbles through the baking mixture causing it to rise as the bubbles get trapped. When the mixture reaches a high enough temperature the yeast is killed and the alcohol produced (bakers' yeast produces far less alcohol than brewers' yeast) evaporates away. Like all microbes the yeast grows and reproduces best when it is warm and has a plentiful supply of food.

Care and protection of the environment

As the future guardians of our planet, children should be taught at an early stage to respect the environment, both the physical environment and the organisms that live there. Human activity has the potential to harm habitats and *ecosystems* (the communities of organisms with their environments) on a local and a worldwide scale. When studying a local environment, pupils should be made aware that they must not intentionally harm organisms living there and if there is need to remove animals then they should be put back as soon as possible and treated with care. Good scientists observe with minimal disruption to what they are observing. When studying such areas the teacher must also take into account the health and safety of the pupils, providing plastic gloves if necessary and making sure they have washed their hands afterwards.

Later on these ideas can be extended by considering how a habitat could be affected by human activity and examples are given in the QCA Scheme of Work (Unit 4B). In addition to those examples provided, consideration could be given to other ideas such as the removal of hedgerows for farming, reclaiming marshland, the building of roads, houses, schools and industrial sites. In the recent past, little consideration was made of the effects of our actions and it is only in relatively recent years that we have come to realize what a potentially devastating effect we can have on habitats and the organisms that live in them. Use of chemicals in the environment is important here as well. Early pesticides such as dichlorodiphenyltrichloroethane (DDT) to help grow crops entered the food chain and affected organisms throughout those food chains, especially the top predators that suffered the effects of increasing concentrations of these chemicals in the food that they ate. Ecosystems are complex and it is often difficult to predict the knock-on effects of tampering with only part of them. On a global scale, issues such as global warming and climate change are big news and the potential changes to habitats that these and other environmental problems make the future of the planet as we know it ever more uncertain.

Links to teaching

More teaching activities

The best way for children to learn about environments is to study them where they occur. However, if school trips prove to be difficult, then smaller environments such as wormeries or ponds can be created within classrooms.

It is difficult to study organisms such as bacteria that are too small to see. However, their effects can be safely studied. One example is to test conditions for keeping slices of bread or apples fresh. For instance, slices can be placed in the fridge or freezer, in the classroom in plastic or paper bags or in airtight boxes.

Other things to do and try

There are a surprising number of environments in a school, and not all are outside. Children can compare the field, the playground, the toilets, the wildlife garden and many other places in the school grounds.

TOP TEACHING TIP

It is important to follow health and safety guidelines when dealing with all living things in the classrooms, from pet rabbits, to earthworms and bread mould.

Some common misconceptions o

- All bacteria are 'bad' for humans.
- Bacteria and viruses have animal characteristics, for example, that a cold can deliberately 'get you'.
- That environments with living things only exist outside (try the toilets!).

AMAZING FACT

The human body is home to more micro-organisms than there are people living on the planet.

9

Grouping and classifying materials

National Curriculum: Attainment Target Sc3, Strand 1 (KS1: 3.1a–1d, KS2: 3.1a–1e)
QCA Schemes of Work: Units 1C, 2D, 3C, 3D, 4C, 5C and 5D

Curriculum requirements

Grouping and classifying materials forms part of the Sc3: Materials and their properties Attainment Target, which is essentially the chemistry element of the National Curriculum for Science. At KS1 and KS2 the programmes of study deal essentially with *bulk* properties, that is, properties of materials themselves, while at KS3 there is a change of emphasis where the nature of these properties is explained by consideration of the particles that materials are made of. By KS4 this section of the National Curriculum is focused on atoms and explains why the materials they are part of behave in the way they do in chemical and physical terms.

The National Curriculum for Science programme of study states that at KS1 pupils should be taught to use their senses to explore and recognize the similarities and differences between materials; sort objects into groups on the basis of simple material properties; recognize and name common types of material and recognize that some of them are found naturally, and find out about the uses of a variety of materials and how these are chosen for specific uses on the basis of their simple properties. At KS2 pupils should be taught to compare everyday materials and objects on the basis of their material properties, including hardness, strength, flexibility and magnetic behaviour, and to relate these properties to everyday uses of the materials; that some materials are better thermal insulators than others; that some materials are better electrical conductors than others; to describe and group rocks and soils on the basis of their characteristics, including appearance, texture and permeability, and to recognize differences between solids, liquids and gases, in terms of ease of flow and maintenance of shape and **volume**.

Particles: the building blocks of materials

Although particles are not part of the Sc3 programme of study until KS3, it is not possible to *explain* the behaviour of materials without considering them. Indeed, *particles* is one of the key themes in the National Strategy for Science. That is not to say that the existence and behaviour of particles necessarily ought to be explicitly taught to younger children, indeed it may be wholly appropriate for those of higher ability at KS2, but an awareness early on that everything is made up of tiny particles that affect how substances behave will not do any harm. Taking this idea too far at an early stage may, however, prove problematic. While a knowledge of particles and how they are arranged and behave in, say, solids, liquids and gases is easy to pick up (we are essentially talking acquisition of facts here – level 4 at most really), there is a considerable conceptual leap in appreciating quite how particles affect the substance they are in and that particles themselves do not exhibit the properties they 'give' the material they are part of. For example, particles do not get warm; the material they are in feels warm because the particles in that material are moving more.

Understanding particles is very important, as it helps teachers support accurate subject knowledge acquisition. In this context particles are bits of matter on the atomic scale. The size of an iron atom (one example of a particle) for instance is about 0.125 nanometres, where one nanometre is 0.000000001 metres or one-millionth of a millimetre – this means that 8,000,000,000 iron atoms lined up will measure one millimetre. Atoms are one type of particle, and there are other entities which we could mean when using the term. Some examples would be:

- molecules
- **protons**
- **electrons**
- quarks
- ions.

Molecules are groups of atoms; a water particle is a molecule containing two atoms of hydrogen joined to one oxygen atom. Ions are particles (atoms or molecules) that have lost or gained one or more electrons. Protrons, which are found *in* atoms, can also be considered particles – *subatomic* particles. These parts of atoms themselves are made of smaller particles called quarks. This all sounds a bit confusing and that is because the term 'particle' is a *general* one. It just means a small part of something and could conceivably be any size. In a scientific context we could say that a particle was something *as big or smaller* than a molecule. When we discuss particles and their role in determining the properties of the material we are talking about we actually mean the smallest part of that material which, if broken up any smaller, would not then retain the properties that it gives to the material it was one part of. This may seem complicated to explain to young children but simply put is made clearer with an example. Pure water contains molecules (as already stated) consisting of a group of three joined atoms (two hydrogen atoms and one oxygen atom). If you could isolate one of these molecules and then allow it to join other water particles the resulting group of particles would behave like water. However, if you were to break the molecules apart so that you freed the oxygen atoms from the hydrogen atoms, the resulting mix of atoms would *not* behave like water; they would behave like a mixture of oxygen and hydrogen. If, on the other hand, you took a piece of pure iron and broke it down into its individual atoms, they would still behave like iron because iron is composed solely of iron atoms. Hence what determines what the particle is depends on whether your material is an element or a compound (in this case iron is the element and water the compound).

Figure 9.1 shows a simplified model for an atom and is typical of what most pupils learn when they first study them. In the centre is a nucleus composed of two types of smaller particle – protons and **neutrons**. These are the heavy parts of the atom and give it its mass. The protons have a positive electric charge and the neutrons are neutral (hence their name), thus the nucleus is positively charged and holds negatively charged electrons in orbit around it (atoms themselves are neutral because they have an equal number of protons and electrons). The electrons define the edge of the atom and there is empty space between the nucleus and the orbiting electrons. When atoms join to others they use their electrons to do this. Some atoms give up one or more electrons to other atoms to form ions. The atoms which lost electrons now have a surplus positive charge and the ones that gained the electrons have a surplus negative charge and so these positive and negative ions attract each other strongly forming an *ionic bond* – this is how sodium atoms and chlorine atoms join together in salt (sodium chloride). Metal atoms join to each other in a similar way but only form positive ions (this is discussed later in the section on electrical conductivity). Other atoms can join by sharing electrons between them. This commonly happens when two non-metal atoms join to one another and the resulting bond (the shared electrons) is called a *covalent bond*. This is how molecules form. Water molecules have covalent bonds between the oxygen and hydrogen atoms. These different bonds are all similar in strength but the type of bonding between atoms will affect the behaviour and properties of that substance. Ionically bonded substances have typically high

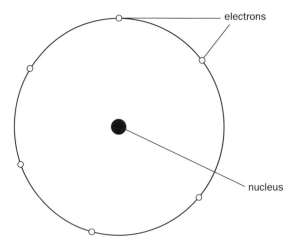

Figure 9.1 A simple model for an atom

melting and boiling points because they are only held together by their ionic bonds and form *giant structures* of billions of atoms rather than in the small groups known as molecules, thus you actually separate the atoms (ions) when you melt or boil the substance. Some covalently bonded substances can form these giant structures as well (such as the carbon atoms in diamond), but most form molecules which tend to consist of much smaller groups of atoms. When you boil or melt molecular substances you are *not* breaking the covalent bonds, you are actually only overcoming weaker forces of attraction *between the molecules*; thus the molecules themselves remain intact but are separated from each other (see Figure 9.2) – water vapour is comprised of water molecules not hydrogen and oxygen atoms.

Pure substances only contain one type of particle (in the way it was defined earlier), hence pure iron only contains iron atoms and pure water only contains water molecules. The difference is that iron is an *element* and water is a *compound*. Elements are the substances that every other substance is made from. There are about 100 known elements (some have only been shown to exist fleetingly in nuclear reactors) and they are shown in the periodic table of elements. Elements contain only one type of atom; hence the element oxygen is only composed of oxygen atoms and is listed in the periodic table. Substances that are not present in the periodic table are compounds, meaning that they comprise the atoms of two or more elements. Hence sodium chloride (salt) is a compound of sodium and chlorine, containing atoms of

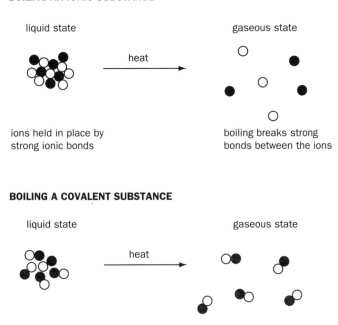

BOILING AN IONIC SUBSTANCE

liquid state

gaseous state

heat

ions held in place by strong ionic bonds

boiling breaks strong bonds between the ions

BOILING A COVALENT SUBSTANCE

liquid state

gaseous state

heat

molecules are held to each other by weak attractive forces

boiling only breaks the weak forces between molecules

Figure 9.2 Boiling ionic and molecular substances

each, sugar (sucrose) is a compound of carbon, hydrogen and oxygen. Strictly, a compound like sodium chloride cannot be referred to in terms of molecules as it does not contain molecules but ions, likewise some elements actually exist as giant structure and others as small molecules (often in pairs which is why the chemical formula for oxygen is O_2); this means we really need a catch-all term for the individual components of a substance as they vary depending on which substance we are considering. As such, the term *particle* is what we use for all these things. Despite the fact that it can refer to a wide range of different things, its use frees us from the minutiae of the chemical world yet is still correct.

Solids, liquids and gases

Prior to KS3 the teaching of the *states of matter*, that is, solids, liquids and gases, is focused on the bulk properties of these states, that is to say, the properties that we can experience and observe of substances that are in one of these three states. At KS3 this is developed by considering the behaviour and arrangement of the particles that make up substances in the solid, liquid or gaseous state and, ultimately, how the behaviour of the particles result in the bulk properties we experience. As has already stated, the ability to do this involves a significant conceptual leap. As an initial exercise it proves useful to look at and consider a range of substances that are in each of the three states, to get a feel for how they behave. However, caution should be exercised here as a number of everyday substances do not always seem to exhibit these properties as they should and can lead to confusion at an early stage. Salt, for instance, is a solid substance, yet it appears to be able to flow and so we can pour it. This is because we are observing the combined effect of many individual pieces of salt acting together, while if we take a single salt crystal then it does behave in the way we expect a solid to (indeed, it is possible to grow a very large salt crystal to demonstrate its solid properties). Also, some common materials contain a combination of substances in their make-up and add to this confusion. A typical property of solids is that they cannot be compressed, so what about a sponge? It seems to be a solid, yet it can be compressed because the solid part of a sponge is quite flexible and there is air in the gaps in the sponge which, as a gas, can be compressed. Another problem is that the substance we frequently refer to when considering the states of matter is water, yet water is actually a very untypical substance. For instance, whereas most substances contract when they freeze, water actually expands so solid water floats on liquid water. Another problem is in terms of language. We have different names for water in each of its three states (ice, water and water vapour or steam) and so pupils can often lose sight of the fact that all of these things are water. It does not change into a new substance when it boils or melts! That said, water is a safe substance that we can easily change from one state to another, which does have some benefits in the classroom.

The typical properties of solids, liquids and gases are summarized in Table 9.1.

These properties can be explained if we consider the particles that make up the substances. Not all substances can actually exist in all three states. This is because some change chemically as their temperature increases. For instance the chemical that makes up the bulk of chalk, calcium carbonate, cannot be melted in normal conditions. When calcium carbonate is heated it will decompose (change into simpler chemicals)

Table 9.1 Typical properties of the three states of matter

Property	Solid	Liquid	Gas
Shape	Fixed	Variable – will take the shape of the *bottom* of any container it is placed into	Variable – will take the shape of the *whole* of any container it is placed into
Volume	Fixed	Fixed	Variable – will *fill* any container it is placed into
Relative density	High	Medium	Low
Ease of compression (that is, how easily is it squashed)	Virtually incompressible	Virtually incompressible	Easily compressed
Ease of flow	Do not flow	Flow easily	Flow easily

and it forms calcium oxide and carbon dioxide. The carbon dioxide escapes into the air and the calcium oxide is a white solid, so the chalk hardly appears to change at all. Simple substances, such as elements can generally exist in all three states and we can measure their melting and boiling points, which are unique to that substance.

Figure 9.3 shows a typical set of representations of the arrangement of particles in solids, liquids and gases. Such diagrams are commonplace in books and can vary depending on what they are trying to show. Few convey the arrangement in the liquid state well and this is mainly due to the constraints of representing a three-dimensional structure with a two-dimensional one. Much better at this are the number of animations that are now available which also help to get across the idea that particles are in constant motion, even in a solid.

It is these arrangements that explain the properties of solids, liquids and gases, and these are summarized in Tables 9.2a–c.

Liquids again can prove to be problematic. The crucial difference between the particles in a liquid and those in a solid is that the particles in a liquid are free to move around each other, whereas in a solid they are held in a fixed arrangement. The actual distance between the particles in the two states is virtually the same, which is why you can not compress a solid or a liquid. Liquids are often regarded as compressible but are not, owing to the fact that the particles are essentially as close to each other as in the solid state. This can be demonstrated simply with a plastic syringe. Draw some air into a syringe, block the end and push and the gas inside can be compressed, but draw some water into the syringe and it cannot be compressed. The incompressibility of liquids is crucial in a car's hydraulic braking system.

Changes of state

Changes of state occur when energy is removed or given to particles in the form of heat. This energy affects the movement of the particles (their kinetic energy). If we

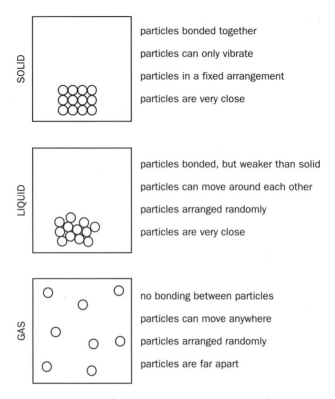

Figure 9.3 Typical arrangements of particles in the three states of matter

start with a solid, the particles are vibrating, but stay bonded to each other so that they remain fixed to their neighbours. On heating the solid the particles begin to move more. More heating eventually provides the particles with enough energy that they can start to loosen the bonds to their neighbours, and once they can start to move around (yet still remain in contact) the liquid state is reached. Continued heating enables some of the particles on the surface of the liquid to fully break free and escape to form a vapour (which happens first on the surface because those particles are in contact with fewer others) and this is called *evaporation*. When the liquid has reached its boiling point, then all the particles have enough energy to escape their neighbours and the liquid changes to a gas (this is why we see bubbles emerging from all places in boiling water, those bubbles containing steam, not air; the air has been driven from the water long before then in the smaller bubbles seen well below the boiling point). The bonds that hold together the particles in different substances have different strengths, which is why each substance has its own unique melting and boiling points. Indeed, temperature is in effect an indirect measurement of the movement of the particles in that substance; the higher the temperature, the faster the particles move. Lowering the temperature by removing heat energy from a substance causes the particles to move slower and hence they stick together better, so a gas cools to a liquid (it condenses) and then to a solid (freezing or solidifying). The names of the changes of state are

Table 9.2a Explaining the properties of solids

Properties of solids	Explanation
Fixed shape	Particles are held in fixed positions by strong bonds
Fixed volume	Particles are held in fixed positions by strong bonds
High relative density	Particles are very close together
Virtually incompressible	Particles are very close together and can not usually be pushed any closer
Do not flow	Particles are held in fixed positions by strong bonds

Table 9.2b Explaining the properties of liquids

Properties of liquids	Explanation
Variable shape	Particles can move past each other
Fixed volume	Although the particles can move around they are still quite strongly attracted to each other, so they stay together
Medium relative density	Particles are very close together although often not quite as close as the particles in some solids
Virtually incompressible	Particles are very close together and can not usually be pushed any closer
Flow easily	Particles can move past each other

Table 9.2c Explaining the properties of gases

Properties of gases	Explanation
Variable shape	Particles are free to move anywhere and have no bonds between them
Variable volume	Particles are free to move anywhere and have no bonds between them
Low relative density	Particles are far apart
Easily compressed	Particles can be pushed together, making the gaps between them smaller
Flow easily	Particles are free to move anywhere

shown in Figure 9.4. Again, water can be a problem in terms of language. Many think of 0 °C as freezing point, which it is for water but iron 'freezes' at 1535 °C.

It should also be remembered that melting point and freezing point occur at the *same* temperature, as does the temperature at which something boils and condenses. Thus water melts *and* freezes at 0 °C and boils *and* condenses at 100 °C.

Another point to consider is the difference between evaporation and boiling. Evaporation of a liquid into a vapour can occur below the boiling point (for water, evaporation can start from 0.15 °C). Evaporation below a substance's boiling point

Figure 9.4 Changes of state

takes place at the surface of that fluid into the surrounding air. Once a liquid is heated to its boiling point it cannot get any hotter. Pure water boils at 100 °C; once at this temperature it cannot get any hotter in the liquid state, even if it is still being heated. Therefore, the boiling point is really the hottest temperature a liquid can reach before it all changes to a gas. At the boiling point any additional energy is used to turn the remaining liquid into a gas; hence using temperature as our way of monitoring the energy given to a material breaks down. The energy we put into a substance when it is undergoing a change of state is referred to as *latent heat* (latent means hidden – hidden because it causes no temperature change). Once all the water has boiled to steam the temperature can start to rise again. In the same way, melting point is essentially the hottest temperature that a solid can reach before it all changes to a liquid, and the temperature of water remains stable at 0 °C while it is melting in the same way as it does when it is boiling, only rising again once all the water (ice) has melted.

Such changes of state are known as *physical changes*. As mentioned earlier, water in each of its three states is still water and physical changes result in a change of physical appearance without a change in substance. In all cases it is how the particles behave, not the particles themselves, which changes. In the same way when we heat substances within a state they usually expand, while cooling them causes the substance to contract. Again, *the particles themselves do not change*. When a substance expands or contracts the particles stay the same size, but the space between them increases or decreases. Except with gases (which have no bonds between the particles so they are free to move anywhere in what contains them), this change in distance is small but if billions of particles move ever so slightly further apart it can have a marked effect on the whole of the substance they are part of.

Grouping materials

As with the classification of organisms (or any form of classification), materials can be classified by their similarities. When classifying materials, we tend to classify by what they are used for, or by their specific properties. Indeed, the uses that we put materials to depend on their properties.

What *is* a material? When we here the word 'material' in everyday language we tend to think of fabrics, and this may be the context where most young children will encounter the use of the word 'material'. In the context of science it could mean any substance. Generally though, we could consider materials as substances that we use for a particular purpose, such as metals, wood, ceramics, and so on. Some materials are often referred to as natural materials, meaning materials which we use in their natural state, such as the wood used to make a window frame or the flint used to build walls. Conversely, we have human-made or synthetic materials which have to be processed before use, such as plastics, ceramics and most metals. These sorts of materials are made from a third group called raw materials, such as oil for plastics, metal ore containing rocks for metals and sand for glass. This method of classification can have its uses but may become rather confusing as some natural materials can also be raw materials for synthetic materials, such as wood for charcoal.

Teaching activity

Simple classification of materials can start with the senses: how a substance feels to the touch, how it looks, what it smells or tastes like, even what it sounds like when hit. Once a feel for these basic characteristics has been gained, then further sorting can start looking at other simple properties. The ways in which individual children will sort materials can vary and depends on the form in which they are presented with those materials. This is commonly done with a selection of everyday items; however, the children may then focus on the uses of the objects they are presented with rather than the materials themselves. As such it is better to provide them with blocks of those materials if the aim is to explore the properties. Where possible the blocks should be of equal size and shape so that they can get an idea of things such as comparative heaviness. There are many materials kits that are available for this purpose.

Examples of properties for consideration are given in the KS1 and KS2 programmes of study, although it is a good idea to present the children with more than one example of a particular type of material to prevent early misconceptions. One such example is **magnetism**. Very few metals are actually magnetic, yet if pupils only experience iron or steel as an example of a typical metal then they may assume that all metals are magnetic. Even then, we should expect that pupils will sort things by different criteria. Like all classification there will be things that are harder to sort than others and they could belong to more than one group. As such, it is important to emphasize when allocating something to group that the materials in that group have a number of things in common and that they will not all share exactly the same properties. How many young children would put mercury in a group with metals on its observable properties? (*Note: mercury should not be used in the classroom* due to its hazardous properties. This is merely a thought to share between writer and reader.)

The types and properties of materials

There are an endless number of different materials and to list them all would take up a lot of space and be pointless. The respective programmes of study suggest a few that could be discussed and no doubt you can think of many more. The KS1 programme of study also raises the point that some materials can be classed as materials which are found naturally (see also above). In addition, it should be remembered that many materials are not pure substances. Rocks, for instance, will contain a variety of minerals (a mineral being a naturally occurring chemical substance, usually inorganic – that is, not from a biological source), wood will contain a variety of chemical substances, alloys such as steel and brass are made by mixing metals with other metals or non-metallic substances and there are different types of glass produced by putting different substances in the glass mixture. It is precisely these mixtures that can give a material its specific properties.

What is perhaps more useful is to consider some of the major groups of materials, their general properties and some examples of each. The specific properties of a material depend on the particles that it is composed of and how those particles are arranged and behave. This is explored in more detail with respect to thermal and electrical conduction later in this chapter.

Metals
About three-quarters of the elements are metallic substances. Mixing metals with other substances (often metals and sometimes non-metals such as the carbon mixed with iron in steel) forms alloys which combine the properties of their constituent metals and are often harder than the pure metal themselves. Metals tend to be *solids* at room temperature, shiny when outer corroded layers are removed (for example, by polishing or scratching), quite *dense* (heavy for their size), *good conductors of heat and electricity*, *malleable* (can be hammered into shape), *ductile* (can be drawn into wires) and *sonorous* (make a ringing sound when hit). Good examples of everyday metals are iron, copper, aluminium, tin, gold and silver. Alloys include steel (iron with principally carbon), brass (copper and zinc) and bronze (copper and tin).

Magnetic materials
Not to be confused with metals! Only *three* of the metallic elements are magnetic: iron, nickel and cobalt. Alloys of these metals will also be magnetic such as alnico (aluminium – not magnetic but used because of its low **density**, nickel and cobalt). Magnetic materials can be magnetized to make permanent magnets and be attracted to magnets themselves, which makes them temporarily magnetized (which is why you can pick up a steel paper clip with another which is already attracted to a magnet). Electrons in the atoms of these three elements can spin, causing the atoms themselves to act like tiny magnets. These atoms are thought to form groups within the material, called domains which can line up to increase this magnetic effect, so forming a magnet. The magnet can exert a force on other magnetic materials around it, without them even touching the magnet, because the magnetism creates an area around the magnet called a magnetic field, where the influence of the magnet can be felt by other magnetic objects. When the material is unmagnetized the domains point in different directions so overall the material is not itself a magnet. The ends of a magnet have quite concentrated magnetism and we call the ends of magnets *poles*. If we take a simple bar magnet with poles at the ends and let the magnet move freely (for example, by hanging it from a string or floating it on water (on a cork or piece of expanded polystyrene) then one of its ends will point to the Earth's magnetic north pole. This end is therefore known as the *north pole* (more fully, the north-seeking pole) of the magnet, while the other end is called the *south pole* (south-seeking pole). Place two of these magnets together (see Figure 9.5) and the north poles of each magnet will push away from each other or repel, as do the two south poles. Place a north pole to a south pole and they will *attract*. Thus we say that like poles attract and unlike poles repel.

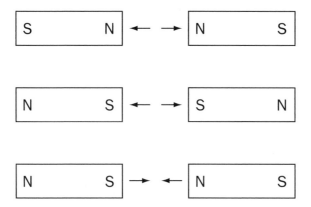

Figure 9.5 The attraction and repulsion of bar magnets

Plastics

These are composed of very long molecules called *polymers* made from joining together smaller molecules. This can occur in nature as well (to make protein molecules for instance), but plastics are made synthetically from small molecules (called *monomers*) mainly obtained from refined crude oil. Plastics are typically low density but very strong for their mass. They also tend to be insulators of heat and electricity, and some are transparent. Some plastics (thermoplastics) soften when heated and can be reshaped, others (thermosetting plastics) remain rigid when heated but may become brittle as a result. Elastomers are plastics that have elastic properties, such as synthetic rubber. Different types of plastic are made from different monomers and each have their own unique properties as well as a result. Good examples are polythene, PVC (polyvinylchloride), PTFE (teflon – used for non-stick pans because of its low friction properties), polystyrene, nylon, perspex and polyester.

Ceramics and glass

These materials are produced from rocks: ceramics from heated clays and glass from heated sand (silica). Often other substances are added to alter the basic properties of the material, especially with glass. They are typically hard, yet brittle, heat resistant, chemically inert and good insulators of heat and electricity. Glass is also transparent. Both types of material are used extensively in homes, especially in the kitchen (cooking vessels, storage jars, plates, cups, and so on) and in the fabric of the house itself (tiles, bricks, underground drains, and so on).

Wood

Woods vary depending on the tree or shrub they are taken from. Wood is essentially the remains of the dead xylem cells in the plant it is taken from (xylem cells conduct water through a plant). As it is made of old cells, a large part of wood is made up of cellulose (another natural polymer composed of thousands of glucose molecules linked together). Xylem cells are also surrounded by a tough substance called lignin and this imparts extra strength to the wood. Woods tend to be relatively hard (even so-called softwood like pine) and can be carved and cut into shape fairly easily by removing or cutting away layers of cells. They are also poor electrical and thermal conductors. These days wood remnants such as chippings and sawdust are combined with glues and synthetic polymers (plastics) to create new materials such as chipboard and MDF (medium-density fibreboard).

Fibres and fabrics

These encompass a wide range of materials both natural and synthetic. Natural fibres such as cotton and wool are another example of naturally occurring polymers, while synthetic fibres such as polyesters and nylons are man-made polymers. These materials are good thermal insulators and, when woven into fabrics, this insulating effect is enhanced by allowing layers of air (an excellent insulator) to be trapped around the body, when worn as clothes. In addition many fibres, especially the synthetic ones, are good at repelling water which also makes them good for use in clothing. Remember there will always be exceptions to the above general properties, and some materials in each group may exhibit these properties more or less than others. For example, copper is a much better conductor of electricity than lead but plastic is a so much poorer conductor than lead that plastic is really classed as an electrical insulator.

The properties of materials and their uses

What we use a material for depends on the properties that it has. More often than not we might exploit only some of the properties of that material, or maybe only one! One problem that pupils often seem to have is in identifying that it is the *material's* properties that we tend to exploit rather than the object itself. There is something in this as design can play a part in the properties of the object as a whole.

Floating and sinking

A good example to illustrate the difficulty in differentiating between the material's properties and the object would be ships. In the past all boats or ships were made of wood. This is undoubtedly due to the fact that most woods float (because they are less dense than water), so if wood floats then something made of wood will float too. However, wood is easily damaged by the buffeting of waves or, in more extreme circumstances, cannon fire so, as iron and steel became available in larger quantities, more and more ships were made from metal. Yet iron and steel are both more dense than water so metal ships should sink (many sceptics said that Isambard Kingdom Brunel's great iron ocean liners would sink). However, it is the design of the ship that allows it to float, as the overall density of all the materials in the ship (and, crucially, the air inside it) is less than that of water. This leads us to two things. First, be careful what objects you choose with which to examine the link between property and use. Second, what is density and how does it affect the ability of something to float or sink?

Density is essentially how heavy something is for its size. Strictly, density applies to a specific material; hence we can look up values for the densities of certain materials. However, we have seen that the density of a whole object results from the densities and relative amounts of the different materials that make up that object.

Thus a milk bottle will float when filled with air, but sink when filled with water (the glass itself, if it were melted into a lump, would sink as well). The density of a material or object can be calculated if we know its mass (how heavy it is) and its volume (its size).

$$\text{Density} = \text{mass} \div \text{volume}$$
(Mass in g; volume in cm^3.)

If we were to measure out 1 cm^3 of water, its mass would be 1 g, hence the density of water is 1 g per cm^3. Objects that have a density less than 1 g per cm^3 will float, those with a density greater than 1 g per cm^3 will sink. This is all very well, but why? This can be explained by displacement. If an object is lowered into water, the water level rises as the object pushes the water away and takes up some space that was originally occupied by the water (think about getting into a bath, like Archimedes). The water will try to resist this movement and push back with a force known as *upthrust*. If the object has a mass smaller than the mass of the water pushed away (the displaced water) then the water can push on it hard enough to keep that object afloat. If, however, the object is heavier than the water it displaces, then the water cannot push hard enough on the object and it sinks. The lower the density of an object, the less it weighs for a particular volume so, if the density is less than 1 g per cm^3, then it will weigh less than the water it displaces and float, with the opposite being true for objects with a density greater than 1 g per cm^3.

Separating property from use and property from object is, as had already been written, sometimes difficult for a child. As such, it is good to model responses to draw out the desired learning outcomes. This should probably start simply with objects made of only one material. This can then be developed to look at objects that consist of a combination of materials. For example, a window pane is made of glass because glass (not a window – you could conceivably fill a window with anything, like the bricks put in to evade window tax) is a transparent material. Glass is also a good thermal insulator which is another good reason for its use here. Light bulbs are also made of glass because glass is transparent and so lets the light out; however, glass cannot conduct electricity so the base of the bulb contains metal because metal is a good conductor of electricity. The filament of the bulb is made of tungsten because it is a metal with a high melting point, so it will conduct electricity but not melt when it gets hot enough to glow white. Clearly there is an endless list of examples to choose from but the teacher should be aware of the different materials and their suitable properties in any examples explored, remembering that some of the properties of a material are not always desirable. Glass may be good for the aforementioned uses, but is brittle and so can shatter – not a desirable property here but one we overlook because its desirable properties far outweigh this undesirable one.

Finally, there may also be something to gain from comparing similar objects made from different materials. Spoons can be made from metal and wood. Metal spoons are easier to keep clean and feel better when placed in the mouth and are easy to manufacture on an industrial scale, but stirring your soup with a metal spoon may result in a burn because the metal is a good conductor of heat. As wood is a poor conductor of heat it makes a far better implement for stirring your soup (either that or put a wooden handle on a metal spoon!)

Electrical conductivity

The ability to conduct electricity is one of the key properties of a metal. Other solid materials such as silicon can conduct electricity but only effectively at certain temperatures. Also, some substances such as salt (sodium chloride) can conduct when molten or when dissolved in water. The ability of metals to conduct electricity is due to how their atoms bond together. Figure 9.6 shows a model for the bonding of metal atoms. In order to bond together the metal atoms lose at least one of their outermost electrons. This leaves the metal atoms with a positive charge and they are now strictly ions (see the first part of this section on particles). The electrons that were lost are free to move around all these ions in what is known as a *sea of electrons*. Since the electrons are negatively charged they attract the ions and this is what keeps the structure together.

An electric **current** is a flow of charge and since the electrons in the sea of electrons are free to move they can be made to flow in one direction when a source of electrical energy such as a battery is connected to the metal. Hence we have an electric current flowing through the wire, and this is what makes metals such good conductors of electricity, their mobile electrons. The only other common solid conducting material that pupils are likely to encounter is graphite (what the 'lead' of a pencil is made from). Graphite is a form of carbon and again the carbon atoms bond in such a way that there is a sea of electrons that can be made to flow as an electric current. Likewise, if we have an ionic substance like salt we can make the electrically charged ions flow to create a current but only when those ions are free to move, either when the substance is a liquid or dissolved in water. In its solid state an ionic substance like salt cannot conduct electricity as its charged ions cannot flow.

Electrical insulators are substances that cannot conduct electricity well either, because they contain no charged particles or any charged particles they might contain do not flow easily. Water itself is a poor conductor of electricity as it does not contain a significant amount of fully charged particles (the ends of a water molecule are partly charged but overall the molecule is neutral), however, most water we encounter does contain dissolved charged particles so will be more conductive than pure water.

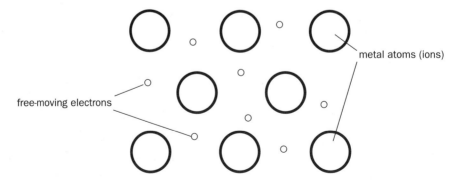

Figure 9.6 A representation of the structure of metals

Many of the problems that occur when touching electrical devices with wet hands result from the ever-present salt that is left on our skin through perspiration and this dissolves in the water to make it more conductive.

Strictly, it is more correct to talk of good or poor conductors rather than things which can conduct and those which cannot. It should also be remembered that different metals will exhibit a variety of conductivity and the same is true of insulators.

Thermal insulation

A thermal insulator is a material that does not conduct thermal energy (that is, heat) very well. Generally, materials that conduct electricity well also conduct heat well. This would seem to indicate that, in part at least, the mobile electrons in a metal also help it to conduct heat. As stated earlier, when a substance is heated its particles move more and the ability for a material to conduct heat well is reflected in the ability of its particles to pass on these increased movements to neighbouring particles. The freely moving electrons in a metal are quite effective at carrying this extra energy through the metal structure. In addition the atoms (ions) in a metal are very closely packed together (this is where Figure 9.6 falls down a little bit as it seems that the ions are far apart, they are not really but the diagram would not effectively show the sea of electrons if it more accurately represented the distance between the ions) and this allows the increased vibrations of one atom to be quickly and effectively passed on to the next set of atoms and so on through the metal's structure. All objects which are heated will lose some of this heat to their surroundings, however, the heat is transferred more quickly through the material than to its surroundings so we are aware of it passing through the material.

Thermal insulators do not pass on these vibrations as effectively so tend to lose any additional heat to their surroundings faster than it can pass through them. They will eventually conduct the heat though, as is evident when hot tea has been in a cup for a while. Part of this lack of conductivity will be due to the way in which the atoms are joined in an insulator. These tend to have covalent bonds which can act like tiny springs and so absorb some of the increased atomic vibrations. As a general rule, solids will conduct heat well, liquids less so and gases even less. This is often utilized in materials which are used as insulators. Many insulators (such as fabrics) trap layers of air and since air is a gas it is a very poor thermal conductor. Expanded polystyrene is a solid foam which has bubbles of gas trapped in it, which again make it a more effective insulator than the same amount of plastic without the trapped air, which is why expanded polystyrene cups keep drinks warmer for longer than thinner, unexpanded polystyrene ones.

Whether we want a good thermal conductor or a good thermal insulator depends on the use we put that material to. Insulators are perhaps more easily understood here, it is conductors that may present a problem. A saucepan is made of metal because we want the heat to pass through it quickly, whereas a casserole dish is made from an insulator because we want it to retain the heat once inside. Radiators are made of metal partly due to manufacturing and strength considerations but also because the metal conducts the heat effectively from the water inside to the air surrounding the radiator. Beware though, hot-water tanks and central heating pipes are made from copper not because it is a good conductor of heat (that is why we should lag the tank with an insulator to stop heat escaping) but because copper is resistant to corrosion and is quite soft so can be bent into shape easily.

Rocks and soils

The topic of rocks and soils is a potentially complex one for primary aged pupils. The substances that we encounter can be scientifically very complex and the processes which create rocks and soils can seem abstract. However, when the pupils learn about the properties of rocks and soils in practical ways learning in this topic can support not just an understanding of geology but also wider scientific ideas.

Rocks

The whole of the Earth's surface (the crust) is covered in rock. This is a fact that some pupils may not be fully aware of since most of that rock is covered with water, soil or built-up areas. We only tend to see the actual rocky surface where it is exposed, such as mountains and cliff faces. Rocks are comprised of minerals (described earlier) which form a solid mass. Sometimes organic remains are also found in the rock, such as shells from long dead animals. Different types of rock contain different mixtures of minerals and are formed in different ways. Pebbles and stones are just small pieces of this rock, often with their outer edges smoothed by erosion. Sand comprises even smaller pieces of rock and its appearance on the coast is a result of erosion of land at the coastline and pieces of rock that have been carried by rivers and eroded into small pieces as they travel.

Rocks are usually classified initially by the method by which they were formed and older rocks are being continually recycled into new ones in a process known as the *rock cycle*, which works on timescales of thousands or even millions of years. The first of these is *igneous* rocks, which are formed by the cooling of hot, molten rock (*magma*) into a solid form. Radioactive processes below the crust generate heat that keeps the lower part of the crust molten. This molten rock is under great pressure and can rise up through weakness in the crust. Sometimes it breaks through the surface and is referred to as *lava*. Lava flows cool on contact with the air or water above the cracks in the surface of the crust and form *extrusive igneous* rocks such as *basalt*. Sometimes the magma never reaches the surface and cools more slowly under the surface to form *intrusive igneous* rocks such as *granite*. As the rock cools it forms crystals in its structure and the rate of cooling affects the size of these crystals. Intrusive rocks cool slowly so the crystals form more slowly and are bigger than those in extrusive rocks where the cooling is much quicker.

The second major group is *sedimentary* rocks. These are formed when pieces of exposed rock are broken up by *weathering*. This can be chemical weathering where chemical reactions (for example, with water and dissolved acids) weaken the rock structure. Physical weathering involves forces breaking off pieces of rock, and biological weathering is due to the action of living things such as the roots of plants. These broken pieces of rock get carried away by gravity and the movement of water, and often end up in rivers, where they can be carried to the sea or some other large body of water. As the flow of water decreases the pieces of rock settle as layers of *sediment*, which gradually build up on top of each other. Over time the water is lost from these layers and the dissolved minerals that were in the water help to bind the pieces together into rock. Good examples are shales, sandstones and limestones (primarily made of mud, sand and the remains of marine animals respectively).

The third group is *metamorphic* rocks. These are formed when sedimentary or igneous rocks are exposed to great *heat* or *pressure* or both, in the crust. The rocks are so altered by these processes that they are significantly different to the rock they formed from. Good examples are slate from shale, marble from limestone and quartzite from sandstone.

Each of these types of rock have very distinctive characteristics. Igneous rocks tend to be hard and crystalline and never contain fossils. Sedimentary rocks tend to be softer than igneous rocks (reflecting the fact they are formed from small pieces) and composed of grains rather than crystal. Sedimentary rocks may also have coloured layers (from the sediments that they formed from) and may also contain fossils. Metamorphic rocks tend to be a bit of a halfway house depending on the rock they were formed from. The colouring of a rock will depend on the main mineral it contains and any trace minerals that are present on the rock. Limestones, for instance, are mainly composed of the white mineral calcium carbonate but can be a variety of colours reflecting the other substances that are present in the rock; a high proportion of iron rich minerals may make the rock more orange in appearance for example. Chalk is an especially pure form of limestone which is why it is usually so white.

Rocks are used for a variety of purposes, depending on the properties of that rock. It should also be remembered that in many places traditional uses of rock reflect the locally available rock. Slate splits easily into sheets and is hard and waterproof so is ideal for roofing. Limestones can be used for buildings but are also used widely to make cement by heating the limestone and chemically changing the calcium carbonate to calcium oxide (quicklime). This can be added to water and forms calcium hydroxide (slaked lime) which can be used to make mortar. Limestone powders are also found in toothpaste and cream cleaners to make then abrasive. Granite is very hard and weather resistant, and so is used where this is an advantage such as steps and gravestones. It should also be remembered that rock can be very attractive, especially when polished, and this is a key property for its use in memorials, statues and elegant buildings, a good example being marble.

In addition to general appearance, rocks can also be classified in other ways and this can be reflected in their use or the avoidance of their use. Rocks that are soft are prone to erosion. This is very evident to those who live in coastal areas where the local rocks are being lost to the sea. The weathering of sandstone buildings and gravestones can also be a problem. Permeable rocks contain small pockets of air which can fill up with liquid. This can be observed by placing the rock in water. Small bubbles may be seen streaming from the rock as the air is replaced by water, and the rock will increase in mass as a result. Permeable rocks may weaken when waterlogged and are susceptible to ice damage, as when the water inside freezes it expands, putting pressure on the solid part of the rock which may result in cracks.

It is possible to obtain small rock kits for use in the classroom, and it is possible to collect samples of rock to study as well. Children should be encouraged to describe what they can see (hand lenses are invaluable here) and to test the properties such as permeability and relative hardness/softness. This may help them to decide what the rocks they are studying could be used for after consideration of what rocks are used for in everyday life. It is also worth remembering that relatively large samples of rock help to get a real feel for what each is like, rather than very small samples.

Soils

Soils are basically a mixture of rock particles, humus, water and dissolved minerals. The nature of a soil is characterized by its balance of these constituents and their origin. The rocky part of soil is composed of broken-down and weathered rock and will depend on the local rocks in a particular area. Typically this will be clay or sand, or both. Humus is the remains of organic matter and will depend largely on the plants growing in that soil. The dissolved minerals will come from both the rocks and the humus. Soils in areas prone to flooding may also be rich in peat or silt.

The nature of a particular soil can affect what can be grown in it and soil characteristics which are commonly studied are their ability to retain water, colour, their overall structure and feel, their pH (acidity or alkalinity) and the levels of mineral nutrients that they contain. All these characteristics will vary, depending on the origin of the rocks and organic matter that the soil is comprised of. Soils have been incredibly important to human development and settlement ever since farming started during the neolithic period. The best general soils for agriculture are loams, which provide good drainage with the ability to retain reasonable amounts of water due to the fact that they have a good balance of particle size (in this context particle means the actual lumps of matter in the soil). Loams also have a good humus and mineral content. Sandy soils tend to have poor water retention and consequently minerals are easily washed out of them, they dry more quickly and they break up more readily. Clay rich soils tend to be the opposite of sandy soils and will not break as easily so are harder to work.

The QCA Scheme of Work (3D) offers suggestions for the analysis of soils by pupils. This can be with pre-collected samples of locally collected samples. Care should be taken, however, when collecting samples locally due to the likelihood of animal faeces being present and litter which could also be harmful, such as glass and discarded metals. Also soils contain a lot of bacteria such as tetanus and so it is advised that gloves are worn when collecting and handling such samples and hands are washed afterwards.

As has already been stated, some soils suit different plants better due to the mineral requirements of that plant and the amount of wetness or dryness they can tolerate. Soils can be improved by various means to make them loamier, and this depends on the nature of the soil. One way to improve sandy soils is through marling, where a pit is dug down to layers of chalk or limestone below the soil and this 'marl' is then spread on the fields and dug into the soil, increasing its water retaining qualities and mineral content and reducing acidity. This accounts for many pits and deep depressions in fields found in areas of traditionally sandy soils. Also manure and compost can be dug into the soil to further improve water-holding capacity and mineral content. Some pupils may be familiar with this on a smaller scale in their own gardens or allotments. Mineral content can also be enhanced by the use of chemical fertilizers which dissolve into the soil water.

Links to teaching

More teaching activities

Sorting and classifying materials is an important aspect of science learning in the primary school. When teaching about the properties of materials it is better to have examples of the materials in blocks rather than objects which are made from the materials (so as to lessen the confusion between the properties of the material and the properties of the object). These blocks can then be sorted according to properties, and *then* objects made of the materials can be located in the school and pupils can link properties to uses.

Other things to do and try

It can be difficult to explain changes that are happening to particles at an atomic level when substances change state form solid to liquid to gas. However, this can be easily explained using tennis balls. Pupils using these as representations of the particles can demonstrate a solid (hold the tennis balls in one place), a liquid (make them flow over one another) and a gas (throw them around).

TOP TEACHING TIP

The weather provides a good practical example of how materials change state. Use rain, evaporating puddles and snow/ice to illustrate how the water in our atmosphere can behave in different temperatures.

Some common misconceptions

- Ice, water and steam are different substances.
- Materials are just fabrics.
- Atoms can be seen through a microscope.
- Snow is frozen rain.
- All sand is made by the sea.

AMAZING FACT

Water is unusual as a substance because its solid form (ice) is actually less dense than its liquid water form, so ice floats. This has had a massive impact on life on Earth as during the ice ages the surface of the seas froze but many living things were able to continue to live in the still liquid water underneath.

10

Changing materials

National Curriculum: Attainment Target Sc3, Strand 2 (KS1: 3.2a–2b, KS2: 3.2a–2e)
QCA Schemes of Work: Units 2D, 5D and 6C

Curriculum requirements

Changing materials is really concerned with how we can change them into new, different materials. Therefore, understanding how materials can change and identifying if this change results in a new substance forms part of the foundation for the study of chemistry. As with the previous section on grouping and classifying materials, at KS1 and KS2 the focus is on substances rather than the particles (developed at KS3 and KS4) that make them up. However, as we have already seen, to gain a fuller understanding so that we ourselves are confident in teaching about these changes we need to consider things at the level of particles. In addition, much of what is required to be taught is descriptive rather than explanatory, because explanations can only really be arrived up by considering two abstract concepts, energy and particles.

The National Curriculum for Science programme of study states that at KS1 pupils should be taught to find out how the shapes of objects made from some materials can be changed by some processes, including squashing, bending, twisting and stretching; and to explore and describe the way some everyday materials change when they are heated or cooled. At KS2 pupils should be taught to describe changes that occur when materials are mixed; to describe changes that occur when materials are heated or cooled; that temperature is a measure of how hot or cold things are; about reversible changes, including dissolving, melting, boiling, condensing, freezing and evaporating; the part played by evaporation and condensation in the water cycle; that non-reversible changes result in the formation of new materials that may be useful; that burning materials results in the formation of new materials and that this change is not usually reversible.

Types of change: chemical or physical?

As an introduction we ought to consider the two general types of change that materials can undergo. These are known as chemical changes and physical changes. When *chemical changes* occur the substances that we start with change to form *new* substances. This is what we commonly call a chemical reaction. All substances are composed of atoms joined together. There are about 100 types of atom, represented by the elements in the periodic table. When a chemical change takes place, the atoms in the original substance or substances (the reactants) break apart and then rejoin in a different way to form a new substance or substances. We can think of atoms rather like Lego bricks. The different types of brick represent the different types of atom and the different things you build represent different materials. To build something new you have to pull apart all your Lego bricks and reassemble them in a different way. Chemical changes can be quite simple, such as the reaction between hydrogen and oxygen (see Figure 10.1). Take a mixture of hydrogen and oxygen gases, put a flame to the mixture to start to break some bonds and there will be a very loud explosion which results from the hydrogen and oxygen atoms reassembling not as hydrogen and oxygen but as water. This releases a lot of energy, hence the explosion.

Some chemical changes are more complex, such as the changes that occur in food when it is cooked.

Generally (although not always) chemical changes are regarded as difficult to reverse. To reverse the water formation reaction above you need to apply an electric current to water, and even then the conversion back to oxygen and hydrogen is a slow one. The second types of change though, *physical changes*, are much easier to reverse. In a physical change no new substances are formed. The substance you are changing only changes in its physical appearance with its particles remaining the same. Good examples of physical changes are the changes from one **state of matter** to another such as melting and boiling. When ice melts to liquid water and water boils to steam, the particles do not change (they are *always* water particles: two hydrogen atoms joined to an oxygen atom), however, the arrangement and behaviour of those particles change (see the section on solids, liquids and gases in Chapter 9, 'Grouping and classifying materials').

Forces and change

Changing the shape of an object can be classed as a physical change as this does not change the material itself, only its appearance. Some materials are easy to change the shape of, such as plasticine; others are much more difficult to change in this way, such as metals and ceramics. This is due to how strongly the individual particles in a material are joined. The bonds between metal atoms are very strong and so are harder to move, whereas others are weaker and so can be moved more easily. However, the amount of force needed to change the shape of something also depends on the form of that object. It is impossible to stretch or compress a block of steel with one's fingers, yet a steel spring can be easily stretched and squashed because all you are essentially doing is moving the coils. However, there is a limit to how far this can be done. When one pulls a spring far enough its coils eventually stop unravelling and it will be

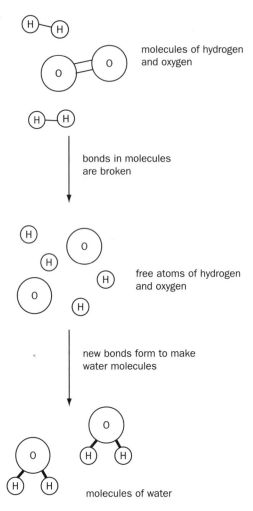

Figure 10.1 The reaction between hydrogen and oxygen

impossible to stretch it further as to do so means trying to pull the metal atoms apart. Rubber can be easily stretched and compressed because its molecules are coiled rather like a spring, but again there will be a limit to how far this can be done for the same reason. In addition different materials have different tolerances to different types of force. Glass is very strong when compressed (try compressing a window pane lying flat and it proves to be very strong, but if you try bending the glass it is likely to shatter). Again this is due to how the particles in the material are arranged.

The effects of heating and cooling

Heating a material involves the transfer of energy to that material, while cooling is the removal of that energy. All particles in all materials move to some degree. Whenever a material is heated the particles inside it start to move more and if it is cooled the particles move less. In a solid the particles are fixed to their neighbours so this movement is restricted to vibrations, while in liquids and gases the particles can move around and sometimes heating and cooling results in purely physical changes such as expansion and contraction and changes of state. This is further discussed in the section on solids, liquids and gases in Chapter 9). Sometimes, however, heating may result in a chemical change occurring, such as burning (see later) or decomposition. The type and extent of change will depend on the material concerned, the presence of other materials and the amount of heating or cooling.

To ascertain and communicate whether a change has taken place involves pupils describing the differences between materials before *and* after they have been heated or cooled. All too often pupils concentrate on what the material is like after the change rather than before, and both are important. Good things to describe include physical state (that is, solid, liquid or gas), colour, shape, size, texture, hardness and any other observable features. Generally (although not always), a physical change such as a change of state will reverse itself when the reverse process occurs, so, if water boils when heated, it will condense back to a liquid when it cools. Examples of materials one could consider are given in the programme of study and these include water, dough, bread, chocolate and clay. Heating and cooling water involves the physical changes state from solid to liquid to gas mentioned above. Heating water also increases the speed at which it can dissolve a substance and how much it can dissolve, with cooling having the opposite effect (the process of dissolving will be discussed later on). Indeed, when water is not pure the dissolved substances in the water affect its boiling point and melting point. Such impurities will tend to lower the melting point below 0 °C – this is why seawater does not freeze at 0 °C and why we put salt on the roads in the winter as the temperature must be lower than 0 °C for the water to freeze. Conversely, impurities will raise the boiling point of water above 100 °C. Heating dough and clay both cause chemical changes that result in the formation of new substances with different properties. These changes are irreversible, for example, bread can be changed by heating when making toast. Water is driven off from the bread as it essentially burns in the toaster. The longer it is heated, the more it burns. Chocolate is interesting as a number of changes occur when it is heated. If heated in a pan the fat in the chocolate melts and this makes the mixture behave like a liquid. In the mouth the same thing happens although additionally, the sugar in the chocolate starts to dissolve in the saliva in the mouth and some of the molecules in the chocolate trigger responses in our taste buds and the olfactory organs in the nose, responsible for smell. All these changes and movements of particles combine to deliver the very satisfying experience of eating chocolate.

Teaching activity

Its always tempting to use foodstuffs in teaching changing materials in the primary phase because they are readily available, cheap and safe, but teachers should bear in mind that chemical and physical changes which take place in foodstuffs are complex and should be carefully described. For instance, eating a fizzy sweet involves the sugar dissolving, the acid and alkalis turning to a salt (the catalyst effectively being water) and other substances in the sweet going into suspension.

Temperature and heat

Temperature is a way of measuring how hot or cold something is. The temperature scale that is most commonly used today is the Celsius scale. All temperature scales rely on fixing two points of reference to base all other temperatures on. The Celsius scale uses the melting/freezing point of water as one reference point (0 °C) and the boiling point of water as the other (100 °C). To calibrate a simple thermometer (that is, to mark it up for use) it should be placed in an ice water mixture and the position of the liquid in the thermometer marked as 0 °C, then placed in boiling water and the new position of the liquid in the thermometer marked as 100 °C. Then the other numbers are placed on the thermometer at regular intervals between 0 and 100. In reality, most cheap thermometers are mass produced to a design and therefore will be subject to some inaccuracy as a result. Electrical thermometers rely on changes of current at different temperatures to give their readings but are still calibrated in the same way, with respect to water. Because of the way in which a temperature scale is derived, it means that the numbers themselves are actually arbitrary – a scale could be based on any two phenomena related to heating and cooling.

Temperature varies with the variation of movement of particles in a material. The higher the temperature, the faster the particles move and vice versa (in theory, the coldest possible temperature is −273 °C, known as absolute zero; actually impossible to reach, at this temperature all particle motion would cease). This means that temperature can give us an idea of the thermal (heat) energy of a substance but it cannot give us an absolute value as that depends on the amount of the substance as well. For example, a bath of hot water can be at the same temperature as a mug of hot water, but the water in the bath will have more energy because it contains more water at that temperature. Strictly speaking, materials cannot possess thermal energy, rather it is energy that moves from one place to another and where it moves from or to depends upon temperature. An idea that many carry with them is that 'heat rises'. This is *not* true. Heat moves from hot objects or areas to colder ones, that is, from an area of higher temperature to one at a lower temperature. This notion of heat rising comes from the fact that when air warms up it becomes less dense therefore it floats up above colder, more dense air, which sinks down below it. So really hot air rises above colder air. This leads us to another misconception surrounding coldness. Coldness is simply an absence of heat (rather like darkness is an absence of light). Cold itself is not a tangible thing (unlike heat) so it is incorrect, for instance, to say that we can give cold to something. A material is made cold by removing heat. When we leave a door open it is true to say that this can let colder air in but it is not true to say we have let cold in – we have lost heat by the fact that some of the warmer air has escaped and some of the heat energy of the warmer air has been transferred to the colder air it is in contact with. Another example of this movement of heat is when we touch hot and cold objects. Hot objects feel hot to the touch because they will transfer heat energy to our skin (which is at a lower temperature), while objects that are colder than our skin feel cold because heat is lost from our skin to the colder object (this also explains the sensation of a cold day). If an object is at the same temperature as our skin it feels neither hot nor cold as no heat will flow in either direction. Heat only flows if there is a temperature difference, in the same way that a ball will only roll on a sloping surface where there is a difference of height and not on a horizontal surface, where there is no difference in height.

Mixing materials

Mixing materials is a physical process. This means that mixing should be relatively easy to reverse. However, sometimes when two materials are mixed a chemical reaction may occur if there is enough energy available to start that reaction. This will therefore be more difficult or impossible to reverse and will produce new substances. A basic definition of a mixture is where there are two or more substances together but they are not chemically joined; meaning there are no chemical bonds between the particles of one substance and the particles of another. This is different to a compound where the atoms of different substances are joined by chemical bonds to one another. Air is a good example of a mixture. It contains many different types of substance (nitrogen, oxygen, carbon dioxide, and so on but they are not joined to each other). If one mixes salt and sand they remain as salt and sand, the individual grains may be mixed up but the salt does not join on to the sand in any real fashion.

Mixing materials may result in different properties than the mixture's individual substances had at the start. These could be simple differences such as colour – mix a blue substance with a yellow one and the mixture may look green, depending on how well they are mixed and the physical state of the substances. There may be more dramatic changes such as when foams form. Foams are an example of a mixture known as a colloid. Colloids also include emulsions and gels. A foam is made by forming a mixture of a gas and a liquid (the gas is dispersed in small pockets throughout the liquid) such as when one whips cream, dispersing small pockets of air through the cream. The whipped cream has different properties to the un-whipped cream such as a lower density and a more solid appearance and feel. In this sort of mixture there is no chemical change as one still has air and cream.

Dissolving

Dissolving is another way of making a mixture. The name of the mixture formed by dissolving is a *solution*. Dissolving involves forming a mixture of a liquid with either another liquid or with a solid or a gas. The liquid that does the dissolving is called a *solvent*, while the substance which dissolves into the liquid is called a *solute*. The resulting solution will have the particles of the solute evenly distributed throughout the solvent. Dissolving is essentially a physical change as it does not result in the formation of new substances; however, this can be confused by a number of factors that make dissolving often seem like a chemical change. Some solutes, for instance, may subsequently react with their solvents, leading to a chemical change (ideally one chooses a solvent that will not react with the solute that is being dissolved). In addition, the process of dissolving can lead to the breaking of chemical bonds and the formation of new interactions between particles – something that is more normally associated with a chemical change.

When a substance dissolves it is broken up into individual particles. The nature of these particles depends on the type of substance dissolving. When compounds composed of molecules dissolve, the molecules themselves remain intact and their chemical bonds are not broken. It is the weaker attractive forces between the molecules that are overcome so that the molecules can mix with the solvent. When substances composed of ions, such as salt, dissolve, then the chemical bonds that hold the ions together do break so that the individual ions move freely in the solvent. When the solute is broken up into particles in both cases the bonds and attractive forces that are lost are replaced by attractions between the solvent and the solute particles. For a substance to dissolve there needs to be a similar amount of these new interactions to replace the bonds or forces that existed originally, as the new forces of attraction release energy which compensates for the energy needed to break the particles apart in the first place. A substance will be *insoluble* if the energy that would be released on forming the solution is insufficient to compensate for the energy needed to break apart the particles in the first place. What we should do to visualize this process is to imagine a substance being placed into the liquid solvent. The particles of the solvent are free to move and collide with the particles of the substance we are trying to dissolve. When this collision takes place, the solvent particles attract the solute particles. If this attraction is strong enough, the solvent particle effectively pulls the solute particle away so that it is now free to mix with the solvent. This can continue until either all the solute is dissolved or there is so much solute dissolved that this process can no longer continue. A solution that contains the maximum amount of dissolved solute is called a *saturated* solution. Solvents can de divided into two groups known as *polar* and *non-polar* solvents. Polar solvents are composed of molecules that have a slight positive charge at one end and a slight negative charge at the other. This makes them good at dissolving substances that are charged as well, such as salts. Water is the most commonly used polar solvent. Non-polar solvents have no charged ends and are better at dissolving similarly non-polar substances. Organic chemicals such as those derived from crude oil are good examples of non-polar solvents, such as petrol. There are many solvents that fall between these two extremes and this allows them to mix with non-polar substances as well as water – propanone (acetone) is a good example here and is the solvent in nail-varnish remover. Thus, just because something does not dissolve in water, does not mean it will not dissolve in another solvent, and vice versa. Also each substance has its own *solubility* in a particular solvent. This is a measure of how soluble it is and solubility varies from substance to substance.

One problem with many solutions is the fact that we have no obvious proof that the dissolved substance is still there, unless that substance was coloured and produced a coloured solution. (*Note*: all solutions are clear, they may be coloured too, but they are *always* clear – cloudiness is due to undissolved solids.)

If we want to speed up the process of dissolving a solid then we can do two basic things. Stirring and shaking helps because it helps the solvent particles to collide with the solute particles. In addition, heating the solvent provides energy to help break apart the solute particles and it increases the speed of the solvent particles so that they collide with the dissolving solute more often. Heating can also increase the amount of solvent that can be dissolved (again by providing extra energy) so that a solution that is saturated at a lower temperature may not be saturated at a higher temperature.

Teaching activity

One way to check that a substance is dissolved is to taste the solution. If this is tried, appropriate steps should be taken to ensure this is done in a safe way so that children are not exposed to any risk. Salt and sugar solution prepared outside any science laboratory should be safe, especially if done in, say, a kitchen using tap water, teaspoons, glasses and salt or sugar straight from an unopened packet which is only used for this purpose. It is also inadvisable for pupils to actually ingest the solutions, especially with the problems that can be associated with salt in the diet.

Solutions

What is the purpose of a mixture like a solution? Solutions are very good mediums for chemical reactions to take place in. This is because the particles in them are free to move around and collide, and particles need to collide in order to react. Thus a substance that is normally a solid may react better with other substances (especially other solids) when in solution. One of the reasons that water is so vital to living things is that many of the chemical reactions that sustain life occur best in solution. Also, dissolved substances travel much more easily through the body, such as dissolved foods in the bloodstream. A solution, therefore, is an easy way to make a substance which is normally a solid or a gas behave in a liquid fashion, if that is a more useful state for it to be in and, unlike melting or condensing, you do not need to heat or cool the substance to achieve this. Solutions are also used to allow dilution to take place so that we create a solution that has as much or little dissolved substance as we desire, depending on our use for that substance. In addition, the fact that some substances are soluble, others are insoluble and that solubility varies from one substance to the next allows us to use solutions as a way of separating substances (for more see Chapter 11, 'Separating mixtures of materials').

As stated earlier, dissolving is classed as a physical change, which means it should be fairly easy to reverse. The simplest way of separating a solvent from its solute is to heat the solution. Unlike solids, gases actually dissolve better in cooler conditions (remember, in their gas form they are already separated, so gases need to be cooled to behave more like liquids). Therefore, heating a solution of a gas will drive the dissolved gas out of the solvent. This is why we see small bubbles in a glass of tap water which has been left to warm up – the dissolved gases such as oxygen are forming bubbles which eventually escape to the surface). When a solid is dissolved it is separated from its solvent by heating the solution sufficiently so that the solvent itself evaporates. When all the solvent has been evaporated, then the once dissolved solid is left behind. Slightly harder to separate is a solution where the solute is a liquid. This is separated in a similar way to that of a dissolved solid except that the heating needs to be more controlled. Different liquids have different boiling points, so the two liquids will evaporate away from the solution at different temperatures. This process is known as distillation and is how water is removed from alcoholic drinks to make them stronger in alcohol (spirits), such as changing wine into brandy.

Reversible changes and non-reversible changes

The idea that some changes can be reversible and some are irreversible has already been mentioned in the context of chemical and physical changes. As a general rule physical changes are readily reversible as they do not involve changing a substance itself. The particles in a substance remain the same but have a different arrangement after a physical change, so reversing such a change is relatively straightforward. We have already met all these changes in this section and in Chapter 9. Examples of these physical changes include dissolving, melting, freezing, evaporating, boiling and condensing. In addition, the expansion and contraction of a material can also be included here and this has already been discussed as well (see Chapter 9).

Many materials can undergo these various physical changes, but not all. For example, some substances may react chemically with water when they have been dissolved. A change like this is given in the KS2 programme of study where the addition of plaster of Paris to water is considered. Plaster of Paris contains a chemical called calcium sulphate, which is partially hydrated (this means there are some water molecules involved in the solid structure as well as the calcium sulphate). Adding more water causes a chemical reaction between that water and the existing partially hydrated calcium sulphate to form fully hydrated calcium sulphate (where more water molecules are joined to the existing material). This new version of the calcium sulphate has a different arrangement of particles which is stronger than when only partially hydrated, making the plaster set in a hard mass. Evidence that this is a chemical change is given by the fact that energy is released by the process, which makes the reacting mixture warm up.

Heating some materials may also trigger a chemical change before they have a chance to change state. One of the most common of these changes is *combustion*, which involves the chemical reaction between a material and oxygen in the air, and is dealt with in more detail later. Substances can also react more slowly with the oxygen in the air. The slow nature of such reactions does not release energy as quickly as burning, so will not cause a flame, but essentially the reaction is the same. Such reactions form new chemicals called oxides, hence a metal left in air will slowly oxidize to produce a layer of metal oxide on its surface. This will have the effect of reducing the shine of the metal as it is the metal itself which is shiny and the oxide layer on its surface is not. As the layer of oxide gets thicker the metal appears less and less shiny as the oxide layer obscures the pure metal below. These sorts of chemical changes are usually hard to reverse and to all intents and purposes are regarded as non-reversible (when we shine a dull metal we remove this oxide layer, not convert it back to pure metal). Examples of non-reversible changes are given in the programme of study and the QCA Scheme of Work and the key ideas here are that non-reversible changes result in a new material being formed and that some of these new materials may be useful. Examples of such useful changes are many and include the plaster of Paris change already discussed, the changes in foods when they are cooked, the formation of plastics from oil and the extraction of metals from the chemicals in rocks (ores).

It should, however, be noted that not all chemical changes are non-reversible. While at this stage it may be inappropriate to consider this idea fully with pupils, it is important to realize this point if one is teaching chemical changes. Some chemical changes are reversible. One of the key reversible reactions studied at KS4 and KS5 is the reaction that produces ammonia from hydrogen and nitrogen. The chemical word equation for this reaction is:

$$\text{nitrogen} + \text{hydrogen} \rightleftharpoons \text{ammonia}$$

The rather unusual arrow signifies that this reaction can easily go in both directions. Hence, when you want to make some ammonia (the vast majority of ammonia made in the world is used to produce chemical fertilizers) some of it will always change back to nitrogen and hydrogen. The problem of limiting the reverse reaction was studied and solved by the German chemist Fritz Haber and the Haber Process is known to many a student of GCSE and A level chemistry.

The water cycle

The water cycle (see Figure 10.2) describes how water is recycled in the environment. Water on the surface of the Earth is *evaporated* by the heat of the Sun. This water may come from the oceans, lakes and rivers or may be lying on the ground as puddles or in the soil. Water also evaporates from the leaves of plants by a process called *transpiration*. As it rises up into the atmosphere this vapour cools and eventually *condenses* into fine droplets which can float on air currents. These droplets of water can congregate into large groups forming clouds. Indeed, if a cloud is high enough, the water will freeze into particles of ice. When these droplets reach a certain critical mass they can no longer be held in the air and start to fall to the ground and, depending on the air temperature and the atmospheric conditions, may fall as rain, sleet, snow or hail. Thus

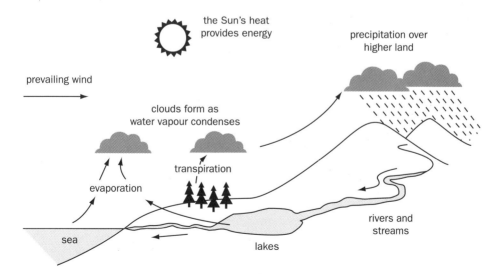

Figure 10.2 The water cycle

the water returns to the surface of the Earth and the seas, lakes, rivers and land from whence it began its journey.

Thus the water cycle involves the reversible, physical changes of evaporation and condensation and is driven by energy from the Sun. Of course, wind can blow rain clouds many miles before they yield their water and the chance of rainfall increases if clouds are blown over hills and mountains as the clouds are forced to rise higher into the atmosphere where the temperature is lower and the rate of condensation of water vapour increases. This explains why the west of the UK gets more rainfall than the east. The prevailing winds come from the west and carry moist air that has just passed over the Atlantic Ocean. This moist air then reaches the high land in the west of the country and rapidly cools and releases its quickly condensing water. In the UK we are often obsessed by our changeable weather, caused by the fact that we are surrounded by water, leading to a very active water cycle.

Burning materials

The idea of *combustion* (the chemical name for burning) as a chemical change has already been mentioned. Some substances when heated may not simply change state but change chemically by burning. When a material is burned it reacts with oxygen in the air. The products of this chemical reaction depend on what is being burned and on how much oxygen is available. Many substances can burn and this can be problematic in situations where we do not want burning to occur. However, we do make use of this when we burn fuels for the heat and light they release when they combust.

Fuels are substances which burn fairly easily to produce a large amount of heat. When a chemical reaction gives out heat (thermal) energy it is said to be *exothermic*. Most of the fuels that we use contain materials that are composed entirely or partly of atoms of hydrogen and carbon. When such fuels burn they form oxides of the carbon and hydrogen. The oxide of hydrogen is water (H_2O), while carbon can form carbon dioxide (CO_2) and carbon monoxide (CO). If combustion occurs in a plentiful supply of oxygen then *complete combustion* occurs. This means that the carbon atoms manage to join to the two oxygen atoms they need to form carbon dioxide. Methane is the main gas in the natural gas that we use in our homes and is an example of a chemical called a hydrocarbon as it contains only hydrogen and carbon atoms (other common hydrocarbons include the propane used in camping gas, the butane used for gas lighters and octane used for petrol). The chemical equation for the complete combustion of methane is shown below:

$$\text{methane} + \text{oxygen} \longrightarrow \text{carbon dioxide} + \text{water}$$
$$CH_4 + 2\,O_2 \longrightarrow CO_2 + 2\,H_2O$$

The equation shows that the carbon atoms and hydrogen atoms in the fuel have joined to the oxygen atoms in the air. For this to happen the molecules of methane (CH_4: a carbon atom joined to four hydrogen atoms) and the molecules of oxygen (O_2: two atoms of oxygen joined together) have to first break apart. The energy for this will come from the spark or flame that is used to ignite the fuel. As the new materials (the carbon dioxide and water) are formed, energy is released. So much energy is released that there is enough to break apart more molecules of methane and oxygen, and the reaction becomes self-sustaining. There is also sufficient excess energy released that it is transferred into the surroundings as heat. It is this surplus energy that we utilize when we burn the fuel. The heat also means that the water produced vaporizes instantly and escapes into the air with the carbon dioxide.

If the air supply (and thus the oxygen supply) to the fuel is limited, then there may not be enough oxygen atoms for all the carbon atoms to become carbon dioxide (the hydrogen atoms will always form water). This results in what is called *incomplete combustion*. In some cases the carbon atoms will form carbon dioxide but some will only join with one oxygen atom and form carbon monoxide (*note*: di- means two; mono- means one). Indeed, some of the carbon atoms may not join with any oxygen atoms at all and will remain simply as carbon, forming soot. The flames that accompany burning fuels are a result of the effect on the heat of the products of combustion. There will always be a little incomplete combustion, whatever the conditions, but where there is predominantly complete combustion occurring the flame will be very hard to see and mainly a pale blue colour (due to hot carbon monoxide which will rapidly form carbon dioxide as it mixes with more air). Where incomplete combustion occurs the flame will be more luminous and have more of an orange colour. This is due to the soot as the carbon atoms it is made up from glow a yellow/orange colour when hot. The more incomplete combustion that occurs, the more luminous the flame is.

Methane tends to burn with little soot because of the relatively small number of carbon atoms in each molecule. However, in many domestic settings there is still some restriction of air flow and, combined with the fact that air is only about 20 per cent oxygen, this means that incomplete combustion can occur which can lead to a build-up of the poisonous carbon monoxide unless rooms are properly ventilated and the vents on boilers and gas fires are in good working order. Larger molecules, containing more carbon atoms, tend to be more prone to incomplete combustion and thus soot production. This, however, is not always a bad thing. While we might burn some fuels for the heat they give out, we also use them for the light emitted by their flames. Candle wax can be made from a number of materials including large hydrocarbon molecules. These large molecules tend to undergo much more incomplete combustion than the smaller ones, but the glow of the soot in the flames they produce make them effective sources of light.

It should be remembered here that the fuel in a candle is the wax. The wick allows melted wax to be drawn away and vaporized in the heat so that it can burn. Fuels need to vaporize before they can burn. If one looks at a burning candle one sees the solid wax and an area of molten wax around the wick. This molten wax is drawn up the wick, where it vaporizes and burns. The flame itself is not in direct contact with the wick and a small gap can be observed around the wick where the vapours are released before they catch fire. One of the reasons a candle is much harder to light than methane is that methane is already a vapour, while the wax needs to melt then vaporize before it can catch alight. The same is true of wood. Wood is a mixture of substances, mostly carbon based. When wood burns, oils from the wood seep out and vaporize before catching fire. This is very obvious with woods rich in oils such as pine (matchsticks are made from pine and a burning match shows this idea very nicely). The ash left behind comprises substances in the wood that did not escape into the atmosphere as it burned. The fact that most of the substances produced when a material burns escape into the atmosphere, and are much more stable than the fuel was in the first place, is why burning is a very difficult process to reverse.

Links to teaching

More teaching activities

The way in which materials change is often taught in primary schools through the use of food substances. This is quite understandable as they are generally safe and readily available. However, teachers need to be aware that food substances are often scientifically complex. A good example of this is melting chocolate. When heating chocolate over a pan of warm water (or, more safely for children, in a microwave) it is actually the fat in the chocolate that melts, while the cocoa and sugar usually remain in a solid state (but suspended in the liquid fat). This can be simply illustrated by melting different types of chocolate, for example, comparing white chocolate with high cocoa dark chocolate. The white chocolate (higher fat content as it contains cocoa butter) becomes more liquid and stays liquid for longer than dark chocolate.

Other things to do and try

Try growing salt or sugar crystals from a saturated solution. Using different salts (available from chemists) can make different coloured crystals.

TOP TEACHING TIP

A useful information technology (IT) tool when teaching this topic is a set of accurate electronic scales. It is a simple procedure to weigh water and see the weight increase as soluble substances are added to it (for example, salt or sugar) – they may seem to disappear but the scales show that they are still present.

Some common misconceptions

- Ice, water and steam are different substances.
- Heat rises.
- You can put cold into something as well as heat.
- When a candle burns it is the wick which burns, the wax just supports the wick.
- A substance 'disappears' when it dissolves.

AMAZING FACT

There is only so much of a substance that can be added to a solute before no more can be dissolved (this is called saturation point). For example 100 ml of water can dissolve about 35 g of salt, depending on the temperature of the water. However, it is possible to dissolve over 200 g of sugar (sucrose) in the same amount of water.

11

Separating mixtures of materials

National Curriculum: Attainment Target Sc3, Strand 1 (KS2: 3.3a–3e)
QCA Schemes of Work: Units 4D and 6C

Curriculum requirements

Separating mixtures of materials forms part of the programme of study for science at KS2 only. A knowledge of separating processes remains important at all levels of science study from this point onwards, especially in the field of chemistry. The various techniques for separating the components of a mixture tend to rely on differences in the physical properties of those components such as solubility, particle size and differences in boiling points. There are chemical separation methods but these tend to be more complex. As your knowledge of these techniques develops, understanding the reasons why these different methods work is important so that you can make decisions about which is best to separate the components of a particular mixture.

The National Curriculum for Science programme of study states that at KS2 pupils should be taught how to separate solid particles of different sizes by sieving; that some solids dissolve in water to give solutions but some do not; how to separate insoluble solids from liquids by filtering; how to recover dissolved solids by evaporating the liquid from the solution; and to use knowledge of solids, liquids and gases to decide how mixtures might be separated.

What is a mixture?

What we mean by a mixture has been discussed already in Chapter 10, 'Changing materials'. To recap, a basic definition of a mixture is where there are two or more substances together but they are not chemically joined, meaning there are no chemical bonds between the particles of one substance and the particles of another so that they still behave chemically as they would when separate. This is different to a compound where the atoms of different substances are joined to one another by chemical bonds. A simple mixture commonly used when teaching separation techniques is one of salt and sand. Air is also a mixture as is crude oil.

Mixtures also include solutions, colloids and suspensions. In a solution one substance (a solid, liquid or gas) is mixed on the level of the individual atoms or molecules that the two substances involved are made from. The liquid doing the dissolving being called the *solvent* and the substance that dissolves is the *solute*. Solutions will always be clear in appearance as the individual particles in the mixture are not big enough to scatter light (more detail on how solutions are formed can be found in Chapter 10).

Colloids are mixtures such as gels, foams, aerosols and emulsions. Unlike solutions they are not formed at the level of individual atoms or molecules; rather, they are a mixture of 'particles' composed of many molecules of one substance (the dispersed phase) grouped together. These dispersed particles are spread out in another substance called the continuous phase. The type of colloid depends on the nature of the two phases: *gels* are a liquid disperse in a solid (for example, jelly); *foams* are gases dispersed in a liquid (for example, beaten egg white); *aerosols* are a liquid or solid dispersed in a gas (for example, fog and smoke); *emulsions* are a liquid dispersed in another liquid (for example, milk). Colloids tend to stay together relatively well over long periods of time but may eventually separate. This is especially true of artificial emulsions such as salad dressing. This mixture of vinegar and oil can rapidly separate out into two separate layers. This is why mustard is added to the mixture as the mustard acts as an *emulsifier* which helps keep the mixture together for a longer period of time.

Suspensions are at the other extreme to solutions. Comprised of a solid mixed with a liquid or a gas, here the groups of suspended particles are so large that they will immediately start to settle after mixing. A good example is a muddy puddle; after mixing, the particles that make up the mud will sink to the bottom of the water that the puddle is made up of. Suspensions are always cloudy as the 'particles' of solid will scatter light passing through. Colloids may be cloudy or clear, depending on the size of the particle groups in the dispersed phase.

Solubility and separation

The idea of solubility has also been mentioned in Chapter 10. Not all substances are as soluble as each other in a particular solvent and different solvents can dissolve different substances to different degrees. These variations in solubility are at the heart of a number of separation techniques, especially when one substance in a mixture is soluble and the other is insoluble in a particular solvent. In addition, solubility means that some mixtures may need more extreme means to separate them, such as the heating of a salt solution to separate the water from the salt. An appreciation of solubility and what this means is, therefore, important when studying separation techniques. It is also important to remember that substances may seem to disappear when they are dissolved but they are still present. A fact that is obvious if one tastes a salt or sugar solution.

Separation techniques

There are a number of different ways to separate materials from one another. Teachers need to give pupils experiences of these methods before they present them with investigations where the best techniques can be selected.

Sieving and filtering

Sieving is a very basic separation technique used to separate solid particles. In this sense we do not mean particles on the scale of atoms or molecules, but much larger particles that will likely be composed many millions of atoms or molecules (we could call these *macro-particles*), such as a grain of sand or a crystal of salt. Sieving only separates substances by the size of these particles, rather than by substance itself.

Teaching activity

Soil is a common substance sieved in school experiments. Greater separation can be achieved by using a range of sieves with different sized holes. To achieve a good separation the size of the holes in each successive sieve should get progressively smaller so that the larger particles will separated out first and the smallest ones last.

Filtering (see Figure 11.1) is akin to sieving as it essentially separates by particle size, although what we actually separate with a piece of filter paper is the aforementioned 'macro-particles' from particles on the atomic/molecular scale. A piece of filter paper is porous with very fine holes that let few, if any, solid (macro-)particles through (some grades of filter paper may let some very small solid particles through)

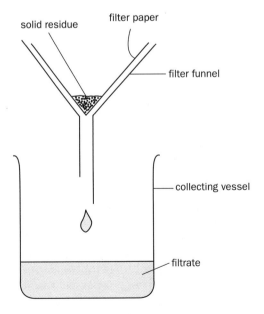

Figure 11.1 Filtration

and some pupils may have come across the filter papers used in coffee machines. Liquids and dissolved substances can flow through a filter paper because the tiny particles (atoms, molecules and ions) they are comprised of are small enough to pass through the holes in the filter paper. Thus filtering is a useful way to separate a suspension, with the solid particles in the suspension being left in the filter paper and the liquid passing through.

In addition, filtering can be used to, indirectly, separate two solids providing that one is soluble and the other soluble. The classic separation of salt and sand from a mixture of the two is a case in point. Adding water to a mixture of salt and sand, then stirring well, will allow the salt to dissolve, while the sand will not, because the salt is soluble and the sand is insoluble in water (warm water will help speed up this process – see the section on mixing materials in Chapter 10 to understand why). If this mixture is then filtered, the undissolved grains of sand will be stopped by the filter paper. However (because it has been broken up into individual atoms/ions by the dissolving process) the salt can pass through the filter paper along with the water molecules. This then separates the salt from the sand (washing the sand in the filter paper with clean water will make sure some of the salt solution does not stick to the sand, ensuring a better separation). All we now need to do is allow the sand to dry and separate the dissolved salt from the solution (see 'Recovering dissolved solids', below). Pupils should learn about a range of soluble and insoluble substances so that they can assess if they can be separated or not by this technique. As such, it is a good idea to introduce other mixtures that can (and, indeed, can not) be separated in the same way to broaden pupils' experience and not just rely on the salt and sand that everyone seems to separate. Safe soluble substances to try might include sugar and bicarbonate of soda and any of a number of insoluble substances, including wood chippings, small plastic objects and chalk. Pupils could be presented with different mixtures as well as the separate substances they are composed of, test each of the individual substances to see if they are soluble or insoluble, and then decide if they can be separated by the technique of adding water and filtering.

(*Be aware*: many culinary substances (especially powders) that are soluble are often mixed with other insoluble powders called anti-caking agents and will give a cloudy mixture due to the undissolved anti-caking agent. Thus dissolving granulated or caster sugar will give a better, clearer solution as they tend not to contain such anti-caking agents, rather than icing sugar which does.)

Recovering dissolved solids

In addition to differences in solubility, the technique mentioned above for separating soluble and insoluble substances also relies on the fact that you can recover the dissolved solid from its solution. This is done by evaporation. The evaporation can be allowed to occur slowly without direct heating, or quickly with direct heating. Particles in the solution are constantly moving around, but some move quicker than others as the amount of energy each particle has varies. In a solution there are usually far more solvent particles than solute particles and sometimes when one of these more energetic solvent particles reaches the surface of the solution it breaks free and escapes into the air – evaporation. This will temporarily reduce the temperature of the solution as the particles which escape are those with more energy, leaving behind those particles with less energy, so the liquid cools down. However, further heat energy will transfer in from the solution's surroundings to sustain the evaporation process if the surroundings are hotter and a greater amount of heat can flow into the solution and so it evaporates faster. Eventually a point will be reached where so many solvent particles have been lost that the remaining volume of solvent is insufficient to keep all the solute dissolved and it starts to come out of solution. This means that groups of solute particles start to bond together again and thus form pieces of solid. Often this occurs at a certain place in the solution called a nucleation site, such as a small speck of undissolved solid that got into the solution or an imperfection in the walls of the vessel used to hold the solution. Once this has started the small lump of solid formed acts as a nucleus for further solute particles to join to and the size of this undissolved piece of solid gets larger as more water evaporates. Many of the substances that dissolve in water form crystals in their solid state, such as salt (sodium chloride). Hence, as the water in a salt solution evaporates, crystals of salt form. In some cases the crystal structure also ends up containing some of the water molecules that were in the solution, and this is known as water of crystallization. As this is part of the crystal structure, if this water is lost then the crystal structure also changes and the solid tends to become powdery. This is one of the reasons why if we force the evaporation of water from a solution by heating it strongly we will not end up with nice, large crystals, but a powdery looking solid, since all the water has been evaporated, including that which would be used for the crystal structure. Some substances, such as sodium chloride (salt) have no water of crystallization anyway, yet this forced evaporation will also result in a powdery solid as the crystals form so quickly they are extremely small.

A final point to note here is that some substances that will dissolve in water might be damaged if we try to heat the solution strongly to recover them. One example is sugar which will turn to caramel if heated too strongly. In such cases it is best to let the water in a sugar solution evaporate naturally, perhaps in a warm room, to see the crystals form.

Other separation techniques
In addition to the separation techniques mentioned above there are a number of other useful techniques that children could use or be aware of at primary level. These include decanting, chromatography and distillation.

Decanting is a very simple technique to separate a solid from a liquid. The solid needs to have had time to have sunk to the bottom of the liquid, and then the liquid is poured carefully so that the solid that has settled at the bottom of the container remains there while pouring. This was used much more in the past for wines and spirits when they often had sediment at the bottom of the bottle and were placed into a decanter before consuming. Similar to decanting is the separation of liquids which do not mix and so form layers (as oil does with water). Such liquids can be separated by pouring too, although using a piece of apparatus known as a separating funnel is better. This has a tap at the bottom which is opened to let out the bottom layer, leaving the top layer in the funnel and so separating the two liquids.

Distillation is a way of separating a liquid from a mixture by boiling the liquid and then condensing it to collect that liquid (see Figure 11.2). This is often done with water which can be distilled to purify it. This distilled water is used a lot in chemistry

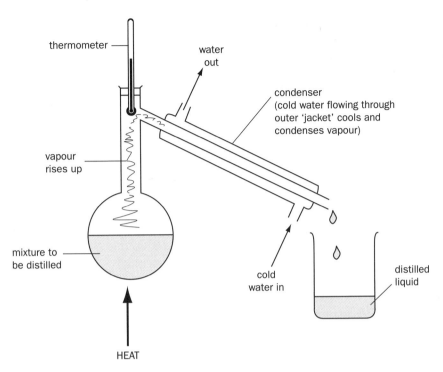

Figure 11.2 Distillation apparatus

laboratories and is the de-ionized water that can be used in steam irons; removing the substances dissolved in the water means that when it is heated in the steam iron it leaves no solid residue (commonly called limescale). Alcohol is also distilled from alcoholic drinks to produce spirits. This works because the water that is mixed with the alcohol has a different boiling point to the alcohol so the alcohol boils off first. This technique can be further refined in a process called *fractional distillation* which is used in the oil industry to separate the substances found in crude oil into a number of useful substances such as petrol and paraffin. Crude oil is a mixture containing many substances, each with a different boiling point. By heating the oil to a vapour it is possible to collect each substance because each will condense at a different temperature.

Chromatography is another technique for separating substances that is often used to determine the substances in a mixture. This is commonly first encountered by pupils as paper chromatography (see Figure 11.3), often by separating the pigments in ink. Some inks are made using a mixture of pigments to produce the desired colour. By placing a spot of water-based ink on the chromatography paper (rather like filter paper), then allowing water to soak up the paper, the different pigments separate out because they move at different speeds across the paper, depending on how well they stick to the paper and how soluble they are in the water. Many black inks are composed of a mixture of red, blue and yellow pigments, and these are clearly seen at different places across the paper once the water has travelled across the whole of that paper. As different substances move at different speeds across the paper, it is also

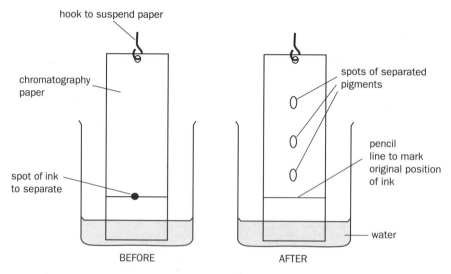

Figure 11.3 Simple paper chromatography of ink

possible to identify them by how far they move and comparing these distances to the results of other experiments where the individual substances are known.

In addition to these there are a number of other techniques or part techniques that are interesting to consider. It is possible, for instance, to separate magnetic materials from non-magnetic materials using a magnet. Centrifuging is a final technique worth considering. This involves spinning a tube containing the mixture at high speed in a piece of apparatus known as a centrifuge. The different substances in the mixture are forced towards the end of the tube in different amounts due to their different densities, thus separating them. This is commonly used to separate out the various components of blood when it is collected from blood donors.

Choosing separation techniques

Once pupils have been made aware of the different separation techniques that are available to them they should then be able to start making decisions on the best technique to separate them. This can be done by trial and error to a certain extent, but an understanding of why each method works will allow pupils to make more informed choices and to make choices when they are not able to try them out, in an examination for instance. Identifying substances as solids, liquids and gases will help here, for instance, when deciding if filtration will work or not. In addition, knowledge of solubility is important since it is not possible to separate two insoluble or two soluble substances by just adding a solvent, such as water, then filtering. Another consideration should be the ease of the method and how time-consuming it might be; it is perfectly possible to separate salt from sand using tweezers but this would take a long time! Allowing pupils access to more unusual mixtures will test their understanding and assess their ability to make informed choices; how would one, for instance, separate a mixture of iron filings, sugar and sawdust and what order should this be done in?

Links to teaching

More teaching activities

Pupils can learn a lot about the properties of materials by separating them. Teachers need to give pupils experience of these techniques as well as the freedom to choose what they think is the best way to separate them. When giving pupils this choice teachers should be willing to allow children to make mistakes, as they will learn just as much from these errors as getting it right. For example, a child who thinks sand and sugar can be separated using a fine sieve needs to see how this will not work!

Chromatography works well when different type of black pens are compared. Dots of black ink should be put onto a filter or blotting paper which is then suspended in a pot of water. More expensive pens tend to have fewer but stronger pigments than less expensive ones.

Other things to do and try

Try to use a wide range of substances rather than just salt and sugar. Coffee is an interesting substance, as is cocoa.

TOP TEACHING TIP

Chromatography is interesting and works best with cheap felt-tip pens. Try several colours and see where the same dyes have been used in different pens.

Some common misconceptions

- A substance 'disappears' when it dissolves.
- The only salt is sodium chloride.
- A foam is a solid.

AMAZING FACT

The kitchen is a good place to find complex substances like colloids. Milk, for example, is a suspension of fats in water, but it is the small amounts of enzymes which cause it to separate (into smelly solids at the bottom and pale green liquid at the top) when it goes off.

12

Electricity

National Curriculum: Attainment Target Sc4, Strand 1 (KS1: 4.1a–1c, KS2: 4.1a–1c)
QCA Schemes of Work: Units 2F, 4F and 6G

Curriculum requirements

Electricity forms the first strand of the Sc4: Physical processes Attainment Target, which is essentially the physics element of the National Curriculum for Science. An understanding of electricity and its uses is an important part of all key stages and is also utilized in many areas of science. It is especially important in society, as electricity is one of our most important energy resources and huge quantities of electricity are used throughout the world.

The National Curriculum programme of study states that at KS1 pupils should be taught about everyday appliances that use electricity; about simple series **circuits** involving batteries, wires, bulbs and other components; and how a switch can be used to break a circuit. At KS2 pupils should be taught (through the use of simple circuits) to construct circuits, incorporating a battery or power supply and a range of switches, to make electrical devices work; how changing the number or type of components in a series circuit can make bulbs brighter or dimmer; how to represent series circuits by drawings and conventional symbols, and how to construct series circuits on the basis of drawings and diagrams using conventional symbols.

The nature of electricity

One of the problems with electricity is that we cannot actually see it, we can only observe its effects. Electricity is caused by charged particles. When we use electricity in a circuit we are using the *energy* that the flow of charge has (electrical energy). *Charge* is a scientific concept that is used to describe how some particles can attract or repel each other.

What is electricity?

Explaining what charge actually is can be a very complex issue, however, we can describe the effects that this charge has. Electric charge comes in two forms which we call *positive* charge and *negative* charge. Some particles are positive, some are negative and some are *neutral*, meaning they have no charge (often, like atoms, because they have an equal amount of positive and negative charges). The amount of charge a particle has is measured in units called *coulombs*. Charged particles can affect other particles around them because they have an electric field around them (rather like a magnetic field). An electric field will cause charged particles to move according to the charge that they have. The field around a positive particle repels other positive charges, but attracts negative charges. In the same way a negative charge has a field around it that attracts positive charge but repels other negative charges. So, in much the same way as the poles of a magnet, *opposite charges attract* each other while *like charges repel* each other. *Static electricity* is caused by a build-up of charge and does not flow, hence its name. It occurs when two insulators (substances which do not conduct electricity) rub together. The friction causes some of the negative electrons in the atoms of one of the insulators to be removed. As these atoms have lost negative charges, they are left with a positive charge and the insulator is said to be positively charged. The other substance will have picked up these electrons and so will become negatively charged. This means that the two insulators, with their static charge, will attract each other as they have opposite charges. This can be very easily demonstrated with a balloon. The balloon is made from rubber (an insulator) and if it is rubbed on someone's hair (also an insulator) electrons will move from one of the insulators to the other. The hair and balloon will now have opposite charges and if the charged balloon is passed gently over the charged hair, it will attract the hair towards it.

It is important to be aware that a number of these ideas are similar to magnetism, which was discussed in Chapter 9, 'Grouping and classifying materials'. To a physicist this would not be a strange idea because electricity and magnetism are, in a sense, two sides of the same scientific coin. For instance, electricity can be produced using magnetism (this is how generators and dynamos work) and magnetism can be produced using electricity (used to produce electromagnets for devices such as doorbells and speakers). Pass a current through a wire made of any metal (not just magnetic ones) and the wire will become magnetic. Likewise, move a wire near a magnet, or vice versa, in the right way and an electric current will be produced. This is because, in metals the causes of magnetism and electrical conduction are the same; the electrons in the metal. Also we see those same rules of attraction and repulsion, where opposite attracts (charges or poles) and like repels.

Any build-up of charge is quite an unstable situation (remember, like charges repel) and the charges will 'seek' any opportunity to come into contact with an opposite charge and become neutral. This is why we sometimes get small shocks from places where static has built up. What happens is that electrons flow from one object to another to balance out the charge on each and this gives us a shock. This is much easier if the electric charge can find a way to flow to the ground in a process known as *earthing*. Let us imagine a situation where you have just walked across a nylon carpet. As your shoes have rubbed against the carpet this has caused some of the electrons to be removed from the carpet and you have picked up a negative charge. You then go to open a door and you feel a shock as electrons race from your hand to the door handle in an attempt to lose the extra charge you have built up. You have been earthed by this process and have lost the charge that you had.

This build-up of charge cannot occur easily on an electrical conductor, unless it is insulated itself, since it would just flow away. A flow of charged particles is called an electric current and is what happens in electrical circuits. For a substance to be able to conduct electricity it must possess charged particles which can move. These particles could be positive or negative, but in most everyday circuits they are negative electrons, since most everyday circuits use metals as their conductors; as such we will focus on conduction and current flow through metals. The reason why metals make good conductors is explained in detail in Chapter 9, but briefly it is because some of the negatively charged electrons in metals are free to move anywhere in that metal. To create a flow of charge in one direction and thus produce an electric current, we need a source of energy that can produce an electric field that will cause the electrons to move around the circuit together, and this is what is provided by power sources such as cells, batteries and mains power supplies. It is wrong to think of the power source as the provider of the electrons, as they are already in the wire. A power supply provides the energy to make the electrons move in the desired direction around the circuit (rather like a central heating system, where the water in the pipes is like the electrons in the wires and the pump that pushes the water through the system is like the power source for the circuit).

This is, perhaps an appropriate time to consider the word *power*. This and the word *energy* are often mixed up and thus misused. Energy is one of the key concepts that has been highlighted in the National Framework for Science (primarily aimed at secondary schools). The concept of energy is one of the underlying bedrocks of the study of science, especially physical sciences. Like charge, it is another imponderable concept in that it is difficult to define what energy actually is; rather, we discuss it in terms of its effects. *Energy* is often described as something that 'makes things happen' and the standard definition found in many sources, is that energy is 'the capacity to do work', meaning that when something has energy transferred to it, that transfer of energy can cause some movement, with work being a measure of the force and distance associated with this movement (work = force × distance). Energy is measured in units called *joules* and can exist in many forms, a number of which we will meet in other sections of this book. One of the key ideas associated with energy is that of the 'conservation of energy'. The law of energy conservation states that energy cannot be created or destroyed, it can only be transformed from one form into another, for example from electrical energy to light energy and heat (thermal) energy in a light bulb. Thus it is wrong to say that energy is used up; rather, when it is used it just changes to another form, but often these forms might be difficult to detect, with most energy eventually being changed to heat energy which is 'diluted' by being absorbed by particles in the surroundings and making them move a little more. *Power* is a measure of how fast energy is being used. This means that it is wrong to say that power is used, it is energy that is used. It is measured in watts, where one watt means that one joule of energy is being transferred every second. In a circuit, the power can be calculated if one knows the **voltage** and current (power = current × voltage).

Using electricity

As has already been stated, electricity and its use is one of the most important factors in our society. Once produced, electricity is, essentially, a clean energy resource and its value lies in the fact that it is easy to convert it to other forms of energy that we find useful. Thus we can convert it to thermal energy using cookers, kettles, electric fires and electric blankets; into light energy using bulbs, fluorescent tubes and televisions; into movement (kinetic) energy using the electric motors found in food mixers, CD players, microwave oven turntables, and into sound using the speakers in telephones, radios and alarms. Thus there are a great many appliances in the home that use electricity, either taking their source of energy from the mains supply or from batteries/cells.

It is appropriate at an early stage to consider the possible dangers of electricity. There is little harm that the electricity from batteries can cause, although the chemicals that the batteries contain are dangerous and pupils should not be encouraged to take batteries apart to examine their contents. It is these chemicals that provide the energy to push electrons around circuits through a chemical reaction occurring between the chemicals. These chemicals are eventually used up, thus giving the battery a finite life (with rechargeable batteries it is possible to reverse the chemical changes and so use the battery again). The word 'battery', in many cases, is actually used inappropriately as most 'batteries' are in fact *cells*. A battery is actually composed of two or more cells working together (a battery of cells). A typical AA type battery is actually a single cell that provides a voltage of 1.5 volts. Probably the most common type of actual battery in use is the rectangular 9 volt battery that one attaches with a clip. Its voltage is achieved because it contains 6 cells inside $(6 \times 1.5 = 9)$.

Mains electricity is a different matter altogether. This has a voltage in the UK of 230 volts and this makes it far more dangerous than the electricity supplied by simple batteries/cells. Thus one must always be vigilant when using mains electricity with pupils. Cells are perfectly adequate for most simple experiments with circuits and they provide the type of current needed for these simple experiments, which is called direct current (dc). Direct current flows through the circuit in one direction only. Mains electricity is alternating current (ac) and this works on a cycle where the direction of the current effectively flows one way then reverses very quickly (50 cycles per second in the UK; also known as 50 hertz). We do not notice this rapid alternating current, although we can often hear the sound it can cause when we hear appliances buzzing – always at a frequency of 50 hertz. If a mains-operated power supply is used in circuits experiments, it will convert this ac electricity from the mains into dc electricity at a much reduced voltage (the latter for safety), since the type of current we tend to study is dc rather than ac (ac is not really studied in any detail until KS4). One reason we often cannot run battery-powered devices from the mains (and vice versa) is the fact that they use a different type of current to mains current and any adaptor that we might use to plug a battery-powered device into the mains will convert the mains electricity to dc so that the device can work.

Electrical circuits

Much of what pupils learn about electricity is through the construction of simple circuits. A circuit consists of a battery/cell or power supply to provide electrical energy, wires, usually at least one switch and at least one component (such as a bulb). In some cases conventional wires are used to connect each component of the circuit directly, but many schools use circuit boards to place the components on and many of these circuit boards use sprung connectors, which consist of a strip of metal which acts as the wire, with the other components also clipping on to the board. Circuit boards are often easier to use as they relate well to the diagrams we draw to represent circuits and reduce the chance of wires getting tangled up. There are two ways in which the components of a circuit can be connected together; in *series* or in *parallel*, with the focus at KS1 and KS2 on series circuits. Before we discuss these two types of circuit though, we need to consider two important concepts which are often confused, namely, *current* and *voltage*. The two types of circuit affect the behaviour of current and voltage in different ways so we need to understand what voltage and current are if we are to understand how the wiring of the circuit causes these differences.

Current

Current is a measure of the flow of the electricity. It is defined as the amount of charge flowing through a particular part of a circuit every second, thus the more charge that flows, the greater the current. Current is measured in units called amps (short for ampere; symbol A). The charge is carried by the electrons in a wire and so current is related to the number of electrons flowing per second. Since it is the electrons in the wires and components that constitute the current and since these electrons are not used up (only the energy they carry is used), this means that current is not used up in the circuit (a common misconception), hence the *total* current measured at one end of the circuit is the same as the total current at the other end. One legacy of the fact that the nature of an electric current in a metal wire was not fully understood when electricity was first used and experimented with extensively in the 1800s, was the idea of the direction in which the current flows. The idea of positive and negative charges had already been established and the assumption made was that in a conventional circuit, the charge flowed from the positive terminal to the negative. Only much later was it discovered that the charge carriers in a metal wire were electrons and that these were negative, hence the charge in a metal wire actually flows from the negative terminal to the positive one. By this time, however, many of the physical laws had been established about the nature of electricity and its relationship with magnetism and so a decision seems to have been taken to largely ignore this apparent anomaly. Hence we now talk of two ideas – *conventional current* and *electron flow*. Conventional current still assumes that current in a circuit flows from *positive to negative*, despite the fact that, in reality, the electron flow is from negative to positive. Many pupils, when they eventually encounter this idea are confused, but it is a quirk of science that we are stuck with. Incidentally, in some situations (such as in solutions) some of the charge carriers are positive and so they do flow from positive to negative. Since many of the rules that pupils will learn in later years rely on the idea of current flow being positive to negative then it is probably best to stick to this idea with them.

Voltage

Voltage (measured in volts) is a measure of the energy carried by the electricity. Strictly it is a comparative measurement and this is reflected by its proper name of *potential difference* (pd). Potential difference measures the difference in the amount of energy that each coulomb of charge is carrying at different points of the circuit. Thus it indicates how much energy is used (transferred into other forms) by the components of the circuit. The voltage of a cell/battery/power supply indicates the amount of energy that it can supply, so a higher voltage causes the charge to have more energy and we can sometimes think of this as the amount of 'push' the current is given.

Circuits

Series circuits contain components which are wired together to form a single loop. As such, all the charge flows through every component. When components are connected in a *parallel* circuit, there are a number of loops, hence only some of the charge passes through each loop.

   Figures 12.1a and 12.1b, shows two circuit diagrams consisting of three bulbs, one wired in series and the other in parallel. Figures 12.2a and 12.2b also show these circuits, but how they might actually look in practice if proper wires are used to build the circuit, rather than a circuit board. Each bulb in the circuit uses the energy provided by the cell to glow and in the series circuit the energy has to be shared between the three bulbs as all the charged particles move through all three of them. In the parallel circuit, however, each bulb has, in effect, its own direct connection to the cell (this is perhaps better seen in Figure 12.2b, rather than Figure 12.1b, as the convention of circuit diagram drawing hides this idea) meaning that each of the charges only has to pass through one bulb and so the energy they carry does not have to be shared. If we were to use a voltmeter to measure the voltage across each bulb (that is, the potential difference between the electricity going into the bulb and leaving the bulb)

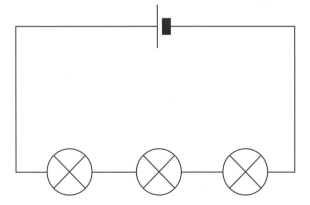

Figure 12.1a Circuit diagram showing three bulbs in series

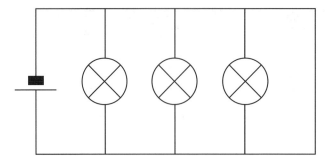

Figure 12.1b Circuit diagram showing three bulbs in parallel

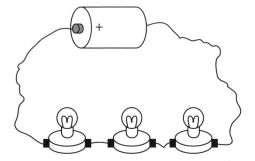

Figure 12.2a Three bulbs wired in series

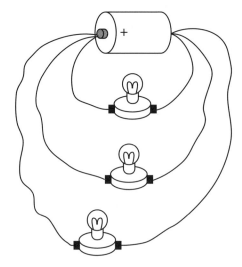

Figure 12.2b Three bulbs wired in parallel

we would notice that in the series circuit the sum of the voltages across each bulb adds up to the total voltage supplied by the cell (in a perfect world they would all have a third of the voltage of the cell if all the bulbs were identical), while in the parallel circuit each bulb would have the *same* voltage as the cell. In terms of current we need to consider each bulb rather like an obstacle to the flow of the charge. When the bulbs are placed in series, each of the electrons have to flow through all three bulbs, thus are impeded three times more than the electrons in the parallel circuit, each of which is only impeded by one bulb. This means that measuring the total current in each circuit would show that it is lower in the series circuit. These ideas are explored a little more later on; however, it might be appropriate to consider one more idea at this time. As a result of how many parallel circuits are drawn (and often constructed) they are seen as one entity, but what they actually are is a number of circuits in parallel with each other. Hence, to appreciate the differences between series and parallel circuits it is often useful to consider a parallel circuit as a number of separate circuits, powered by the same cell/battery/power supply, thus all the bulbs in the parallel circuit in Figures 12.1b and 12.2b behave as they would in *three separate circuits* containing one bulb.

Electrical components

Electrical components are what we use to build circuits. There are a number of electrical components that pupils will encounter during their school studies, with perhaps the most common being cells, batteries, power supplies, wires, crocodile clips, switches, bulbs, buzzers, motors, voltmeters, ammeters, resistors and diodes (with the latter four possibly only beyond KS2). Every component has a function within the circuit (see Table 12.1) and will also affect the way the current flows and how the energy is used in that circuit. It is important that children get the chance to use a variety of different components in their circuits since all too often they only really get to use bulbs and thus are deprived of the experience of relating to these devices and comparing their effects on the circuit with bulbs.

Table 12.1 The functions of some electrical components

Component	Function
Wire	Connects components together
Cell/battery/power supply	Provides energy to 'push' the charge around the circuit
Switch	Allows the current to flow/stops the current flowing
Bulb	Changes electrical energy to light energy
Buzzer	Changes electrical energy to sound energy
Motor	Changes electrical energy to movement (kinetic) energy
Resistor	Controls the current flow
Ammeter	Measures the amount of current flowing
Voltmeter	Measures the difference in electrical energy between two points in a circuit

Circuit diagrams

Circuit diagrams are a simple, clear way of representing electrical circuits. Drawing a circuit in a realistic way can be rather confusing and the idea of a circuit diagram is that it can be easily followed to connect a circuit quickly. A good analogy for a circuit diagram is the map for the London Underground which was originally designed in the same way as a circuit diagram. The London Underground map uses straight lines rather like the way we show wires, and stations like components with some lines intersecting, as wires may do in a circuit. The idea of the Underground map is to see quickly how to get from one station to the next but it does not accurately represent the geography of London, or the distance between stations. Likewise, a circuit diagram does not show a realistic picture of the actual circuit or the lengths of the wires. This abstract nature of a circuit diagram can sometimes be confusing to pupils and unless they are taught how to use such a diagram they can find them difficult to use when constructing a circuit, or to draw a circuit they have made, especially as those circuits get more complicated. Figure 12.3 shows a simple circuit diagram for a series circuit containing one bulb, one cell and a switch.

It can be useful to get pupils to physically trace the circuit diagram with their fingers in a series of stages, to work out how to connect their actual circuit properly. So in the example shown in Figure 12.3, they should see that they start with the cell/battery, then connect a wire to the positive connection of the cell/battery; next they connect a switch to the wire, then another wire to the other side of the switch; a bulb is connected to the end of this wire and, finally, a wire leading from the other side of the bulb to the cell/battery. The fact that we tend to use a perpendicular set of lines on the right hand side of the diagram can be confusing as it looks a bit like three short wires joined together when it is actually just one. Although the study of parallel circuits is not statutory before KS3, they are sometimes taught to some pupils and constructing these circuits from diagrams can be tricky too, especially if a circuit board is not used.

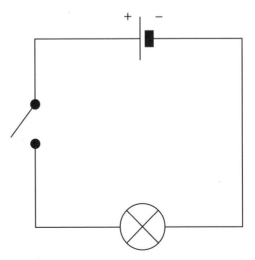

Figure 12.3 A simple diagram of a series circuit

One tip here is to get pupils to construct them one loop at a time, rather than in one go; this is especially useful if a voltmeter is attached to the circuit, which it is advisable to leave until the end, when the main circuit has been constructed.

Another feature of circuit diagrams is that we use a common set of symbols to represent each component of the circuit. This means that anyone can understand how the circuit is constructed. Figure 12.4 shows the most common circuit symbols that pupils will encounter when they first start using circuits and a few they may meet a little later.

Finally, it is good to get pupils into good habits from the start and so in addition to using the correct symbols they should be encouraged to use rulers for the wires as this aids clarity, and preferably a pencil for drawing so that mistakes can be easily rectified. Also they should ensure that there are no unintentional gaps between wires and components – apart from being good practice this also reinforces the idea of a complete circuit.

Making changes to circuits

Once we have built some simple circuits, then experimentation will allow pupils to explore how making changes to that circuit, in terms of the components used, the number of components and the way that they are connected, will affect how the circuit works. Before we start our discussion though, it is important from a safety point

component	symbol	component	symbol
wire	 ————	bulb	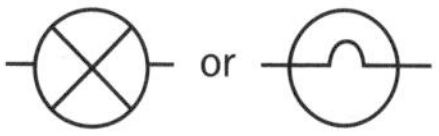 bulb symbol or bulb symbol
cell	 cell symbol (+ −)	buzzer	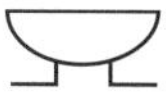 buzzer symbol
battery	 battery symbol	motor	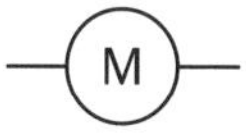 motor symbol (M)
power supply	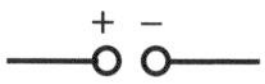 power supply symbol (+ −)	resistor	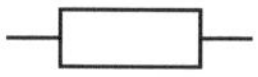 resistor symbol
switch (open)	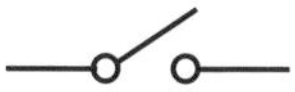 switch open symbol	ammeter	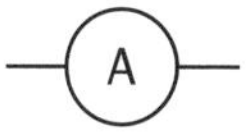 ammeter symbol (A)
switch (closed)	 switch closed symbol	voltmeter	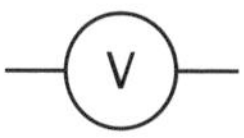 voltmeter symbol (V)

Figure 12.4 The circuit symbols of some electrical components

of view that pupils are made aware of the potential hazards associated with the use of electricity. As has already been mentioned, if one is using cells as a power source then there is little to worry about, but a good rule of thumb is to ask pupils to have their circuits checked before they use them, and having a switch in the circuit will help here. If mains electricity power packs are to be used this checking is vital, and pupils should also be warned not to make up a circuit unless either directed to do so or advised by the teacher that it is safe (this could also be a useful way of developing circuit diagram skills as they could first draw the circuits they intend to make).

All components, even wires, affect how a circuit works. To consider why they affect the circuit in the way that they do it is useful to reconsider what *current* is and the idea that an electric current is a flow of particles is fundamental and really ought to be taught to pupils. That way they will have a physical model in their minds of what electricity really is and they can then talk about it with more confidence and develop their ideas further. All the effects of components on circuits can be described in terms of the current flow and therefore pupils should be encouraged to use this, rather than the more abstract idea of 'electricity.'

Switches

The simplest starting point is probably the *switch*. The current in the circuit cannot easily jump across gaps (if the voltage is high enough it may jump across small gaps, but with the types of voltages that we get from cells this is not going to happen). Hence, when a switch is open it creates a gap in the circuit that electrons cannot jump across. For a circuit to work there needs to be a positive connection at one end *and* a negative correction at the other, and creating a break in the circuit means that one of the wires at the switch is no longer affected by the positive terminal of the cell and the other wire is no longer affected by the negative terminal of the cell, hence the current cannot flow. This might be better understood if we consider the circuit in a straight line, rather than as a loop (see Figure 12.5).

Closing the switch re-establishes the connections to the cell and the current can flow again. This is almost instantaneous, so any bulbs and so on in the circuit will start to work straight away. Arranging switches in different ways can provide a variety of effects and this is especially apparent in a parallel circuit. With the two circuits shown in Figure 12.6, the switch on the left-hand circuit is placed in such a position that it will cause all of the bulbs to light at once, but the arrangement of switches in the right-hand circuit allows each bulb to be operated separately.

Power supply

Cells, batteries and mains power supplies, as has already been mentioned, provide the *energy* to 'push' the current through the circuit. They each have a positive terminal

Figure 12.5 An alternative view of a simple series circuit with an open switch

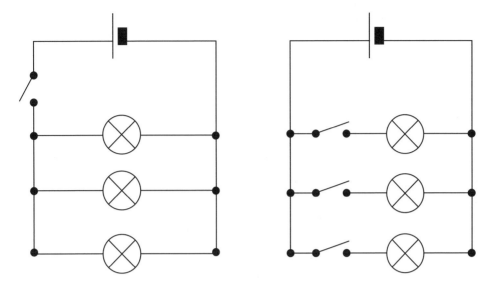

Figure 12.6 Two different arrangements of switches in a parallel circuit

and a negative terminal, one attracting the particles that make up the flow of current and the other repelling them. If we increase the voltage of these power sources then we increase their attractive/repulsive force and so the electrons are 'pushed' harder and thus move faster through the circuit. As the current is a measure of the amount of charge passing through the circuit (or a point in that circuit) every second, its value increases also. Decreasing the voltage will have the opposite effect. The result of this increase of current is that more energy can be supplied to the devices in the circuit so that, for instance, bulbs are brighter, buzzers are louder and motors spin faster. There may be a limit to this effect though, since the flow of current also heats up the devices (this is how a bulb actually works, with the heat of the filament inside causing it to glow) and excessive heating will damage the device by causing the wires inside to melt, thus breaking the circuit.

Increasing the voltage using cells is achieved by connecting more cells in series. This combines their attractive/repulsive force (the total voltage being the sum of the voltages of each cell) to increase the current flow. However, to do this we must connect the positive terminal of one cell to the negative terminal of another. If we connect the cells so that either the two positive terminals or the two negative terminals are connected, then they will cancel each other's effect. Two cells connected in this way will cause no current to flow and three cells connected, with one of them connected the wrong way round, will therefore behave like one cell, and so on.

Wires

Wires also affect the behaviour of a circuit. Like all other components wires heat up as current passes through them. This is due to their *resistance*. Resistance is a measure of how much a conductor resists the flow of charge through it. As electrons flow through a metal wire they will encounter the atoms in that wire and these atoms act as an obstacle to the flow of the electrons. Electrons will collide with the atoms and transfer some of their energy to them, causing the atoms to vibrate more and thus heat up the metal itself. In some metals this effect is more pronounced than in others and they are said to have more resistance. This effect is inevitable, thus the more wire in a circuit, the greater the resistance and the more energy is lost as heat. To reduce this effect low-resistance metals are used to make the connecting wires in circuits and, especially if the current is low, (increasing the current causes more of these collisions per second so more heat is lost) the heat loss due to resistance is negligible. Copper is used for most wiring as it has a very low resistance. Sometimes, however, we actively encourage this heating effect by deliberately using higher-resistance metals and this is how electrical heating devices work, such as the element in a kettle, hob or electric fire. Wiring devices in different ways also affects the resistance of a circuit, with the resistance increasing when we connect devices in series and decreasing when we connect them in parallel. This idea will be explored in more detail later when we consider bulbs, but the reason that wiring in parallel decreases resistance is because there are multiple pathways for the current to flow through, hence more charge can flow at once. Since resistance is the measure of the opposition to current flow, this means that if we compare two circuits with the same voltage supply, but where one has more current flowing through it, it must therefore have a lower resistance. The study of resistance in detail is not really encountered until KS4, but a simple appreciation of it is vital if pupils are to understand the effects of adding components to circuits in particular ways. Resistance is measured in units called ohms (symbol: Ω) and is found by knowing the voltage across and current flowing through either the whole circuit or parts of that circuit then dividing the voltage by the current:

$$\text{Resistance} = \text{voltage} \div \text{current}$$

In addition to the material it is made from, the length, thickness and temperature of a wire are also important in determining the amount of resistance it has. A long wire offers more opportunities for electrons to encounter the atoms restricting their flow, thus it will have a higher resistance than a short wire. A thick wire will contain more electrons that can flow than a thinner one, so more current can flow through a thicker wire than through a thinner one, even if we use the same voltage (since each electron is affected by the voltage *individually* and *independently* of the others). When a wire is hot, its atoms vibrate more, therefore it is more likely that an electron will hit these atoms than the atoms in a cooler wire, hence resistance increases as temperature increases. As a general rule, if the current is high, then the resistance is low, although this is only a fair comparison if we are dealing with circuits with the same voltage.

A final point worth considering here is the idea of a short circuit (see Figure 12.7). This is when a loop in a circuit contains no components such as bulbs and other devices.

Since current will flow easily through most connecting wires, creating a part of a circuit like this (effectively a parallel circuit) will have the effect of a very large current flow through the lone wire and a much reduced current flow through the part(s) of the circuit which do contain devices. The result is that the devices in the other parts of the circuit will not work due to the low current and the short-circuiting wire will get very hot. This is therefore hazardous as it can lead to burns and fires, so unintentional

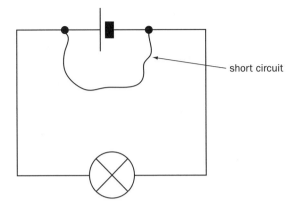

Figure 12.7 A short circuit

short circuits should be avoided – another good reason to check pupils' circuits before allowing their use.

Bulbs

Bulbs are probably the most common device used to explore the nature of simple circuits and how they behave. On reason for this is because they provide an instant visual effect which is easy to compare qualitatively. Inside a bulb is a very thin wire, commonly made of the metal tungsten, called the filament. The filament is designed to have a high resistance so that it heats up to the point at which it glows. The greater the current flow though the bulb, the more energy is delivered to it per second, hence the hotter it becomes and the brighter it appears. If the current flow to the bulb is too high it will get hot enough for the wire to melt and this will cause the bulb to stop working and create a break to the circuit at that point. If the circuit is a series circuit, this will cause the whole of that circuit to stop working as the current will no longer be able to flow, but if it is part of a parallel circuit then only the loop that that bulb is part of will stop working and the other loops will continue to work as they are independent pathways through the whole circuit. One way of increasing the current flow to bulbs is to increase the voltage supplied to the circuit, hence a higher voltage means brighter bulbs. The brightness of bulbs is also affected by other components in the circuit which may be drawing energy from the current. In addition, the way in which the bulbs are connected (series or parallel) will affect their brightness. All components have a certain amount of resistance associated with them and in a series circuit the total resistance increases as we add more bulbs. This means that adding more bulbs decreases the flow of current so each bulb receives less energy per second and they appear dimmer. If, however, we reconnect all the bulbs so that they are in parallel with each other, then each parallel circuit only has the resistance associated with one bulb, so the current can flow faster through each loop, more energy is supplied to each bulb per second and the bulbs are brighter than in the series circuit (the same brightness as one bulb in a series circuit). One point to note here is that we are talking about using identical bulbs. Different types of bulb have different resistances, so they will have different brightness with the same voltage (this is why a 40W bulb is dimmer than a

100W bulb, despite the fact that they are both using 230V). So when conducting such experiments, make sure the bulbs are all of the same type! Hopefully it will also be clear that in the parallel circuit, as more current in total is supplied, then any cell connected to such a circuit will become exhausted more quickly than in the equivalent series circuit. Figure 12.8 demonstrates these ideas by considering the current flow at different parts of a number of series and parallel circuits (the current values are arbitrary, but relate to each other appropriately).

It can be seen that the current is the same at all points of a series circuit and decreases as more bulbs are added. With the parallel circuits, each additional bulb receives the same current as the others, thus increasing the total current flow through the circuit as a whole. The last example shows a combination of a series and parallel circuit, which combines the ideas discussed.

If a bulb in a series circuit is removed, the effect is the same as if it had its filament

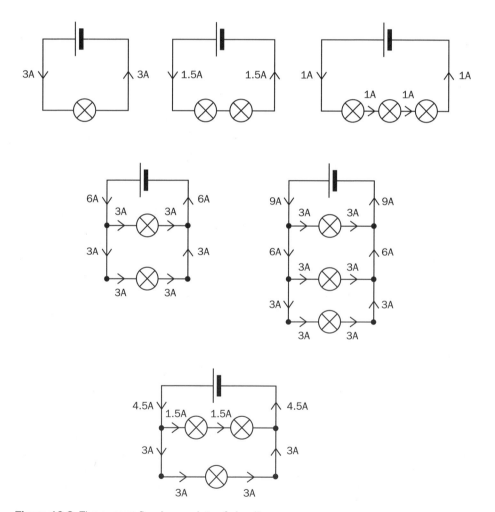

Figure 12.8 The current flow in a variety of circuits

damaged, namely, that the whole circuit will stop working. This is the same as used to be the case with the old-style Christmas tree lights, which were wired in series. Removing (or losing to damage) a bulb from a parallel circuit has no effect on the other bulbs (unless there is more than one bulb in that loop); they continue to work and have the same brightness – they do not get brighter as some may think. This is the same as the wiring in the home. Switching on one bulb (or other appliance) connects a new loop in the parallel circuit around the house, without affecting the others. Also, if we turn off a light, or a bulb stops working, all the other bulbs continue to work in the same way.

It might also be possible at this stage to consider the voltages associated with each bulb in a circuit, although commonly this extra layer of detail can confuse many pupils, especially if introduced at this stage, when they are just getting to grip with current. It may, therefore, be prudent to leave teaching this for another occasion, but for completeness it is discussed briefly. Figure 12.9 shows a number of circuits with voltage measurements for each bulb. What these values indicate (although are not equal to) is the amount of energy each bulb uses. For ease of understanding, each bulb is identical, so will use energy from the current in the same way.

What can be noticed is that in the series circuit each bulb 'uses' an equal portion of the available voltage (the voltage is 'shared'), whereas in the parallel circuits, each loop 'uses' the same voltage as the battery; the assumption here is that the wires do not use up any of the voltage. Most pupils can learn this idea, but find it hard to accept because it seems that the bulbs 'seem to know' when they have to 'share' the voltage and when they do not. This is one of the reasons why voltage should be regarded as a higher-level concept and its study is only statutory in later key stages. The fact is that they do not know how much energy to use up. The amount of energy they use is related to their resistance. Putting extra bulbs in series reduces the *current flow* in the whole of that part of the circuit and thus the amount of energy the bulbs are receiving in a given period of time. Since identical bulbs have the same resistance they will transfer the electrical energy at the same rate as each other and so it seems that they share out the energy equally. Add a bulb of a different resistance to the others and the amount of heat and therefore light it can release at that current is different and so it glows brighter or dimmer, and thus effectively uses the energy at a different rate and the voltage drop across it will be different accordingly.

Other devices, such as motors and buzzers will affect a circuit in a similar way to bulbs, but they convert the available energy to different forms (for example, kinetic energy for motors and sound for buzzers) although all will release some heat as well. Some of these other devices, however, only allow the current to flow through them in one direction, so the way we add them to the circuit is important. Put a buzzer in a circuit for instance and it may stop the circuit working if connected the wrong way round! Experimentation with a variety of different components and varying their numbers or the voltage supplied to them will reinforce their effects in pupils' minds and allow them to consider their effects in situations where they will not get the chance to actually experiment, such as when answering questions in tests.

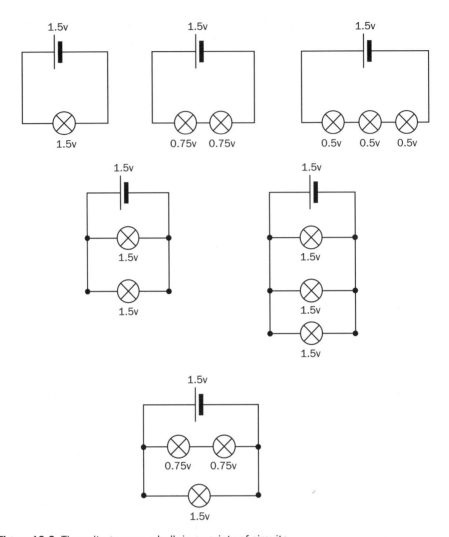

Figure 12.9 The voltage across bulb in a variety of circuits

Links to teaching

More teaching activities

Pupils will quickly get the hang of building a circuit that works. To extend this activity, allow them to experiment with using different numbers and types of bulbs, buzzers, wires and batteries.

Other things to do and try

Many construction kits now allow pupils to build models using motors, lights and power sources.

Another good activity is to build a battery from a potato. If you push a copper coin into potato and connect it with wires to multimeter it will show some current.

TOP TEACHING TIP

It is important to use a unit on electricity to emphasize the dangers of mains electricity.

Some common misconceptions

- Batteries provide the electrical particles for a circuit.
- Components use up energy.
- Components use up current.
- Batteries 'hold' electricity.
- All electricity is dangerous.

AMAZING FACT

Lie detectors use electricity. When you lie you sweat more and this makes the electricity flow better.

13

Forces and motion

National Curriculum: Attainment Target Sc4, Strand 2 (KS1: 4.2a–2c, KS2: 4.2a–2e)
QCA Schemes of Work: Units 1E, 2E, 3E, 4E and 6E

Curriculum requirements

Forces and their effects, particularly in terms of motion forms another of the bedrocks of scientific study, with forces being highlighted as one of the key themes of the National Framework for Science. Study at KS1 looks mainly at movement and the cause of movement, while this is developed at KS2 by considering specific examples of forces, measuring forces and considering the direction of force.

The National Curriculum programme of study states that at KS1 pupils should be taught to find out about, and describe the movement of, familiar things; that both pushes and pulls are examples of forces; and to recognize that when things speed up, slow down or change direction, there is a cause. At KS2 pupils should be taught, through the concept of types of force, about the forces of attraction and repulsion between magnets, and about the forces of attraction between magnets and magnetic materials; that objects are pulled downwards because of the gravitational attraction between them and the Earth; about friction, including air resistance, as a force that slows moving objects and may prevent objects from starting to move; that when objects are pushed or pulled, an opposing pull or push can be felt; and how to measure forces and identify the direction in which they act.

What is a force?

The word 'force', like many words connected to concepts in physical science, is difficult to define easily. While we can experience the effects of forces, they are sometimes acting in situations where we are not aware that they are. There are also many types of force and what we can say about all of them is that they influence the motion of objects, from the smallest subatomic particle to huge objects like **stars**. A related idea is also that forces can (through the movement of particles) affect the shapes of objects (this has been considered in Chapter 10, 'Changing materials'). Another key idea is that forces work in *pairs*; for instance, if we consider the force of gravity between a person and the Earth, then not only does the Earth exert a force of attraction on the person, the person also exerts a force of attraction on the Earth. Most general introductions on forces tend to focus on what forces can do in terms of movement and changes of shape as well as considering forces in terms of *pushing* forces and *pulling* forces. Many forces can be described in this way, but sometimes it is more difficult; for example, what kind of force is involved in slowing down a car or a bike by applying the brakes? Nevertheless, this idea of pushes and pulls as an introduction does help pupils start to appreciate what effects forces can have on objects and that forces are applied in a particular direction, with a certain magnitude.

Describing motion

The way that scientists describe motion is in terms of speed, velocity and acceleration. Speed and velocity are essentially the same, except that velocity also takes into account the direction of motion. Speed and velocity measure the distance a moving object travels in a given amount of time (with velocity that is the distance in a particular direction). In reality these will usually be averages as, say, with a car journey, the speed will vary during the course of that journey. The standard unit for distance is the metre and that for time is the second. To calculate speed, distance travelled is divided by time taken:

$$\text{speed} = \text{distance} \div \text{time}$$

This gives us the speed in metres per second (m/s), so tells us how far the object will move every second.

Acceleration is a measurement of the rate of change of speed (or more correctly, velocity), in other words, how fast the speed is changing. It is found by considering the amount of time taken for the speed to change from one value to the next. It is calculated thus:

$$\text{acceleration} = \text{change in speed} \div \text{time}$$

or

$$\text{acceleration} = (\text{final speed} - \text{initial speed}) \div \text{time}$$

This gives us a measurement of acceleration in metres per second^2 – in other words, metres per second per second, so tells us how much the speed is changing every second. If the value is negative then this indicates that the object is slowing down, or decelerating. A knowledge of these ideas will help when we consider how forces affect the movement of objects.

Movement and force: Newton's laws

One of the most significant works in science was that of Isaac Newton concerning forces and their effect on motion. While in later years it was found that his *laws of motion* break down at the atomic and subatomic level, for most of our everyday experiences of force and motion they still work. Newton distilled many ideas from the work of earlier scientists and his own imaginative ideas into three basic ideas that describe how forces act. To appreciate this, he had to also consider forces that were not readily apparent, such as friction.

His *first law* essentially says that an object will continue to move for ever at a fixed speed and in a fixed direction, unless it experiences another force. The idea of a change in direction seems pretty straightforward since if we push an already moving object in another direction to the one it is moving in, it will change its direction of movement (such as when playing tennis). The idea of the constant speed is less intuitive and is more apparent if we consider a few things. First, when an object is stationary it does have a speed, but that speed is zero. Next we have to consider forces that we cannot see, such as friction, which only arises when objects are moving or trying to move, and will tend to slow things down – 'another force acting on the object'. We also need to be clear about *when* a force is acting on something. A common misconception involves the forces involved in throwing an object such as a ball. A force is exerted by the arm of the person throwing the ball, but the ball only experiences that force before its release. Once it has left the thrower's hand it moves because of that force but *it no longer experiences that force*. Such forces are commonly called *contact forces* because the force is only felt when the object is in contact with whatever is exerting the force (frictional forces are also contact forces). Forces like magnetic force and gravitational force can be exerted on objects without being in contact so are not contact forces and are often called *field forces* Finally, we have to consider the idea of *balanced* and *unbalanced* forces. Newton's object that moves at a constant speed in a constant direction may have forces acting on it (in reality it always will), but the forces are *balanced*. Figure 13.1 lets us look at this in more detail.

If we consider a stationary box on level ground then it will experience the force of gravity pulling it towards the ground and the ground will also push up on it (the box pushes on the ground because of the gravity, so the ground pushes back – remember, forces work in pairs). Since the box does not move, the size of the upward and downward forces must be equal, hence they are balanced and the box does not move. If the box is on a gentle slope another force comes into play, namely, friction. The upward force from the ground is only fully felt at right angles to the ground, so a slope causes the box starts to experience less upward force which will not fully balance the force of gravity. These unbalanced forces will allow the box to start moving down the slope, but as it tries to do so it will immediately encounter a frictional force, which if large enough will replace the 'lost' upward force to keep the forces on the box in balance. If the slope becomes greater then there will be even less upward force to prevent the box slipping and eventually not even the friction can exert a force large enough to keep the box in balance and it will start to slide. This leads us to another misconception, namely, that balanced forces only arise when an object is stationary,

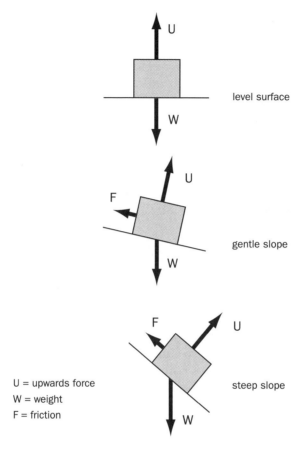

U = upwards force
W = weight
F = friction

level surface

gentle slope

steep slope

Figure 13.1 Looking at some balanced and unbalanced forces

which is not true. When an object is moving at a constant speed (remember a stationary object can be considered as having a constant speed of zero), it also has balanced forces on it, if they were not balanced then the object would start to speed up or slow down.

So, balanced forces will mean an already stationary object will remain stationary and an already moving object will remain at constant speed. Unbalanced forces, however, will cause the speed or direction of motion (or both) of an object to change. This brings us nicely to Newton's *second law of motion*. This can be summarized with two basic statements. The greater the force exerted on an object the faster its *speed will change* and the heavier an object the *more force is needed* to make its speed change. Fortunately for us as teachers, this seems entirely logical to pupils. Newton's second law is summarized with a mathematical relationship connecting the force exerted on an object, the mass of that object and its acceleration:

$$\text{force} = \text{mass} \times \text{acceleration} \ (F = ma)$$

Acceleration, the rate of change of speed, can mean either speeding up or slowing down (deceleration) since a force applied in the direction of motion will speed an object up and a force applied in the opposite direction to the motion will slow the object down. It should be noted though that this acceleration will only occur while the force is being exerted; if this stops, the object will continue at the speed it reached when the force was removed, unless it experiences another force. *Mass* is one of those words that often brings problems in the teaching and learning of science. Mass is measured in *kilograms* and is often confused with *weight*. Mass is a measure of the amount of matter that something contains, while weight is actually a force that results from the force of gravity on the object. Hence, weight is measured in *newtons* (the unit of force) and the conflict arises from our everyday use of the word weight. To understand this better we could consider an object on the Earth and that same object on the Moon. The effect of the Earth's gravity means that every kilogram of mass on the Earth feels a force, due to gravity, of about 10 newtons. On the Moon however, the force of gravity is much less (why this is will be considered later in the section on gravitational forces) and every kilogram will feel a force of about 1.67 newtons. Hence an object with a mass of 100 kg on the Earth has a weight of 1000 newtons, but that same object on the Moon will still have a mass of 100 kg, but a weight of about 167 newtons.

Newton's *third law of motion* states that to every action there is an equal and opposite reaction. This describes the *forces working in pairs* idea. What this means is that when something exerts a force on something else, the second body exerts a force back on the first object that is equal in size, but in the opposite direction. This was encountered when considering the box on the flat surface earlier. The box exerts a force on the ground below it and the particles in the ground push back equally. This idea explains why, when we pull on an elastic band, it pulls back (the harder we pull, harder it pulls back), why when we push something along the ground we feel it push back, why rockets take off by ejecting hot gases downwards and why a gun recoils backwards when a shell is fired forwards.

The forces that pupils need to know about include the contact forces we have mentioned and the two field forces of magnetic force and gravitational force. Related to the magnetic force is the force created by electric charge, and knowledge of this force will help in the understanding of electricity. All can, of course, cause movement and changes in movement, and children should be given the opportunity to identify and experiment with a variety of different forces to gain experience of their effects on motion. They should consider which forces are causing the changes that we see in everyday situations such as vehicles, falling objects, floating objects, springs and rubber bands and objects in the **solar system** such as the Earth and the Moon.

Magnetic force

Much of the theory of magnetism has been discussed in Chapter 9, 'Grouping and classifying materials'. Magnetic materials are actually quite few in number. In this sense we are technically talking abut a type of magnetism called *ferromagnetism* (ferro-pertaining to iron). There are only three magnetic elements: the metals iron, cobalt and nickel. Alloys of these metals (alloys being mixtures of metals) such as steel (an alloy of iron) will also be magnetic. Permanent magnets can come in a variety of forms but the most commonly used magnet in the classroom is a bar magnet. The ends of a bar magnet are called poles, one the north pole and the other the south pole, and the magnetic field around a bar magnet (see Figure 13.2) is such that it is these parts of the magnetic that *seem* to have the greatest effect (this is not actually true since cutting a magnet in two will produce two new magnets, each with a north or a south pole that was originally in the middle of the larger magnet). The shape of the field can be demonstrated by sprinkling iron filings around the magnet and gently agitating them (it is possible to buy iron filings in a plastic casing to observe this effect in a much tidier way). The iron filings become arranged around the magnet in a very particular way that reflects the shape of the field around the magnet. This can be further explored using a small plotting compass to show individual lines of force around the magnet. The arrows in Figure 13.2 show the direction the north-pointing needle will point at that position.

If two magnets are brought close together then their fields interact with one another, creating forces of attraction and repulsion on each other. If two north or two south poles are brought close together then the resultant force is one of *repulsion* and if the magnets are free to move (for example, if they are suspended or on a low-friction surface) they will move apart. The resultant force when two opposite poles are brought together is one of *attraction* and the magnets will move together and, if they are allowed to, will 'stick' to each other.

Objects made of magnetic material, but which are unmagnetized will also be affected by the magnetic field of a magnet. However we will only see a force of *attraction*. This is because the magnet causes temporary magnetism (called induced magnetism) in the object in such a way that the north pole of the magnet will temporarily magnetize the object so that a south pole will be facing it, and vice versa with the south pole of the magnet. The effect of this is that we can only show if a material is

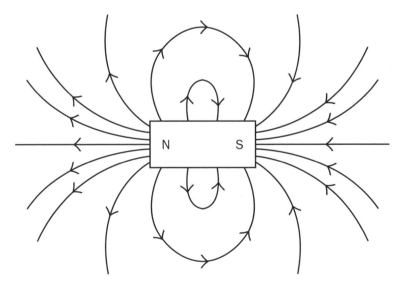

Figure 13.2 The field around a bar magnet

magnetic by attraction; a magnet itself should be able to demonstrate attraction *and* repulsion. Once the object is removed from the magnet it will lose its magnetism, especially if it is made of a soft magnetic material like iron. Soft magnetic materials gain and lose magnetism easily. Hard magnetic materials (like steel) are harder to magnetize but it is also more difficult for them to lose their magnetism, hence a steel paper-clip may retain some of its induced magnetism for a while after being removed from a magnet.

The stronger the field around the magnet, the greater force it can exert on other magnets or magnetic objects. In addition, the strength of the field gets weaker with distance. The field itself can penetrate matter so that it can exert its force through other materials. This clearly happens through air but also through other gases, liquids and **solids**. This is important and can be investigated quite effectively. The fact that magnetism has this property also means that it adds some mystery to their study and children tend to be fascinated by them, which is something to be exploited. Magnets and their effects can be introduced into classroom study in many imaginative and often quite simple ways, such as the mysterious movement of a paper-clip on a surface.

Gravitational forces

Gravity, another field force, works in a similar way to magnetism, except that it *only produces attractive forces*. Indeed, this similarity can sometimes be useful when describing the effects of gravity, provided that pupils do not think they are the same force. As forces go, gravity is actually only a very weak force (it can take a lot more force to separate two magnets, than to jump upwards), but it can act over huge distances, and herein lies its importance in the universe. One of the first things that many children learn about forces is that objects fall downwards because of gravity. This seems a sound enough everyday observation, but it has flaws. First, the notion of falling supposes that this is a passive action, whereas a force is involved (OK, so gravity is mentioned as the cause). Second, is the notion of downwards. Which way is down depends on your perspective. Down in the UK might seem the same as down in Australia, but the actual direction in which an object moves when it is 'falling' in the UK is very different to the direction it is moving in Australia, or India or Jamaica! Unfortunately the National Curriculum uses the word downwards. We could improve this by saying that falling objects are actually pulled towards the Earth because of gravity, gravity being a force of attraction between the object and the Earth. This idea of the Earth pulling on/attracting things is fundamental to a wider understanding of gravity and how it works. We have already mentioned the work of Newton on motion, and wrapped up in these ideas are gravitational forces. One of the major genius moments that Newton had was to realize that the force which makes objects fall was the same as the force that keeps the Moon in orbit around the Earth and the planets in orbit around the Sun. What Newton said was that all objects exert a force of gravity on other objects. Normally these forces are too weak to detect, but when you have an object with a very large mass, like the Earth, this force is very strong. Hence the size of the gravitational force between two objects depends on *both* of their masses (since both of them exert a force of gravity on each other). This means that the force of gravity, due to the Earth say, on an object with a mass of 10 kg is ten times the force exerted on an object of 1 kg, hence the 10 kg object is being pulled towards the Earth with ten times the force and it is more difficult to pick up. The force which the Earth is exerting on the object is *weight*, which was discussed earlier. The other thing that determines the strength of this gravitational force is the distance between the two objects: the further away they are the weaker the force (rather like magnets). So someone at the top of Everest will feel less gravitational force than when they are at the bottom, so they will weigh less. In this last example, of course, the difference in weight will be small (I think everyone probably loses weight scaling Everest anyway), but in both cases the person is still on the Earth, so why does he or she feel less force on the mountain. This is because it is the distance from the centre of the objects that is crucial, so, in this case the distance from the centre of the Earth.

One major piece of work that Newton drew on was that of Galileo who, among other things, studied falling objects. In Galileo's time the accepted theory of falling objects was that proposed by the Greek philosopher Aristotle, that heavy objects fall faster than lighter ones. This seems entirely logical but Galileo was not convinced, supposedly conducting experiments from the top of the leaning tower of Pisa with cannon balls to test his theory out. In many cases the heavier balls did hit the ground slightly ahead of the lighter ones, but not enough for Galileo to be convinced he was wrong. He realized that the air was getting in the way of his experiment as it produced a force of its own (what we now call air resistance) which was affecting his results. This is often the problem with physical relationships, in the real world there are other forces that interfere with the ones we are concentrating on. He eventually solved this by constructing a low-friction slope set at angle to make the effect of the air resistance negligible and balls of different masses all travelled down the slope at the same speed. Indeed, he was vindicated by the astronaut David Scott who famously dropped a hammer and a feather on the surface of the Moon at the end of the Apollo 15 mission – they both hit the ground at the same time as there is no atmosphere and therefore no air resistance on the Moon. The air resistance is a frictional force that has the effect of slowing down a moving object and is discussed in more detail later. Put simply, when objects fall, the lighter the object, the greater, proportionally, the effect of the air resistance, hence they will tend to fall more slowly than heavier ones. In addition, the shape of an object also affects its air resistance, which further explains why a hammer will hit the ground quicker than a feather on the Earth. It was Newton that really explained why Galileo's ideas were correct, and to see this for ourselves it helps if we do not consider objects as falling but as being pulled towards the Earth. It might also help if we take a step back from the world and view this idea from space as in Figure 13.3.

For an object to 'fall' it must be *pulled* to the Earth's surface by gravity. The significance of this fact, that gravity is exerting a force, might be best appreciated by us northern hemisphere dwellers by looking at the southern hemisphere dweller in Figure 13.3. If that person drops a heavy object it should, according to Galileo, fall as fast as a light one; in other words, they will accelerate at the same speed. However, a heavier object, according to Newton, should have a larger force exerted on it by gravity, so why does it not move faster? Newton's second law of motion says that if there is more force on an object, it should accelerate faster, however, his second law

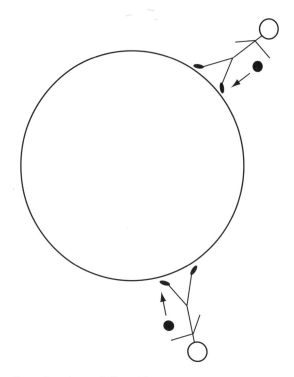

Figure 13.3 The effect of gravity on falling objects

also states that a heavier object needs more force to accelerate it than a lighter object. For example, if the heavy object is twice the mass of the lighter one it may have twice the force due to gravity than the lighter one, but it *needs* twice as much force to accelerate it as fast as the lighter one, hence they both accelerate at the same rate. The rate of this acceleration on Earth is nearly 10 m/s², so every 10 seconds the speed of an object will get 10 m/s faster. This value is known as g, the acceleration due to gravity, and explains why the force of gravity on an object (its weight) is nearly ten times its mass. Using Newton's equation:

$$\text{force} = \text{mass} \times \text{acceleration}$$

if the force here is the force of gravity (that is, weight), the mass the mass of an object on the Earth in kilograms and the acceleration is the acceleration caused by the Earth's gravity (or g), then:

$$\text{weight} = \text{mass} \times g$$

and, since g is 10 m/s²:

$$\text{weight} = \text{mass} \times 10$$

When Scott carried out his experiment on the Moon (there is video footage of this available on the NASA website, www.nasa.gov/), the feather falls much more quickly than it does on Earth, showing that there is less air resistance, and the hammer falls more slowly, demonstrating that there is less gravity. This is because the Moon exerts a weaker force of gravity than the Earth. It is a common misconception that there is no gravity on the surface of the Moon. It does, of course, like all objects, exert its own force of gravity, but because the *Moon is about one-sixth of the mass of the Earth*, so it only exerts a force of gravity one-sixth of the strength of that of the Earth. Thus the hammer was not pulled as hard as it would have been on the Earth and it accelerated at a slower rate.

It was said earlier that as well as causing falling objects to move towards the surface of the Earth, gravity keeps the Moon in orbit around the Earth and the planets in orbit around the Sun. Indeed, there is a force of gravity between all the stars (and other objects) in our galaxy, the Milky Way, and between all the galaxies of the universe. Hence gravity can be said to hold the universe together. Newton realized that if the force that pulled objects to the ground could extend far enough away from the Earth's surface then it could affect the motion of other objects like the Moon, keeping it in orbit around the Earth. All objects in the solar system are affected by the huge gravitational force of the Sun (the Sun contains over 99 per cent of the mass of the solar system, which is why this force is so large), but when an object is close enough to another heavy body it will be affected more by its gravity, which is why the Moon orbits the Earth rather than directly orbiting the Sun. Also, gravity is the force that was responsible for the formation of the solar system and other bodies outside it, for it was the force of gravity between gas and dust particles that grouped them together into the pieces of matter that would eventually become stars, planet, moons, and so on.

Frictional forces

Frictional forces are those that tend to oppose movement. They are contact forces and only arise when there is some motion, or attempted motion, of at least one of the bodies that are in contact. Frictional forces are found in a variety of situations, some of which we find useful and some we find a nuisance. It is friction that means that our shoes grip the floor so that we can walk, likewise it is friction that causes the soles of those shoes to wear down; sandpaper is useful because its high-friction surface *does* wear things down. Let us first consider the friction between solid surfaces. All surfaces, no matter how smooth they feel, have a certain degree of roughness. With some surfaces this is obvious (such as the surface of sandpaper), others (such as glass) less so. This is because the 'rough' surface of glass is on a scale so small that we cannot see or feel it. When the surface of one object moves over another it is the 'bumps' on the surface that cause the friction by making it difficult for one surface to slide over another (see Figure 13.4).

The larger the bumps and the more of them there are, the greater the amount of friction produced, while low-friction surfaces have fewer and smaller bumps. Friction is useful in situations where you want one surface to grip another, such as the brakes of a car or bicycle or when rock climbing. The amount of friction can be increased by

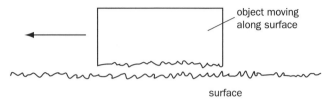

Figure 13.4 How friction arises from two surfaces

making surfaces deliberately rough and even more so by using projections such as spikes on running shoes and football boot studs.

In situations where friction is a problem it is possible to reduce it by various means. One way is to polish surfaces to make them smooth by wearing away some of the bumps on the surface or filling in some of the dips between them with something like wax. The latter method is how lubrication works. Oils and greases reduce friction by coating the surfaces they are applied to, which has the effect of making them smoother and separates them a bit, allowing them to slide over each other more easily. Water can act in this way too, which is why wet floors are slippery and one is more likely to skid when driving on a wet road. The tread on car tyres is designed in such a way that it causes water to be directed away from the bottom of the tyre where it touches the road to prevent the water lowering the friction between the tyre and the road. Another common way to reduce friction is by placing round objects between the two surfaces, such as ball bearings and wooden rollers, which can roll, so allowing more movement between the two surfaces than would be achieved without them.

Friction produces two effects on surfaces which can also be useful or a nuisance. The first is wear. As one object moves over another some of the particles on each surface are removed by the frictional force, causing the surface to wear down; useful when polishing metal to remove the corroded surface, a problem with car tyres. Also, the friction causes the particles on the surface to move more, releasing heat. This is why rubbing your hands together on a cold day warms them up, and why racing car drivers zigzag over the track before the race, to warm up the tyres, so increasing the pressure inside which makes sure that the bottom of the car does not drag on the ground.

Another frictional force is *air resistance* (or *drag*). Whenever an object moves through air it pushes on the air particles and they push back (Newton's third law again) and this will oppose the movement of that object. This force is called air resistance and like all frictional forces can be useful in some situations but not in others. The size of this force depends on two factors and the first of these is speed. When an object is stationary it is not pushing on the air particles, so there is no air resistance. As it starts to move, a small force is experienced, which increases with speed as more air will be pushed away every second. Thus when we stand still we feel no force, when we start to walk we may not feel the air resistance as it will be quite small, if we run we can definitely feel the air resistance pushing on us and if we place a hand out of the window of a moving car we can feel a substantial amount of force. The second factor that determines the size of air resistance is the size of the surface pushing on the air. The larger the surface, the more air particles are pushed on, so the greater the air resistance. Hence the flat front of a lorry will present a large surface to the air and create a lot of air resistance, while a racing car provides a much smaller surface that directly hits the air and the shape of the car allows that air to pass over it easily. Such shapes are called streamlined shapes and the reduction in air resistance means that the car can move faster with less force from the engine and so a lower fuel consumption. The need for streamlining is a way of overcoming air resistance when it is a problem, another example being the all-in-one body suits that some sprinters now use. Air resistance can also be useful, the classic example being the parachute which creates large amounts of air resistance because of its size and the number of air particles it can push on.

Earlier we discussed Galileo's work on falling objects, with air resistance being the force that interfered with his results. It may now be possible for us to see why this was the case. Before an object is dropped it experiences no air resistance, only the force of gravity and the force used to hold it. Once the object is released it experiences the gravitational force, loses the force that was holding it in place but now has a new force exerted on it, air resistance. As we have seen, an object being pulled towards the Earth accelerates, so as its speed increases so does the air resistance it experiences. This will tend to make the net force on the object less, so it will accelerate more slowly. If the object falls for long enough the air resistance will become so large that it *equals* the weight of the object (that is, the gravitational force on it) and at this point the forces on the object will become balanced and it will stop accelerating. The speed it reaches at this point is called *terminal velocity*. A heavier object will need more air resistance than a lighter one to reach terminal velocity, which is why it tends to hit the ground first, as it is continuing to accelerate at a faster rate than a lighter one.

Objects moving through water also experience a frictional force like air resistance, called *water resistance*. This force arises in the same way, although the forces involved are greater due to the fact that water particles are much closer together than the particles in air, so many more particles are pushed against by something moving through water. Animals that live in the water tend to be streamlined to reduce the amount of water resistance they create, allowing them to swim faster to avoid predators or catch prey more easily. As with other frictional forces we can make use of water resistance, such as with our hands when swimming and with the oars of a rowing boat. One important point to note here is that this is not the same force as upthrust, which is the force involved in floating (see Chapter 9).

Measuring forces and representing forces in diagrams

The unit of force is the *newton* (abbreviated to N), named after the man himself. Pupils measuring forces will do so with a *forcemeter* or *newtonmeter*. These devices contain a spring that stretches or compresses a certain amount, depending on the size of force applied. Indeed, a set of bathroom scales is a forcemeter, which measures the force your body applies as a result of gravity (your weight), although it will actually give you a reading of your mass in kilograms rather that your weight in newtons (scales like these can be obtained for use in science lessons with the units in newtons rather than kilograms). Forcemeters can be obtained that allow pushing or pulling forces to be measured and it is important that pupils gain experience of doing this and reading the values accurately. A range of forcemeters is needed since some are designed to measure only small forces (for example, up to 1 N), while others can measure larger forces (they will have a stiffer spring inside). Care should be taken with forcemeters though, as the springs inside can be damaged by overstretching. Lifting an object with a forcemeter will tell us its weight and pupils can also get a feel for the sizes of forces by pulling objects along surfaces (this will indicate the size of the frictional force involved), opening doors, and so on.

In addition to measuring forces, pupils also need to be able to identify the direction that a force is acting, either experimentally or using diagrams. Force diagrams are a simple way of showing the forces acting on an object. Figure 13.5 shows the forces acting on a car. When the car is stationary there are less forces as there is no forward force from the engine or frictional forces. At a constant speed the force from the engine is balanced by the frictional forces and when the car accelerates the force from the engine and the frictional forces are unbalanced.

The forces and the direction in which they act are indicated by the arrows. These really should be drawn so that they are touching the object concerned, although they do not have to necessarily be at the point at which the forces act (the frictional forces in this example for instance, occur in many places, such as the tyres and the surface of the car, and in the car itself, such as in the engine and wheel axle), although pupils are sometimes asked to do this in test questions.

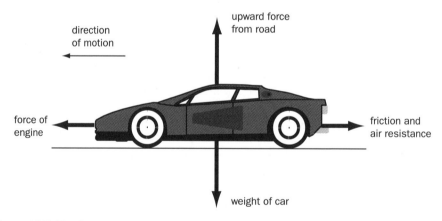

Figure 13.5 The forces on a moving car

measure the time taken to travel a distance. Time cannot be measured in a sufficiently accurate way with stopwatches in this case, because the times and distances are so short.

Sometimes forces that are not involved in changes to the object concerned are left out of diagrams to stop them from being too cluttered or to allow greater focus on the forces that are of most interest. This should not be a problem as long as the teacher and, crucially, the pupils are aware of this. The sizes of the forces can be indicated in two ways. The first is to use different-sized arrows, with longer ones representing larger forces and vice versa. If we want to indicate the actual size of the forces then we place their values, in newtons, by the appropriate arrows. Force diagrams are also a very quick and useful way to illustrate ideas about forces and how they work, and are a good teaching tool. Pupils should also be encouraged to use them to help with their own explanations, as they often convey information far more effectively than words alone. Figure 13.6 shows three diagrams to represent a ball which has just been thrown upwards and is still moving up – which one is correct? Only one of these diagrams correctly show the forces on a ball that has just been thrown upwards. (The answer is a; the balls weight/gravitational force acting downwards and air resistance also acting downwards.)

Links to teaching

More teaching activities

It is very important for young children to experience forces in a number of ways in order to begin to understand them. Therefore visits to the park, ride-on cars and bikes and toy cars and slope are all very important for children to experience. Teachers need to support children's learning by talking about the concepts discussed in this chapter while the children are playing. Talk about pushing, pulling, speed and direction is appropriate right from the Foundation Stage.

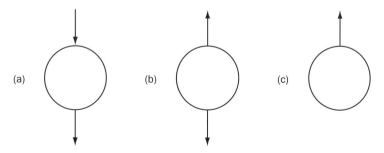

Figure 13.6 Forces on a thrown ball

Other things to do and try

Magnetize a paper-clip and turn it into a compass. This can be done by straightening the paper-clip out and stroking it in one direction, with one of the poles of a bar magnet. Then float the paper-clip on a disc of polystyrene on some water and it will line up north–south.

TOP TEACHING TIP

Videos and simulations are important to expand pupils' understanding of forces. There are some useful ones on the BBC schools website, www.bbc.co.uk/schools/.

Some common misconceptions

- When we throw an object, it still experiences the throwing force once it has left our hand.
- Only stationary objects have balanced forces on them.
- There are no forces acting on stationary objects.
- There is no gravity on the Moon.
- If something goes a long distance it must have been travelling fast.

AMAZING FACT

The weight of a typical apple is about 1 newton.

14

Light and sound

National Curriculum: Attainment Target Sc4, Strand 3 (KS1: 4.3a–3d, KS2: 4.3a–3g)
QCA Schemes of Work: Units 1D, 1F, 3F, 5F and 6F

Curriculum requirements

Light and sound forms the third strand of the Sc4 Attainment Target of Physical processes. These two forms of energy are often studied together as they are both transmitted by *waves* and so share common characteristics, however, the KS1 and KS2 programmes of study do not really highlight this and the comparison between the two only really starts to emerge in the KS3 programme of study.

The National Curriculum programme of study states that at KS1 pupils should be taught to identify different light sources, including the Sun; that darkness is the absence of light; that there are many kinds of sound and sources of sound; that sounds travel away from sources, getting fainter as they do so, and that they are heard when they enter the ear. At KS2 pupils should be taught that light travels from a source; that light cannot pass through some materials, and how this leads to the formation of shadows; that light is reflected from surfaces; that we see things only when light from them enters our eyes; that sounds are made when objects vibrate but that vibrations are not always directly visible; how to change the pitch and loudness of sounds produced by some vibrating objects and that vibrations from sound sources require a medium through which to travel to the ear.

Introducing light and sound

As stated above, light and sound are often studied together. Both are forms of *energy* and thus can be transferred to and from other forms of energy. Both also travel in the form of waves, so have similar properties, and comparisons of sound with light are often made to explore these similarities and the differences in the way that their waves behave. It seems prudent at this stage to discuss what we mean by a wave, before looking at light and sound themselves. Waves are formed by oscillations (vibrations) and can transmit some forms of energy.

There are two types of wave, *transverse* waves and *longitudinal* waves. What differs between them is the way in which the vibrations that cause them relate to the direction of motion of the wave. Transverse waves are perhaps easier to start with as most of us have seen them in the form of water waves. The vibrations that cause transverse waves are perpendicular (at 90° to) the direction in which the wave is travelling, thus with a water wave the water moves up and down and the wave travels perpendicular to this, across the surface of the water. One should note that although the wave seems to move forward, the water itself does not, it merely moves up and down. The so-called 'Mexican wave' that is a common sight at many large sports events is another example of a transverse wave and demonstrates the idea that whatever is vibrating (in this case the people creating the wave) does not actually move around the stadium with the wave. Light travels as these transverse waves, although what is vibrating is quite difficult to understand, as the waves are the result of oscillating magnetic and electric fields.

Sound waves are longitudinal waves. In contrast to transverse waves, the vibrations which cause longitudinal waves are *parallel to* the direction of motion of the wave. Thus when a sound wave travels through air, it is a result of vibrations of the particles in the air. As a result of these vibrations, in some places the particles are pushed together and this is called a *compression*, while in other places the particles are spread out and this is called a *rarefaction*. Like transverse waves though, there the particles do not move along with the wave, rather as the wave passes through it causes the vibrations which sustain it.

Teaching activity

Both longitudinal and transverse waves can be demonstrated nicely with the use of a slinky spring (see Figure 14.1).

In addition to these two types of wave, waves can vary in other ways. *Wavelength* is simply how long a wave is. It is measured from one point of a wave to the same point on the next wave. Wavelengths can vary considerably with some X-rays having wavelengths of about 1 millionth of a millimetre and some radio waves having wavelengths of a kilometre. The *frequency* of a wave tells us how many waves are produced each second and this is measured in hertz (Hz). It is frequency that affects the pitch of a sound. The third property of a wave that can vary is its *amplitude*. The amplitude of a wave tells us how large the vibrations causing it are. Thus the amplitude of a sound wave affects how loud the sound is and the amplitude of a water wave affects how high it is. The idea of waves allows us to fully explain the behaviour of light and sound, although we can *describe* how they behave without these ideas, which is what pupils need to do to fulfil the KS1 and KS2 programmes of study. Light and sound are very important to us as they stimulate our senses and so provide us with information that helps our survival. Light is a form of electromagnetic radiation of which there are a number of other types. The word 'radiation' simply means something that is given off,

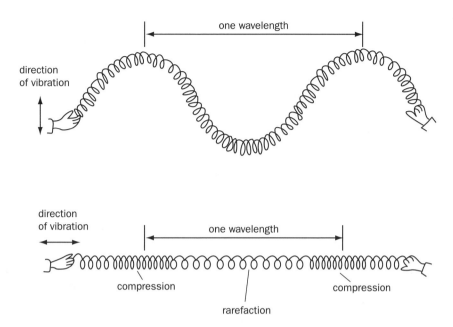

Figure 14.1 Using a slinky spring to show transverse (top) and longitudinal waves

or radiated, from a source and can cause problems as it is used in different contexts (such as nuclear radiation). Other types of electromagnetic radiation are radio waves, microwaves, infrared, ultraviolet, X-rays and gamma rays. All travel as waves, at the same speed (the speed of light). They differ in the frequency of the oscillations that cause them and this gives them different energies and properties. Thus light (strictly, *visible light*) only forms a small part of this family of related waves; it is the type which we can see.

Light

There are many sources of light, some natural, some human-made. In many cases it is hot objects that give off light, such as the Sun (and other stars), flames, light bulbs and heated metals. The light results from the movement of electrons in the atoms of the hot substance (see Chapter 9, 'Grouping and classifying materials' for a description of an atom). When the substance is heated, these electrons gain some of the available energy and move further away from the atom's nucleus; when they return to their original positions they give out their previously gained energy as light. Some light is also given out as a result of the energy released by chemical processes, including biochemical processes in living things such as glow-worms and bioluminescent algae. *Luminous* refers to something which gives out its own light. The light then moves away from its source in all directions, unless it is blocked by something, which is why a light bulb illuminates a whole room and we can see the Sun from all points of the Earth's orbit, provided that our part of the Earth is facing the Sun. Light travels incredibly fast and the speed of light is, indeed, the fastest possible speed. In a vacuum (that is, a space containing no particles) light travels at just under 300 million metres per second (about 186,000 miles per second) and travels marginally slower in air. When it passes from air into other, more dense, transparent media such as water and glass, it slows even more. Einstein described the nature of the speed of light in his famous studies on relativity, and one very odd feature of light is that its speed is always a constant value. Let us imagine that we are in a train travelling at 60 miles per hour (mph) and we throw something along the carriage towards the front of the train at 5 mph. To someone outside the train looking in, the thrown object would appear to move at 65 mph, but light does not do this, it always travels at the same speed, regardless of who is looking at it and from where.

When light travels away from a source it does so as *rays* of light, which travel in *straight lines*. Thus when pupils are starting to draw rays of light, it is a good idea to get them to draw them as straight as possible from the off (preferably with a ruler or other straight edge). Identifying the source of the light is also useful in determining the *direction* in which the light is travelling, since its speed means that it appears to travel instantaneously, and arrows can be added to drawings of light rays to indicate the direction of movement. Some pupils often draw light rays as a series of dotted or dashed lines and this should be discouraged as it implies that there are gaps in the light ray which are not there (if so, we would see a series of flashes).

One final point is that some apparent sources of light are not. A good example is the Moon. Indeed, the word moonlight is often used in everyday language. The Moon is not luminous, it only appears to give off light because it is *reflecting* the Sun's light from its surface. Against the backdrop of a dark night sky, the effect is such that it does appear to be luminous; however, if we compare it to its appearance when seen during the daytime, we can see that it is non-luminous, and if it were luminous then we would always see it as a disc, like the Sun.

Light, dark and shadow

As with all forms of energy, light travels from where there is a lot of it, to where there is less of it. Many pupils (indeed, many adults) become confused with the idea of dark, seeing it as something itself, when it is actually an *absence* of light. This is similar to the idea of cold, which again, is not something in itself, rather it is an absence of heat. It is actually unusual to experience total darkness. Even if we live in remote areas, light will reach us from somewhere to enable us to see at night-time. One of the easiest ways to experience true darkness is inside a cave, venturing to a point where no daylight can reach.

Another phenomenon caused by an absence of light is a shadow. This is an area of darkness caused by light being blocked by an object. The type of shadow will depend on the light source, the nature of the object blocking the light and the distances between the light, source, the object and the surface that the shadow is cast on.

Some materials are classed as transparent, some as translucent and others as opaque. *Transparent* objects allow light to pass through them relatively unhindered, thus will only tend to create very pale shadows which are often imperceptible. Very little of the light is scattered and so, when we view something through a transparent object such as a pane of glass, we see that object clearly. Scattering is when the rays of light are reflected in random directions and do not stay together. *Translucent* objects allow some light through as much more of the light is scattered and this leads to darker shadows. When we view something through a translucent object we tend to only see it faintly and it often appears shadow-like. *Opaque* objects scatter light from their surface and none penetrates the object, thus these create the darkest shadows.

When a shadow is formed (see Figure 14.2) it often consists of two regions: a very dark area in the middle, called the *umbra*, where none of the light from the light source causing the shadow can reach, and a paler area around the umbra, known as the *penumbra*, which has some light from the light source reaching it. The relative size of these two areas depends on the type of light source and the distance of the object from the surface onto which the shadow is cast. If the light source is concentrated in a very small point then the penumbra will be very small or non-existent. If the light source is more spread out, then there is more chance of some of the light passing around the object and so a larger penumbra is created. Likewise, the further away an object is to the surface on which the shadow is cast, the more chance that some light will be able to pass around it and so create a larger penumbra and smaller umbra. The size of a shadow depends on where the object casting the shadow is in relation to the light source and the surface onto which the shadow is cast. The nearer it is to the light source, the more light will be blocked and so the greater the shadow.

Of course, what we see also depends on any other light sources around. Shadows will be paler during the day because there is much more light reflecting off other surrounding surfaces that can partially illuminate the area of the shadow, so it will not be as dark.

Shadows are also good evidence that light rays travel in straight lines, for if they did not they could curve around an opaque object and reach behind it and thus there will be no area of darkness. This and other properties of light are considered in more detail in the next section.

The properties of light

As has already been stated, light rays travel in straight lines. This is apparent with a number of observations from nature, such as the straight edges to beams of sunlight streaming though the trees in woodland and through breaks in clouds. We can also

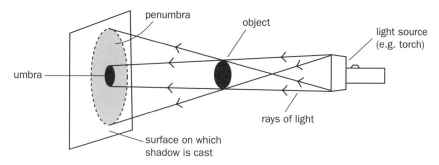

Figure 14.2 The formation of shadows

demonstrate this with simple experiments. One such example that is widely used is to take two pieces of card with a hole in (see Figure 14.3). If the cards are held a few centimetres apart then it is only possible to see things through both holes if they are lined up or partially overlap. If there is no overlap, then a straight line cannot be traced from the observer's eye to the object being viewed and the object will not be seen since the rays of light from the object will be travelling in straight lines.

As light travels away from a source, it spreads out as can be seen with the light from a torch. Since the rays are spreading out, their energy is also spread out and so the beam of light gets dimmer. If light has travelled a long distance from its source then some of the rays, those that were originally very close together, act as if they are travelling parallel to each other rather than spreading out.

Another key property of light (and all other forms of electromagnetic radiation) is that it *does not need a medium* to travel through. A medium is essentially something containing particles; so an object is a medium, so is air and water, and so on. Some waves move by vibrating the medium they are travelling through and so rely on that medium to move, but light waves do not, so they can travel through a region with no particles, known as a vacuum. If light were not able to do this then it would not be able to travel through space (which is essentially a vacuum) and we would not receive the light and heat of the Sun.

When a light ray hits a surface, some or all of that light will be reflected; in other words it 'bounces' off that surface. How much light actually reflects depends on the nature of the surface it strikes and the angle at which it hits that surface. If a light ray hits a transparent object, for instance, then a lot of that light will pass into the object and only some will be reflected (you can see your **reflection** in a pane of glass despite

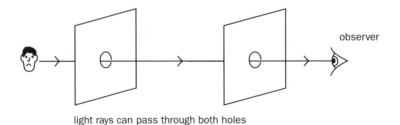

light rays can pass through both holes

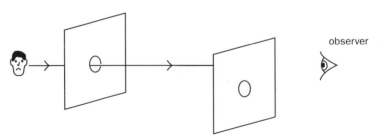

light rays cannot pass through both holes

Figure 14.3 Showing that light travels in straight lines

the fact that much of the light passes through the glass). When light reflects from a rough surface the rays scatter in different directions, however, when it reflects off a very smooth surface, the rays reflect so that they keep together, and therefore we see an image (reflection) from the smooth surface, but not from the rough one (see Figure 14.4).

Mirrors can be treated as perfectly smooth surfaces. A flat mirror is known as a *plane mirror* and light reflects off it in a particular way. A light ray hitting a surface is known as an *incident ray* of light. The angle that this incident ray makes with an imaginary line at right angles to the surface (known as the *normal*) is known as the *angle of incidence* and when the ray is reflected from a plane mirror, the angle of the *reflected ray* (the *angle of reflection*) is the same as the angle of incidence (see Figure 14.5). When initially teaching this fact, it is common to not overcomplicate the situation with a normal line since the angles the two rays make with the mirror will also be the same, however, as one delves deeper into the behaviour of light rays the use of a normal is essential. As all rays hitting the plane mirror behave in the same way the resulting image that we see is undistorted. The image also seems back to front but this

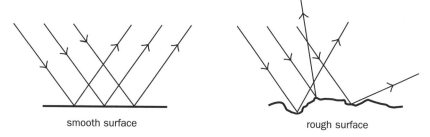

smooth surface   rough surface

Figure 14.4 Light reflecting from rough and smooth surfaces

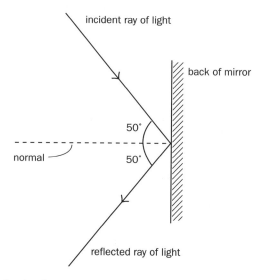

Figure 14.5 Light reflecting from a plane mirror

is really just an illusion and involves no actual swapping over of the rays of light (if you think about your image in a mirror, the rays from the left-hand side of your face are still on the left in the reflection).

Curved mirrors do produce distorted images, since the reflected light rays either separate out or are brought together, depending on whether the mirror curves out-wards (convex) or inwards (concave). Figure 14.6 shows how light rays from distant objects are reflected by these two sorts of curved mirror. We can see how this works if we imagine the curved surface as an infinite number of tiny plane mirrors placed at a slightly different angle to the previous one.

The colour of a surface also affects how the light is reflected. To understand this we need to think a bit about what colour is. As stated earlier, light travels as waves and it is differences in these waves that account for different colours. The waves can be thought of as varying in two ways, their length and their frequency. Different colours of light have different wavelengths, in turn they will also have different frequencies and this means they will have different amounts of energy – the longer the waves, the lower the frequency and the lower the energy. With visible light, red light has the longest waves, the lowest frequency and the lowest energy. Different colours stimulate the eye differently and so appear different when seen.

Coloured light

A prism can be used to separate out different colours of light which are mixed. The light from the Sun is known as white light and contains light of all colours. Light bulbs are also designed to give out white light. Each colour represents light of a different wavelength and the prism refracts (see later) each colour by a different amount, causing them to separate, or disperse. The best spectrums are produced by a 60° prism, the design of which gives full dispersal into a spectrum. Usually seven colours are identified in a spectrum: red, orange, yellow, green blue, indigo and violet and are often remembered with the mnemonic 'Richard Of York Gave Battle In Vain'. In

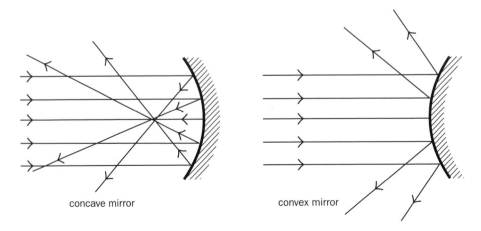

concave mirror   convex mirror

Figure 14.6 Light reflecting from convex and concave mirrors

actual fact it is sometimes difficult to make out all these seven colours in a spectrum and they all merge to form a continuum in any case, so you cannot actually say where one colour ends and another begins.

In the same way as paints, all colours of light can be produced from three *primary colours*, however, the primary colours of light are different to those of pigments and are red, blue and green (rather than yellow). Mixing two of these colours equally will produce the secondary colours of magenta (red and blue), cyan (blue and green) and yellow (red and green). An equal mix of all three will produce white light. This latter idea is not, at first, logical to some because they relate it to their experiences of paint where the more colours you mix, the darker the paint becomes. However we need to consider that we are mixing *light* together and so if we add more light together it does make sense that what we should see will get brighter and, so, whiter. Other colours are achieved by mixing the light in different proportions. The colour that an object appears depends upon which colours it is reflecting. Thus white objects reflect all three primary colours equally. Blue objects reflect blue light only, red objects red only and green objects green only. A yellow object will reflect red and green light but not blue and so on. Of course, most objects are not necessarily a 'pure' primary or secondary colour and so will reflect a particular mix of the three primary colours.

The reason that objects reflect certain colours depends on the pigments they contain. A pigment is a chemical that causes colouration by reflecting some colours of light and absorbing others. As we have seen, the light from the Sun is white light, thus it contains all three primary colours. When this white light hits an object the pigments in that object will absorb some of the colours and reflect others, and it is the reflected colours that we see. Thus grass looks green because the blue and red light from the Sun is being absorbed by the pigment in it (chlorophyll) and so this only leaves the green light left to be reflected. Strictly speaking, in most cases, all the colours of light are absorbed, but then some of it is re-emitted and this re-emitted light behaves as if it has been reflected. Taking this a stage further, objects will appear a different colour depending on what types of light they are exposed to. This can be achieved using filters which only let certain colours of light through and are commonly used for lighting effects on theatre stages. If we place a blue filter over a light then only blue light can get through the filter (the red and green light is absorbed by the pigment in the filter). Thus only objects that can reflect blue light (blue, cyan, magenta and white objects) will appear to have any colour and since there is only blue light available they will all appear blue. Objects that cannot reflect blue light (for example red, green, yellow objects) will not have any other light to reflect so they will appear *black*. This brings us to another point, namely, that blackness indicates that light is not reflecting off a surface, so all colours are absorbed by the pigment. Conversely objects that reflect all colours will appear white or, possibly, silver. A mirror reflects light so well (it will truly reflect rather than absorbing and then re-emitting light, which is why it does not look white) that we see an image that is lifelike. This is because not only are all colours reflected by the 'silvered' surface at the back of the mirror, the smoothness of this layer is such that virtually no light is scattered and the rays reflect from the surface with the same arrangement that had before they hit it, causing the image.

A final property of light that might be worth a brief mention (despite the fact that it only starts to be considered at KS3) is *refraction*, since it plays a role in the creation of a spectrum from a prism. Refraction occurs when light travels from one medium into another, such as from air into glass or air into water. When this happens the light changes direction and this is why a pencil looks bent if it is placed in a glass of water. The pencil will seem to bend at the surface of the water, where the light is changing direction. This change of direction is caused by the speed of the light changing as it moves from one medium to another. This is commonly studied using a rectangular glass or perspex block and shining rays of light at one edge (see Figure 14.7).

When the ray of light enters the block at an angle other than 90°, it changes direction. This is because some of the ray enters the block before the rest and so slows down, while the rest of the ray is still travelling at the faster speed. This causes the fronts of the waves to swing round (rather like a long line of people walking arm-in-arm abreast of each other – if you held the person at one end, the line would swing round) and so the ray changes direction. When the rays leave the block at the other side, the reverse happens and the ray changes direction back again. If the light ray hits the block at 90°, then the whole of the front of the ray hits the block at the same time, so it all slows down at the same time and there is no change of direction. The refraction of white light through a prism causes the colours that the light is composed of to disperse as they are each slowed down by slightly different amount and the shape of the prism means that when they enter the air again they are refracted even more, rather than back to their original direction (as in the rectangular block). A rainbow is also caused by the same effect and it is round because it is a refracted image of the edge of the Sun, and the heat haze that we see above the land on a hot day is also the result of refraction. Refraction is also the basis of how lenses work and this will be important when we consider the eye. A lens is designed to refract different rays of light by different amounts and in different direction so that those rays either come together or spread apart once they have been through the lens (see Figure 14.8).

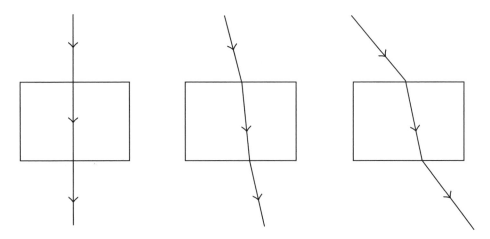

Figure 14.7 Investigating refraction

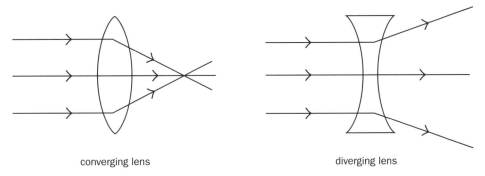

converging lens   diverging lens

Figure 14.8 A converging and a diverging lens

Seeing and light

The function of the eye is also considered in Chapter 5, 'Humans and other animals'. Without light we would not be able to see things. This is why it is harder to see things when there is less light (that is, when it is dark). Most of the light rays our eye receives are those that have been reflected off an object, although sometimes they may come directly from a light source. Thus when you read from a computer screen, you are receiving light directly from the screen, but when you are reading this book, you are receiving light from the Sun or another light source that has reflected off the pages of the book and into your eyes. The direction in which the light moves is important to get right from the start. Many pupils, when asked to draw light rays to show how we see something, draw arrows on their light rays pointing in the wrong direction, out of the eyes. If this was the case then we would never have problem with the dark as when we entered a dark room and opened our eyes, light beams would stream forward like the headlights of a car and illuminate the room! When light hits an object, light rays reflect off it in all directions, which is why we can see that object from all angles. Some of that reflected light then enters the eye through the *cornea* (see Figure 5.7 in Chapter 5).

The eye

The shape of the cornea and the liquid behind it (the aqueous humour) refracts the light so that the rays start to converge towards a single point. The light then passes through a hole called the *pupil*, in the *iris*. This iris is the coloured part of the eye and its function is to control the size of the pupil and, thus, how much light gets in. Too much light might damage the retina at the back of the eye and so when it is bright, the iris constricts the pupil, making it smaller. In low light the iris dilates the pupil (makes it larger) so that more light can enter, making it easier to see. Behind the pupil is the *lens* which more finely focuses the light to get a clear image. The shape of the lens is altered by muscles so that images at all distances can be seen in focus, and this is called accommodation. The closer an image is, the more the light the eye receives from it is spreading out, so the lens needs to be fatter to focus it. The light we receive from more distant objects is not spreading out so much, so the lens is made thinner to focus it. The combined effects of the cornea, aqueous humour, the lens and the jelly-like vitreous humour cause the image to be focused on the *retina* at the back of the eye. This contains millions of light-sensitive cells that produce pulses of electricity when light falls on them. Some of the cells, the *rods*, detect brightness and others, the *cones*, detect colours (there are three types of cone, one for each of the primary colours; colour blindness results from cells not being able to produce the necessary pigments for one of the types of cone). Cones work better when light levels are higher, so in dark conditions distinguishing colours is much harder to do. The electrical impulses produced in the retina are transmitted to the brain via the optic nerve where they are processed as an image. Two eyes allow more information to be collected and with humans this produces two images (alternately open and closing each eye shows this) which the brain overlaps to create a three-dimensional image since the eyes point forward in the same general direction. This is true of many predators, where the ability to judge distance is crucial. Prey, such as rabbits, have less need for this and have more need for all-round vision so they tend to have eyes on the sides of their head to achieve this at the expense of true stereoscopic vision.

It is possible that students with sight problems may want to find out more about eyes. Short sight and long sight result from the inability of the eye to focus an image on the retina (see Figure 14.9), often because of the shape of the eye either being too long or too short. This can be corrected with a lens in a pair of spectacles or a contact lens, which helps to focus the light in the correct place. People with short sight have difficulty viewing distant objects since they are focused in front of the retina. A diverging lens is used to spread the light rays out before they enter the eye to correct this. Long sight arises when light from near objects cannot be focused before it hits the retina and this is corrected with a converging lens which starts to bring the light rays to focus before they enter the eye.

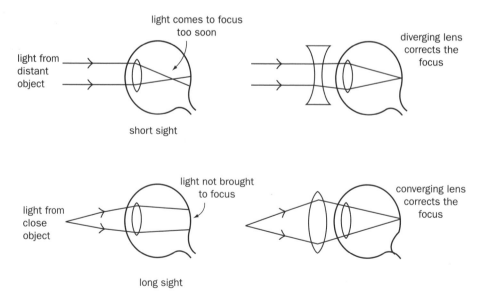

Figure 14.9 Short sight, long sight and their correction

Sound

Sound is produced by vibrating particles. Knocking on a door, for instance, causes particles in the door to vibrate, setting up sound waves. These vibrations are then transferred to the air surrounding the door. As the sound waves travel through the air they vibrate the air particles and some of these waves will enter our ears, which detect the sound. Thus anything that causes particles to vibrate will generate a sound of some kind, and so sources of sound are vibrating. Loudspeakers such as those for hi-fis, radios and televisions contain a vibrating cone, usually of card or plastic, that vibrates the air in front of it and you can easily feel these vibrations. Musical instruments set up vibrations in the air inside them, in some cases through the vibrations of strings. In many cases the vibrations that produce the sound are so fast we cannot see them (middle C is caused by vibrations which occur at 262 times a second) and a good way to experience this is with a tuning fork, which vibrates so fast you cannot see the prongs move. Musical instruments also produce their own unique sound waves. Figure 14.10 shows two sound waves, the first from a tuning fork and the second from an imaginary musical instrument. This is how the wave might look on a cathode ray oscilloscope (like those used to monitor heartbeat patterns in a hospital), which converts the longitudinal sound wave into a transverse wave which can be studied more easily. Both notes being produced are the same as the number of waves produced (in effect the frequency) are the same in each case, however, while the tuning fork produces perfectly smooth waves, the instrument produces a different shape wave. This is unique to the instrument and is what gives the instrument its distinctive sound, or *timbre*. Each instrument produces a different shape of wave, which is why, even though they may be playing the same note, we can tell one instrument from another.

A source of sound that many are familiar with is the buzz of electrical equipment which is plugged into the mains. Although the timbre of the sound is different from one device to another, the pitch is always is the same and corresponds to the frequency of the alternating current that flows through the circuit, oscillating at 50 Hz (50 times a second).

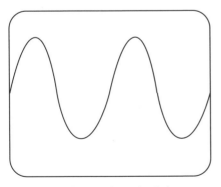

sound wave of a tuning fork

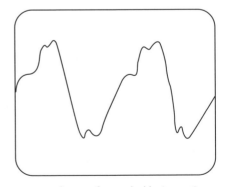

sound wave of a musical instrument

Figure 14.10 Comparing the sound waves produced by a tuning fork and a musical instrument

The properties of sound

Since, like light, sound travels as waves, it behaves in a similar way to light. Sound can be reflected and this is what an echo is. Echoes are more distinct when they occur from a hard, smooth surface, rather than a soft one and this is noticeable in buildings which echo more when they have no carpets and less soft furniture. A hard surface absorbs less of the sound energy and a smooth surface causes less scattering of the sound. Sounds travel away from their source, spreading out as they do so and so getting fainter with distance (like the light from a torch). Like light, we can have sound waves with different wavelengths, frequencies and amplitudes. As the frequency of a sound increases, its wavelength gets shorter and so its pitch increases. To change the pitch of a sound one must change the frequency of the vibrations causing it. This is not always easy to discern when striking an object to create a sound, partly because the particles in an object have a natural frequency (or resonance) that they tend to vibrate at when given some energy and it is difficult to hit something with enough of a varying frequency to easily tell the difference.

Teaching activity

One good, visual way to demonstrate the link between frequency of vibration and pitch is to hold a plastic ruler on the edge of a table and 'twang' it to produce a sound. When more of the ruler hangs over the edge it vibrates more slowly and produces a lower sound than when less of it hangs over the edge. With instruments pitch is changed in a similar way. With wind instruments the column of air inside is altered so that it vibrates at different frequencies. With string instruments the tightness and length of the string affects how fast it vibrates and thus the pitch of the note produced. As with the strings on a guitar, the skin on a drum can be tightened so that it vibrates faster and thus produces a higher sound. Just like the ruler where only a little of it is vibrating, with a small instrument, the air or string will vibrate faster and so the notes it produces will be higher than those produced by a larger instrument (compare a double bass with a violin for example).

As the amplitude of a sound wave increases the sound becomes louder as the vibrations causing the sound get bigger. If the sound is created by striking something, then hitting it harder will increase the size of the vibrations and thereby create a louder sound. With a speaker, greater movement of the speaker cone backwards and for-wards will create a louder sound. With instruments, hitting harder, blowing harder or plucking the string harder will have the same effect.

Comparing light and sound

In addition to the similarities with light there are also some differences. Unlike light, sound needs a *medium* to travel through. Sound is generated by and propagated by the vibrations of particles; hence it cannot travel through a vacuum. This is often demon-strated with the bell in a bell-jar experiment. An electric bell is placed inside a glass bell jar and switched on. We can hear the bell because the vibrations it creates travel from the bell through the air inside the jar, through the glass and finally through the air around the bell jar to our ears. The air is then sucked out of the bell jar with a vacuum pump to create a vacuum around the electric bell. As this happens the sound of the bell gets fainter and fainter until it can no longer be heard, but we know it is still working as we can see the hammer hitting the bell. The reason this happens is because we have removed the air that transmitted the sound waves from the bell to the glass. Letting the air back in provides the particles to transmit the sound waves and so we hear the bell again, gradually getting louder as more air particles are let in. Also, in the same way that the speed of light varies when travelling through different media, so does the speed of sound. Sound travels fastest through solids, slower through liquids and slowest through gases. This is because the particles in a solid are much closer together and so the vibrations can be passed on more quickly. With a gas, the large gaps between the particles mean that it takes much longer for the sound to travel. In air sound travels at about 330 metres per second compared with light which, at about 300 million metres per second, is nearly a million times faster. This accounts for us seeing things happening at a distance before we hear them, such as seeing lightning before we hear it (thunder), the delay between a firework exploding and the bang, and the sound of a football being kicked arriving long after it has moved up the pitch.

One final difference between the behaviour of light and sound that we can consider is the fact that we can hear around corners but not see around corners. The reason this occurs involves a process known as *diffraction*, which is far too complex for consideration at primary level, but may be of interest to the reader. It is possible, for instance, to hear the sound coming from a room without being able to see inside it. The reason why we can't see inside is because the light rays all travel in straight lines and if there is no line of sight through the open door into the room, then no light rays can pass straight to the observer. This should be essentially true for the sound waves, however, as the sound waves pass through the gap, they spread out rather like the waves created by dropping a stone in water. This enables the sound waves to travel from the doorway as if they were created at a single point there (see Figure 14.11, where the lines represent the peak of each wave).

As has been stated, all waves have a wavelength and the closer the wavelength to the size of the gap they get through, the more they diffract. If the wavelength is much smaller than the gap then the waves do not diffract as well. Audible sound waves have wavelengths that are similar to the width of a doorway, hence they diffract well, although the higher the pitch of the sound, the smaller the wavelength and the less well they diffract, making them harder to hear round a corner. Light waves have a much smaller wavelength than audible sound waves and the gap provided by a doorway is far too big for them to be able to diffract, so we cannot see round corners. Make the gap small enough, though, and you can achieve the same effect with light. This is commonly done with a piece of scored glass called a diffraction grating, however, the 'gaps' the light diffracts through are tiny (about 0.01 mm across at their biggest – that is, 100 gaps per millimetre). The phrase 'audible sound' is quite important here as there are some sounds that the human ear cannot detect and this is looked at as part of the next section on hearing.

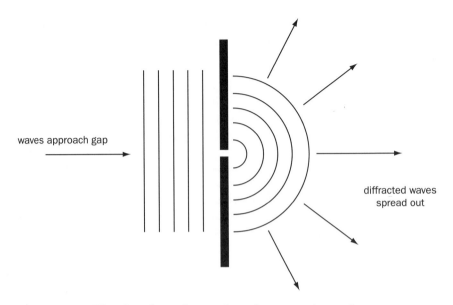

waves approach gap

diffracted waves
spread out

Figure 14.11 The diffraction of sound waves through a gap such as a doorway

Hearing and sound

The function of the ear has also been considered in Chapter 5, 'Humans and other animals'. Ears are designed to pick up sound waves and channel them inside the head, where the vibrations are passed between a variety of structures before being turned into electrical signals that the brain can interpret. Not all sounds are audible by the human ear and we can typically hear sounds with frequencies between 20 Hz to 20,000 Hz (that is, sounds caused by vibrations occurring 20 times a second to 20,000 times a second). The upper and lower frequencies of this range are known as the hearing thresholds and are usually examined during a hearing test along with the ability to hear sounds of a certain quietness (low amplitude sounds). Other animals can detect sounds outside our hearing range, with good examples being dogs which can hear sounds higher than humans can (ultrasounds) and elephants which can produce and hear sound much lower than humans can (infrasounds). This means that just because we cannot hear a sound, does not mean it is not generated. Indeed ultrasound scans of babies in the womb use the echoes generated inside the body of sounds far too high for us to hear. Indeed, some sounds we can hear are generated by vibrations so fast that we cannot see them occurring, even if we can see the object that is vibrating.

The human ear (see Figure 5.8 in Chapter 5) has three main sections to do its job; the *outer ear*, the *middle ear* and the *inner ear*. The outer ear consists of a flap of cartilage called the *pinna*, the shape of which is designed to funnel in sound waves to a point, so amplifying them (rather like an old-fashioned ear trumpet). There is also the ear canal, which directs the waves further into the head by vibrations in the air it contains.

The vibrating air in the ear canal causes the eardrum (a thin membrane) to vibrate and this passes the vibrations into the middle ear. The middle ear also contains air but the vibrations from the eardrum are passed on by three small bones called the *ossicles*, known commonly as the *hammer*, the *anvil* and the *stirrup*. The pressure of the air in the middle ear needs to be the same as that in the ear canal to achieve the best sound transmission and this is achieved with the *Eustachian tube*, which is connected to the back of the throat, and can open and close causing the ears to 'pop'. This is often experienced when rapidly ascending or descending, such as on a car journey in a hilly area or, even more so, during an aeroplane flight. When we ascend the pressure of the air surrounding us, and so the pressure in the ear canal decreases and is now lower than the pressure in the middle ear. This causes the eardrum to be pushed out and it cannot move as much as it should, muffling the sound we hear. Moving the jaws helps the Eustachian tube to open slightly, letting air out of the inner ear to restore a balanced pressure and allowing the eardrum to move freely again and causing the 'popping' sensation. Descending will have the opposite effect and the eardrum will be pushed in as the external air pressure is higher than the internal air pressure. The Eustachian tube lets air into the middle ear to once again restore the balance and so the hearing to its proper level. The sound is passed from the middle ear to the inner ear into a spiral structure called the *cochlea*. This contains a fluid which vibrates when the stirrup hits a point on the cochlea known as the *oval window*. On the walls of the cochlea are tiny hair-like structures called *cilia*, which move back and forth in the vibrating fluid, generating electrical signals which are then passed along the *auditory nerve* to the brain. Also connected to the cochlea are another set of fluid filled tubes called the *semi-circular canals*, which give the brain information about balance when the fluid they contain moves inside. An inner ear infection will often cause dizziness as it will affect these semi-circular canals. Two ears allow us to ascertain the direction of a sound, since they both will hear a sound differently and the brain makes use of this.

Damage of one or more of the many parts of the ear can result in hearing problems. This is usually as the result of infection, a sharp blow to the head or just the wear and tear that comes from old age. Some of these problems can be compensated for such as the use of hearing aids which use a small microphone and a loudspeaker to direct amplified sounds into the ear canal. Nowadays it is also possible to have surgical implants which correct problems with the cochlea. Damage to the nerve, however, is rarely treatable and will result in complete deafness.

Links to teaching

More teaching activities

If you can get one, show an exposed loudspeaker with some polystyrene or paper balls on the speaker cone to show how the vibrations change as the sound changes.

Cover a large bowl with some cling film, sprinkle some salt over it and beat a stick on the table nearby, watching the vibrations of the salt.

Other things to do and try

Dataloggers are good for recording levels of light and sound.

TOP TEACHING TIP

When studying light and sound and the sense, be aware that some pupils will have hearing or visual impairments and it is not appropriate to compare the hearing or vision of different children or make value judgements about good or bad hearing or eyesight.

Some common misconceptions

- The Moon is a source of light.
- Light rays leave the eye when we see things.
- Sounds come from the ear.

AMAZING FACT

If light rays could bend they would be able to travel around the Earth nearly seven and a half times every second.

15

The Earth and beyond

National Curriculum: Attainment Target Sc4, Strand 4 (KS2: 4.4a–4d)

QCA Schemes of Work: Units 5E and 6F

Curriculum requirements

The Earth and beyond forms the final and smallest strand of the Physical processes Attainment Target, but is often one of the more interesting parts of the curriculum for children. The ideas taught here focus on the Sun, the Earth and the Moon, and form the basis of more detailed study at KS3 and KS4 and link closely with the topics of forces and motion and light.

The National Curriculum for Science programme of study only deals with this area of science at KS2, where pupils should be taught that the Sun, the Earth and the Moon are approximately spherical; how the position of the Sun appears to change during the day, and how shadows change as this happens; how day and night are related to the spin of the Earth on its own axis; that the Earth orbits the Sun once each year, and that the Moon takes approximately 28 days to orbit the Earth.

The solar system

The solar system consists of a number of bodies, including the Earth, in *orbit* around the Sun (so it is the 'system' of the Sun – many forget that point). It is thought to have formed about 4.6 billion years ago from a spinning disc of dust and gas. Over time most of this dust and gas started to be drawn together by the force of gravity to form the Sun, the planets and their moons. Other, smaller bodies also formed, such as the **asteroids** and comets. Everything in the solar system is affected by the huge gravitational force exerted by the Sun, which keeps the planets and other, smaller bodies in orbit around it. The solar system is believed to be at least one light-year across. A *light-year* is the time it takes for light to travel in one year and is approximately 9,460,000,000,000 km (5,880,000,000,000 miles). It is this huge distance and, indeed, the huge distances between all the major parts of the solar system that make its size and the relative positions of the planets hard to really comprehend.

Traditionally the number of planets in the solar system has been nine and, in order of distance from the Sun they are Mercury, Venus, Earth, Mars, Jupiter, Saturn, Uranus, Neptune and Pluto. This is often remembered by the mnemonic 'My Very Easy Method Just Speeds Up Naming Planets'. However, in 2006 the International Astronomical Union reclassified Pluto as a dwarf planet, rather than a true planet, due to its small size and the existence of other similarly sized objects in orbit around the Sun. Of course, Pluto will still be considered a planet for sometime yet until textbooks are rewritten on the subject. Indeed, Pluto has always been something of an oddity. All the other planets orbit the Sun in a single plane (which means that if you could view the solar system from the side you could draw a single line through all the planets and the Sun), while Pluto's orbit is at an angle to this plane. All planets orbit in a slightly *elliptical* (oval) path, but Pluto's orbit is so elliptical that this causes it to sometimes be closer to the Sun than Neptune. The inner planets (Mercury, Venus, Earth and Mars) are composed of rock, while Jupiter, Saturn, Uranus and Neptune are composed of gas and are much bigger than the four inner planets, hence the phrase 'the gas giants' (Pluto is thought to be mainly rock and ice). In between the orbits of Mars and Jupiter is the asteroid belt, composed of smaller lumps of rock (*asteroids*) also orbiting the Sun, which may be the remnants of proto-planets that never became as large as the actual planets. We have gained much of our knowledge of the planets through obser- vations using telescopes (especially in more recent years with the Hubble space tele- scope in orbit around the Earth) and through the use of spacecraft that have been sent to explore other planets. The gas giants were first visited in the 1970s and 1980s by the Pioneer and Voyager space probes, which took about 30 years to reach the edge of the solar system, which is another indication of the huge distances involved when dealing with the solar system. Indeed, we often have a distorted view of the relative distances of each planet as many representations of them often show them to be equidistant from each other, which is simply not true (Saturn for instance is nearly twice the distance from the Sun that Jupiter is). It is just that it is not possible to produce a good scale diagram of the solar system on a single page of a book.

Besides the planets there are a number of other relatively large bodies. In orbit around most of the planets (the exceptions being Mercury and Venus) are smaller bodies known as *moons* or natural satellites. There are the asteroids that have already been mentioned. There are also the *comets*, which are lumps of dust and ice that orbit the Sun in a highly elliptical fashion where the Sun is not at the centre of the orbit, but towards one end. Some comets remain in the solar system and orbit the Sun at regular intervals, with perhaps the most famous being Halley's Comet which has a 76-year orbit and is shown on the Bayeux Tapestry. Others only orbit the Sun once, and then leave the solar system. As a comet approaches the Sun it seems brighter and begins to vaporize, forming its characteristic tail. Since the tail is 'pushed' out by the Sun it always points away from the Sun. This means that once a comet has passed round the Sun its tail precedes it. A final body worth considering is a *meteoroid*. These are small objects (they can be as small as a grain of sand) that are often fragments of larger objects such as asteroids or comets. We see them when they enter the Earth's atmos- phere, when they are called **meteors**. They heat up so much that they glow, hence the common name 'shooting stars' (they are, of course, not stars). Most meteors completely vaporize in the atmosphere but some larger ones will impact on the Earth's surface as a *meteorite*.

The Sun

The only *star* in the solar system, the Sun, is a roughly spherical ball of hot gas and it is the ultimate source of most of the Earth's energy. Contrary to popular belief it is not burning (burning is a chemical reaction involving something and oxygen) but releases its energy through a process known as nuclear fusion. It contains over 99 per cent of all the matter in the solar system and like all stars is mainly composed of hydrogen gas. When the Sun formed, this hydrogen was drawn together by gravity with such force that the resulting temperature and pressure caused the atoms to fuse and become a new type of atom, namely, helium. This process of *nuclear fusion* can also cause even larger atoms to occur, so stars are the source of many of the elements. Indeed, most of the atoms in our own bodies were produced in stars that exploded long ago, scattering these atoms across space and forming the material that the solar system is now composed of. Fusion releases vast amounts of energy, some of which radiates from the Sun as light and heat. As this light and heat spreads out as it travels away from the Sun, it means that the further a body is from the Sun the less light and heat it will receive so the colder it will be. One planet that does not seem to follow this pattern is Venus, which is hotter than Mercury, despite being further away. This anomaly is due to the intense greenhouse effect caused by the atmosphere of Venus. The Sun will eventually start to exhaust its hydrogen supply and at this point will enter a new phase (thankfully not for at least about 4 billion years), swelling up into a *red giant* that will take its edge to a point between the current orbits of Earth and Mars. After this phase it will lose its outer layers, forming a *planetary nebula* and this will leave only its core as a *white dwarf* that will gradually cool and fade.

Its huge mass means that the Sun's gravitational pull is greater than anything else in the solar system and this is why the bodies in the solar system orbit it. Observations by some early astronomers of the movement of the planets and the *apparent movement* of the Sun made them realize that it was the Sun that was at the centre of what we now call the solar system, however, religious and other beliefs that the Earth was at the centre of everything meant that these ideas were only accepted slowly. The apparent movement of the Sun through the sky is caused by the rotation of the Earth, and this is illustrated in Figure 15.1. During the summer months the tilt of the Earth means that the path the Sun seems to take through the sky is higher and so takes longer than during winter months. Noon is the point at which the Sun appears to be at its highest. Since the Sun is higher in the sky around noon, the shadows it creates are at their shortest and they are at their longest at sunrise and sunset. The fact that sunrise occurs in the east and sunset in the west means that the Earth is rotating west to east, a fact that is true of all the planets, except Venus.

As it is the only object in the solar system that produces its own light, the reason why we see other planets, moons, comets, and so on is because they reflect light that originated from the Sun. The light emitted by the Sun is white light (see Chapter 14, 'Light and sound'), however particles in the Earth's atmosphere scatter this light and

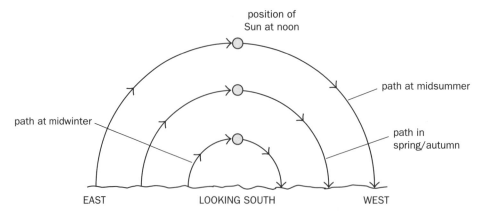

Figure 15.1 The apparent daily motion of the Sun in the sky in the northern hemisphere

some colours are scattered more than others. Blue light is scattered the most and this is why the sky appears blue and why the Sun appears so yellow (it is actually white). At sunrise and sunset the sunlight travels through more of the Earth's atmosphere and so it is scattered even more, so the sky looks even bluer and the Sun appears more of an orange or red colour.

The Earth and marking the passage of time

Like all planets, the Earth is roughly spherical in shape and, as already mentioned, is largely composed of rock. It is unique in the solar system in that it is the only place where life is known to exist (indeed it is the only place in the universe where we know that life exists). The Earth is situated about 149.5 million kilometres (about 93 million miles) from the Sun and is nearly 13,000 kilometres (roughly 8,000 miles) across at the equator. Most of our awareness of time has its roots in the movement of the Earth. The Earth spins about an imaginary *axis* through the north and south poles and a *day* is the time it takes the Earth to rotate once. This is divided by us into 24 hours, although the way that time is measured scientifically these days is by reference to the speed of light, hence a 'day' is actually measured as being slightly less than 24 hours. Daylight occurs when that part of the Earth faces the Sun and night when facing away from the Sun. A *year* is the time it takes the Earth to orbit the Sun once, which takes about 365 and one-quarter days to complete. This can sometimes be confusing to children but if one thinks about it, there is no reason why the time it takes the Earth to complete an orbit should coincide with an exact number of rotations. The leap year was devised to rectify this anomaly, even before it was understood why it happened, to keep observable events like equinoxes at the same date in the calendar.

   Another way of observing the passing of time is the *seasons*. The seasons occur because the Earth rotates at an angle of 23.5° to the plane of its orbit. This means that as the Earth orbits the Sun the northern and southern hemispheres experience variations in the *intensity* of the sunlight they receive. If we consider Figure 15.2 then we can see that on 21 June the Earth's position in its orbit is such that the northern hemisphere is tilted fully towards the Sun. This means that it receives light (and

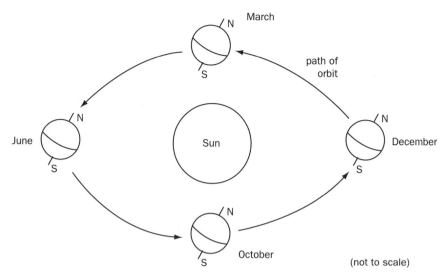

Figure 15.2 The tilt of the Earth as the cause of the seasons

effectively heat) of a greater intensity than that received by the southern hemisphere, so it is hotter. Also the northern hemisphere has longer hours of daylight, so it receives that light for longer than the southern hemisphere. Hence, in June it is summer in the northern hemisphere and winter in the southern hemisphere. As the Earth continues on its journey around the Sun this difference is lessened as the relative positions of the Earth and the Sun are such that tilt has less and less effect on the light received by either hemisphere until the equinox in October when day and night are of equal length and the light received is of equal intensity. During the next three months the Earth's tilt starts have an effect again, leading up to the 21 December when the northern hemisphere is fully tilted away from the Sun and the southern hemisphere tilted towards the Sun. Now it is the north which receives lower intensity light than the south and fewer hours of daylight, so it is winter in the north and summer in the south. Finally, via another equinox in March we are back where we started in June. It is often wrongly assumed that it is the distance each hemisphere is from the Sun which causes this effect, but the difference in distance of each hemisphere at any time, compared with the distance the Earth is from the Sun is negligible.

The Moon

The Moon is the Earth's *natural satellite*. Its actual origins are still uncertain, although it is believed that it was formed at about the same time as the Earth. Like the moons of other planets, our moon has a name, Luna, and is the only body in the solar system humans have visited. Like the Sun, the Earth and other planets, the Moon is roughly spherical and it orbits the Earth at a distance of about 384,400 km (nearly 239,000 miles). The Moon takes nearly 28 days to orbit the Earth and it takes the Moon the same length of time to complete one rotation on its axis. The result of this coincidence is that the *same side* of the Moon always faces towards the Earth. The far side of the Moon, which we never see is sometimes erroneously described as the dark side, which it is not, because it receives as much light from the Sun as the side we see.

The Moon does not give off its own light, so we see the Moon because it reflects light from the Sun. During its orbit the relative positions of the Earth, the Moon and the Sun mean that part of the Moon that is visible to us is in shadow, and this causes the phases of the moon (see Figure 15.3). This cycle occurs approximately every 29.5 days (not the same as the orbit time as the Earth's position in its orbit will have moved on as well) and this is the origin of the timescale of a month and probably of weeks and fortnights.

The cycle is considered as starting when the whole of the Moon is in shadow, a new moon, continues through the waxing phase to the full moon and, finally, through a waning phase until the next new moon.

Eclipses (see Figure 15.4) result when the orbits of the Earth and the Moon are such that they line up exactly. Eclipses of the Sun (solar eclipses) always occur during a new moon and the Moon lies between the Earth and the Sun. The Moon is about 40 times closer to the Earth than the Sun and about 40 times smaller, which means that they appear to be about the same size in the sky and the Moon can completely cover the Sun during an eclipse, causing a shadow on the Earth. The centre of this shadow (the umbra: see Chapter 14 for more on shadows) is where a total eclipse is observed, while partial eclipses occur at the edge of the shadow (the penumbra). The Sun is only totally blocked for a short period of time and an eclipse will not occur at every new moon as the Earth, Sun and Moon will not always be in total alignment. Eclipses of the Moon (lunar eclipses) occur when the Earth lies exactly between the Sun and the Moon. They only occur during a full moon when the Earth casts a shadow over the Moon. The Moon is still visible during a lunar eclipse as it receives reflected sunlight from the Earth, which is then reflected back to Earth and it takes on a reddish-brown appearance.

It is wrongly assumed by many that the Moon exerts no force of gravity. All objects exert gravity by virtue of their mass (see Chapter 13, 'Forces and motion' for more on gravity) so the Moon does have a gravitational pull, but because it is much lighter than the Earth it only exerts a force about one-sixth that of the Earth at its surface. One effect witnessed on the Earth of this gravitational pull is the *tides* (see Figure 15.5).

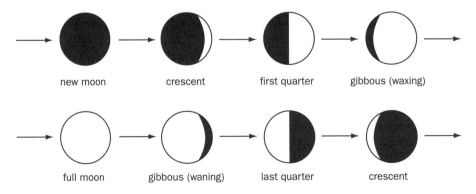

new moon   crescent   first quarter   gibbous (waxing)

full moon   gibbous (waning)   last quarter   crescent

Figure 15.3 The phases of the Moon

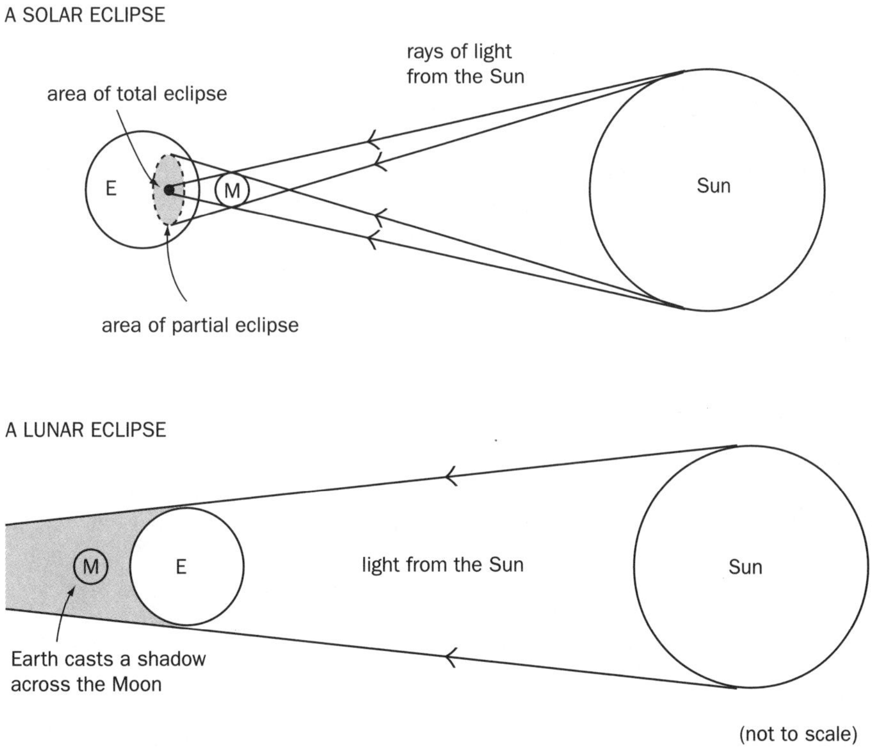

A SOLAR ECLIPSE

rays of light
from the Sun

area of total eclipse

E   M   Sun

area of partial eclipse

A LUNAR ECLIPSE

M   E   light from the Sun   Sun

Earth casts a shadow
across the Moon

(not to scale)

Figure 15.4 How eclipses occur

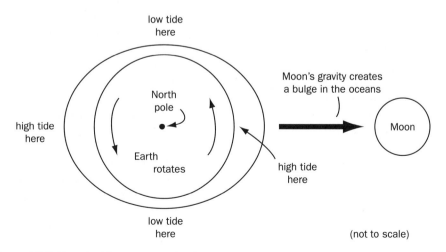

low tide
here

Moon's gravity creates
a bulge in the oceans

North
pole

high tide
here

Moon

Earth
rotates

high tide
here

low tide
here

(not to scale)

Figure 15.5 How the Moon causes the tides

The Moon pulls the water in the oceans towards it with varying strength and because the water is a liquid and can flow, a bulge of water is created on the sides facing towards and away from the Moon. The water on the side facing the Moon is pulled more than the water on the side facing away from the Moon. Areas of the Earth where the bulges of water are experience high tide and the resulting drop of water level on the other sides causes low tide. As the Earth rotates different parts of it will encounter the risen and fallen water levels, experienced as the changes of the tide. This results in high tides approximately every 12 hours, although the time changes slightly as the Moon will have progressed little further in its orbit around the Earth. The Sun also has an influence in the tides, but less so due to its much greater distance.

Beyond the solar system

Although the KS2 programme of study concentrates on the Sun, the Earth and the Moon, it is common for other bodies in the solar system to be studied as well. It is not expected that pupils at this stage study what lies beyond the solar system, however, the following ideas are presented for the interest of the reader and because misconceptions in children's minds can result from a misunderstanding of how the solar system fits into the rest of the universe.

We have already discussed what the solar system contains, however, something very apparent in the night sky are the *stars*. The Sun is the *only* star in the solar system and the others that we observe are well outside our solar system; indeed, many will be at the centre of their own solar systems and there is already evidence for planets in orbit around other stars. If the solar system seems big, it is nothing compared to the scale of the universe. The nearest star to our own solar system is about 4.3 light years away and the galaxy to which it and our own sun belongs contains billions of stars and is about 100,000 light years across. Our galaxy is called the *Milky Way* and the solar system is near the edge of it. On a clear night it is possible to see a faint band of very close stars across the sky and this is a view through the edge of the galaxy. Indeed, all the individual stars that are seen at night are part of the Milky Way galaxy. What we actually see are the stars as they were when the light they emitted left the star, so if we view a star we are seeing it as it was then, not how it is now. The star Betelgeuse (on the 'shoulder' of the constellation of Orion) for instance, is about 427 light years away, so we are seeing it as it was 427 years ago (at the time of writing, when Elizabeth I was on the throne of England).

Constellations are patterns that the stars seem to make in the sky, although it would be wrong to think of these as groups of stars as they tend to be long distances away from each other and only seem to be in a group when we see them. Constellations seem to move during the night because of the same reason that the Sun seems to move, namely, the rotation of the Earth. The only star which does not seem to move is the Pole Star (or North Star) as it lies directly above the North Pole and thus the axis about which the Earth rotates.

True groups of stars are *galaxies* and there are now thought to be many billions of these in addition to the Milky Way. It is not possible to see the individual stars of a galaxy with the naked eye due to their great distance, so galaxies appear as fuzzy blurs of light. Measurements of the light from galaxies indicate that they seem to be moving away from each other and so the universe is *expanding*. This discovery and other findings such as microwaves emitted from around the universe lead to the *Big Bang* theory of the formation of the universe. If all the galaxies are moving away from each other then at some point in the past it is reasonable to suggest that they started at the same point. The Big Bang theory suggests that about 13.7 billion years ago everything that is now in the universe was concentrated at a single, infinitesimally small point called a singularity and for some, as yet unknown, reason a rapid expansion occurred, releasing huge amounts of energy and creating the basis for the early universe. This is the point where most of us are unable to understand why things happen. With the Big Bang the universe began and the universe is just what its name suggests, that is, everything. All the laws of physics were shaped at that moment. There was no 'before' the Big Bang, as time itself started then.

What will happen in the future is still cause for much debate. Fortunately for us, apart from a basic knowledge of the possible fate of the universe and of what the Big Bang was and some of the evidence for it, such advanced physics has yet to be made part of the National Curriculum at any level. The universe may continue to expand for ever or gravity may have its way and start to slow down this expansion, then gradually start to pull everything together again in a 'Big Crunch'. This seems a fitting note upon which to end the final chapter of this book!

Links to teaching

More teaching activities

- Make a sundial.
- Make a scale model of the solar system in the classroom or outside – pupils could wear hats and represent the planets and you could measure distances using a toilet roll scale and, if the space is big enough, the pupils could act out their orbits.
- Use a torch and a football to demonstrate the phases of the Moon.
- Use the Internet to get the dates for forthcoming astronomical events the pupils could observe.

Other things to do and try

Simulations are useful in this topic. The National Aeronautics and Space Administration (NASA) website allows you to view the solar system for many different perspectives, using what their spacecraft have recorded over the years.

TOP TEACHING TIP

Looking at the Sun directly is very dangerous. It is important to emphasize this when studying this topic.

Some common misconceptions

- Stars (other than the Sun) are part of the solar system.
- The Sun is a planet.
- There is no gravity on the Moon.
- The Moon makes light.

AMAZING FACT

On Venus you would be crushed by the great pressure, if you were not burnt to death by the heat and the sulphuric acid in the atmosphere first.

Glossary: key scientific vocabulary for primary school children

Animal – one of the five kingdoms of living things. Examples of animals include mammals, fish, reptiles, birds, amphibians, insects, arachnids, crustaceans and molluscs.

Asteroid – a piece of rock debris in space. Many are found in the asteroid belt between Jupiter and Mars.

Atom – the smallest unit of a single element.

Breathing – in humans it is the process of air being taken in and out of the lungs so that oxygen can enter the bloodstream. Not to be confused with respiration.

Carnivore – an animal that eats other animals for nutrition.

Cell (biological) – sometimes known as the building blocks of life, one cell is the smallest viable unit of living matter, although many living things have many different types of cells.

Circuit – a power source and other components (such as bulbs) joined by wires so that electricity flows through them.

Circulation – the flow of blood around the body, carrying materials to cells which they need and carrying waste away from them.

Current – the flow of charged particles, for example, through a circuit.

Density – the amount of material (mass) in a given volume of a substance.

Earth – the third planet from the Sun in our solar system. Our home!

Ecosystem – groups of organisms from different habitats, together with their physical surroundings (their environment) which interact, for example, a woodland.

Electricity – the word we use to describe electrical charges which either move (current) or stay still (static).

Electron – a negatively charged particle in an atom, orbiting the nucleus.

Environment – a place where living things coexist; their surroundings.

Evolution – the development of living things into new species over long periods of time through minute changes. This is generally accepted to occur by natural selection (a theory developed by Charles Darwin).

Excretion – removal of waste substances that have been produced by processes occurring in cells.

Feeding – process by which an organism obtains its nutrients.

Flower – part of a plant which is adapted for sexual reproduction.

Food chain – a representation of how food energy flows from one organism to another by showing what eats what.

Food web – a collection of food chains in an ecosystem.

Fungi – one of the five kingdoms of living things. One common example is the mushroom.

Gas – a state of matter where the substance will expand to fit the container in which it is stored, the substance has no fixed shape or volume.

Genus – the penultimate category in the sorting of living things. For example lions, tigers and leopards are all part of the Panthera genus of big cats.

Growth – the process by which living things regenerate cells. This may mean that parts of the living thing get bigger, or that parts are repaired or replaced.

Habitat – a place where living things are found.

Herbivore – an animal which eats plants for nutrition.

Human – an animal; the common term for our own species. The scientific name is homo sapiens.

Leaf – the part of a plant where most of its food is made.

Life processes – the collective name for the processes which take place to keep an organism alive. There are generally acknowledged to be seven life processes: movement, respiration, sensitivity, growth, reproduction, excretion and nutrition.

Liquid – a state of matter in which the substance flows, and has a fixed volume but no fixed shape.

Magnetism – a property of a material that means it attracts other magnetic materials such as iron.

Mass – the amount of matter in an object or substance (measured in kilograms).

Material – a general term used to refer to substances.

Meteor – a scientific term for what are sometimes called falling or shooting stars. Meteors are bodies (usually rocks) that collide with the atmosphere. The friction of the body colliding with the atmosphere results in the glowing 'tail' that characterizes them. Not to be confused with comets, which orbit the Sun.

Molecule – a group of atoms that are held together by chemical bonds. An example is a water molecule, which is made from two hydrogen atoms and one oxygen atom.

Moon – a natural satellite; the general name for a body which orbits a planet. We use this word to refer to our own moon, as well as the satellites of other planets, for example Callisto that is a moon of Jupiter.

Neutron – a particle in the nucleus of an atom; it carries no electrical charge.

Nutrition – the process by which living things obtain what they need to stay alive from their food.

Omnivore – an animal which eats both plants and animals for nutrition.

Particle – a general term for a small amount of matter. Examples include atoms and molecules as well as the smaller units of which these are made.

Plant – one of the five kingdoms of living things. Plants are characterized by their ability to make their own food from nutrients through the process of photosynthesis.

Predator – an animal which eats another animal in a given ecosystem.

Proton – a particle in the nucleus of an atom; it carries a positive electrical charge.

Reflection – an image created by reflected light.

Refraction – the change in direction of light rays as they pass from one transparent material into another. An example of this is the way a straw seems to bend when placed in a glass of water.

Reproduction – the process by which living things create new living things.

Respiration – a living process where energy is obtained from food. Often this involves oxygen (aerobic respiration).

Seed – an embryonic plant, stored in a protective case with some initial food to support the first stages of growth once the seed is in the right conditions.

Sensitivity – a life process which means a living thing responds to its surroundings in some way.

Solar system – the system of planets and other bodies orbiting our Sun. Until recently this was regarded as having nine planets, but most astronomers now regard the former planet Pluto as a dwarf planet in the Kuiper Belt on the very edge of the solar system.

Solid – a state of matter in which the substance has a fixed shape and volume.

Species – often the final level when living things are sorted. A species are a group of living things that share many characteristics and can reproduce to produce fertile offspring. Some members of the same genus can produce offspring (for example, lions and tigers, members of the Panthera genus) but the offspring are not fertile.

Star – a massive ball of super hot gas in space. There are different sorts of stars including yellow dwarfs (like our Sun) and red giants.

State of matter – there are three states of matter: solid, liquid and gas. The state a material is in is affected by the way in which the matter it contains behaves, which itself depends on the temperature of the material.

Sun – the star at the centre of our solar system.

Temperature – a measure of how hot or cold something is.

Voltage – a measure of the electrical potential difference in two places in a circuit (that is the difference in its energy).

Volume – the amount of space a substance fills.

Weight – the measurement of gravitational force on an object; measured in newtons; not to be confused with mass (measured in kilograms).

Useful websites

Section 1

www.qca.org.uk/7659.html – the Qualifications and Curriculum Authority (QCA).
www.ncaction.org.uk/subjects/science/levels.htm – National Curriculum in Action.
www.standards.dfes.gov.uk/schemes2/science/?view=get – the Standards site – Schemes of Work.
www.nc.uk.net/nc_resources/html/download.shtml – the National Curriculum.
www.ase.org.uk/ – the Association for Science Education.
www.newscientist.com/lastword.ns – The *New Scientist* questions and answers.
www.wsu.edu/DrUniverse/Contents.html – Dr Universe – questions and answers for children.
http://en.wikipedia.org/wiki/Main_Page – wikipedia online encyclopedia.

Section 2

www.rspca.org.uk – the Royal Society for the Prevention of Cruelty to Animals.
www.food.gov.uk/ – the Food Standards Agency.
www.bbc.co.uk/science/humanbody/ – BBC human body homepage.
www.bbc.co.uk/sn/ – BBC science and nature homepage.
www.bbc.co.uk/schools/websites/4_11/site/science.shtml – BBC schools science website.
www.nhsdirect.nhs.uk/articles/article.aspx?articleId=448 – NHS drugs website.
www.nasa.gov/ – NASA official site.

Bibliography

Section 1

Arnold, C. (2003) *Observing Harry: Child Development and Learning 0–5*. Maidenhead: Open University Press.

Clarke, S. (2005) *Formative Assessment in Action*. London: Hodder Murray.

Coltman, P. (1996) In search of the elephant's child: early years science, in D. Whitebread (ed.) *Teaching and Learning in the Early Years*. London: RoutledgeFalmer.

Feynman, R.P. (1963) *The Feynman Lectures on Physics, Mainly Mechanics, Radiation and Heat*. London: Addison-Wesley.

Jarvis, T. and Woods, L. (2002) Fruit salads and wild gardens! developing investigative and thinking skills in children, in J. Moyles and G. Robinson (eds) *Beginning Teaching: Beginning Learning in Primary Education*. Maidenhead: Open University Press.

McNaughton, G. and Williams, G. (2004) *Teaching Young Children: Choices in Theory and Practice*. Maidenhead: Open University Press.

Office for Standards in Education (OFSTED) (2005a) *Primary National Strategy: An Evaluation of Its Impact in Primary Schools 2004/05*. London: OFSTED.

Office for Standards in Education (OFSTED) (2005b) *Science in Primary Schools*. London: OFSTED. http://live.ofsted.gov.uk/publications/annualreport0405/4.1.12

Qualifications and Curriculum Authority (QCA) (2007) QCA website. www.qca.org.uk.

Qualifications and Curriculum Authority and Department for Education and Skills (QCA/DfES) (2002) *The Foundation State Profile*. London: QCA.

Section 2

The following list provides details of a number of relevant texts and websites, some of which were used to check on some of the data and ideas for the Key Concepts chapters and some that are suggested for further reading. There is no substitute for a good dictionary of science for quick and easy reference and there are a number of good websites that do the same and are source of good diagrams and animations to use in the classroom, plus have links to other useful sources.

Carey, J. (1995) *The Faber Book of Science*. London: Faber and Faber.

Clugston, M.J. (2004) *The New Penguin Dictionary of Science*. 2nd edn. London: Penguin.

Daintith, J. (2005) *A Dictionary of Science*. Oxford: Oxford University Press.

Gannon, P. (2004) *Key Stage Three Science: The Revision Guide*. Newcastle upon Tyne: CGP Publications.

Hart-Davis, A. (2005) *Why Does a Ball Bounce?* London: Ebury Press.

Lafferty, P. and Rowe, J. (1993) *The Hutchinson Dictionary of Science*. Oxford: Helicon.

Nuffield Advanced Chemistry (1984) *Nuffield Advanced Science Book of Data Revised Edition*. London: Longman.

Porter, R. and Ogilvie, M. (2000) *The Hutchinson Dictionary of Scientific Biography*. Oxford: Helicon.

Websites

BBC Bitesize Revision website, www.bbc.co.uk/schools/revision

Science Photo Library website, www.sciencephoto.com

Wikipedia online encyclopedia: www.wikipedia.org

Index

Page numbers in *italics* refer to figures and tables; *g* indicates glossary.

EARLY EXPLORATIONS IN SCIENCE
SECOND EDITION

Jane Johnston

Reviewers' comments on the first edition:

> Jane Johnston communicates a sense of effervescent enthusiasm for teaching and science, and her treatment is comprehensive.
>
> *TES*

> At last! A serious attempt to explore the scientific potential of infant and pre-school children . . . The author explains how scientific skills can be developed at an early stage, stimulating the natural inquisitive streak in children. This book . . . will start you thinking about science in a much more positive light.
>
> *Child Education*

This accessible and practical book supports good scientific practice in the early years. It helps practitioners to be creative providers, and shows them how to develop awe and wonder of the world in the children they teach. The book highlights the importance of a motivating learning environment and skilled interaction with well-trained adults. In addition, fundamental issues are explored such as the range, nature and philosophical underpinning of early years experiences and the development of emergent scientific skills, understandings and attitudes.

New features for this edition include:

- An extended age range encompassing early learning from 0–8
- Updated material for the Foundation Stage Curriculum for 3–5-year-olds and the National Curriculum 2000 for 5–8-year-olds
- A new chapter focusing on conceptual understanding and thinking skills in the early years
- An emphasis on the importance of informal learning and play in early development

The book introduces and discusses new research and thinking in early years and science education throughout, making it relevant for current practice. This is an indispensable resource for all trainee and practising primary school teachers and early years practitioners.

c.208pp   0 335 21472 X (Paperback)

DEVELOPING TEACHING SKILLS IN THE PRIMARY SCHOOL

Jane Johnston, John Halocha and Mark Chater

Teaching is a complex process which involves the development and utilization of subject knowledge and teaching skills. Containing reflective and practical skills, this book supports such development, focusing specifically on teaching skills, considering what they are, how they develop and how they differ between age and subject.

The book contains three sections – Planning, Doing and Reviewing – which demonstrate effective classroom practice. It uses examples of practitioners at different stages of their professional development to link theory and practice, and includes discussions on contemporary issues in primary education, such as:

- Constructivist teaching and learning
- Thinking skills
- Creativity
- Teaching and learning styles
- Child-centred learning

The authors provide a critical analysis of the issues, practice and problems faced by primary school teachers, which is supported by reflective tasks throughout the book. Emphasizing the child as a partner in the learning process and highlighting the importance of teaching for child-centred learning, the book ultimately develops and strengthens the teacher's skills.

Developing Teaching Skills in the Primary School provides essential guidance and support to trainee, beginner and developing primary school teachers.

Contents

List of figures and pictures – Acknowledgements – Acronyms – Developing teaching skills in the primary school – **Section 1 – Planning** *– Planning for creative teaching – Classroom organization – Planning for citizenship – Behaviour management –* **Section 2 – Doing** *– Questioning – Differentiation – Using ICT in teaching – Supporting children in recording work – Developing investigative work/enquiry –* **Section 3 – Reviewing** *– Assessment for learning – Target setting – Professional communication – Developing as a reflective practitioner.*

2007 208pp
978–0–335–22096–0 (Paperback)   978–0–335–22095–3 (Hardback)

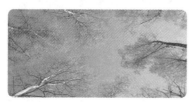